How to Do *Everything* with

Microsoft® Office InfoPath™ 2003

P9-BYN-240

David McAmis

McGraw-Hill/Osborne

New York Chicago San Francisco Lisbon
London Madrid Mexico City Milan New Delhi
San Juan Seoul Singapore Sydney Toronto

The McGraw·Hill Companies

McGraw-Hill/Osborne
2100 Powell Street, 10th Floor
Emeryville, California 94608
U.S.A.

To arrange bulk purchase discounts for sales promotions, premiums, or fund-raisers, please
contact **McGraw-Hill**/Osborne at the above address. For information on translations or
book distributors outside the U.S.A., please see the International Contact Information page
immediately following the index of this book.

How to Do Everything with Microsoft® Office InfoPath™ 2003

4567890 FGR FGR 019876

ISBN 0-07-223127-0

Publisher	Brandon A. Nordin
Vice President &	
Associate Publisher	Scott Rogers
Acquisitions Editor	Nancy Maragioglio
Project Editor	Elizabeth Seymour
Acquisitions Coordinator	Athena Honore
Technical Editor	Todd Carter
Copy Editor	Bill McManus
Proofreader	Mike McGee
Indexer	Jack Lewis
Composition	Tara A. Davis, Kelly Stanton-Scott
Illustrators	Kathleen Edwards, Melinda Lytle
Series Design	Mickey Galicia
Cover Series Design	Dodie Shoemaker
Cover Illustration	John Sledd

This book was composed with Corel VENTURA™ Publisher.

Dedication

To Lisa and Lorie, for their boundless support, love, and encouragement.

About the Author

David McAmis is an enterprise architect and partner in a consulting firm in Sydney, Australia. In his varied career, he has held the roles of consultant, technical trainer, university lecturer, and consulting services manager, and has served as vice-president of a software and services company in the U.S. He has written a number of computer books and enjoys helping organizations of all sizes find technology solutions to common business problems. He can be reached at david@infopathdeveloper.com.

Contents at a Glance

Contents

Acknowledgments

As with any book project, there is a long list of people involved who make things happen and they all deserve credit for pulling this project off. My thanks go out to the entire team at Osborne, including Nancy, Athena, Elizabeth, and everyone else who was involved in this project.

To my friend and agent, Neil Salkind: my sincere and humble thanks for his support and encouragement.

And, as always, to my worldwide support network of family and friends (including everyone who put up with me during the writing of this book): my very special thanks, as I couldn't have done it without you.

Introduction

Welcome to *How to Do Everything with Microsoft Office InfoPath 2003*. Since InfoPath was introduced in a beta release, end-users and developers alike have been excited about the prospect of electronic forms and how they can be used to gather and consolidate information previously held in traditional paper-based forms or in other electronic documents.

It has been a long time coming—over the past few years, paper-based forms and electronic documents (Excel spreadsheets, Word documents, etc.) have grown at a staggering rate as end-users struggle to create processes and systems using the tools at hand. While this enables organizations to quickly implement new processes and systems, it means that there has been a proliferation of "dead" documents, where the data held within the document can't be used for any other purpose.

These documents range from spreadsheet forms (where the information is formatted to the point where it becomes useless) to Word documents with reams of information in them that is unstructured and unusable. Even worse is the proliferation of paper-based documents. Millions of dollars are spent each year scanning and storing documents, when it is only the data contained in the document that is important.

This is where InfoPath really shines—forms created within InfoPath capture information in a way that makes the data usable with almost any application or data source, from simple Access databases to complex workflow applications and web services. That's just the tip of the iceberg—InfoPath has a host of features geared toward improving business processes and the quality of the data that is collected.

So if there is one goal for this book, it is that it will give you the skills you need to effectively use the features and functionality within InfoPath to get rid of the "dead" documents in your organization and gather real, relevant information.

Toward that end, this book will show you how to use InfoPath to create your own forms and integrate them into your existing business processes. The text has been arranged in logical sequence, starting with basic material, background information, and information on filling out a form, moving on to developing and publishing your own forms.

Chapter 1, "Introducing InfoPath" gives an overview of InfoPath's features and how they are used. In this chapter, you'll install InfoPath on your computer and then discover what makes up an InfoPath form.

One of the core technologies that InfoPath relies on is XML. If you are new to XML, Chapter 2, "XML Primer" is your starting point. Here, you'll learn to recognize the components of an XML document and understand how InfoPath uses XML. If you would like to delve a bit deeper, there are recommendations for further reading at the end of the chapter.

For end-users who will fill out the forms they create, Chapter 3, "Work with InfoPath Forms" is essential reading, as it looks at InfoPath from the end-user's perspective. In this chapter, you'll take a first look at the user interface, and learn how to fill out InfoPath forms. From there, we'll also see how you can print, save, and distribute those forms.

If you are a developer who wants to get down to brass tacks, you'll want to have a look at Chapter 4, "Get Started with Forms" which starts our discussion on form design. A brief form design methodology is given, followed by walk-throughs to create and format a simple form.You'll also find out how to preview and save your forms.

For integrating InfoPath with different data sources, read Chapter 5, "Work with Data Sources." This chapter begins with instructions on how to create forms from an existing XML schema or file, followed by a lesson on creating forms from an existing SQL Server or Access database. It finishes with a look at forms created from XML web services.

Once you have created a form, what to put on it? Chapter 6, "Work with Data Entry Controls," has the answer to that question, and more. This chapter covers everything you always wanted to know about form controls that are used for data entry, including how to create and modify controls, use plain and rich text boxes, create drop-down lists and list boxes, and other topics. The chapter also covers material on how to select dates using the Date Picker, and how to use check and option boxes on your form.

As if that wasn't enough, Chapter 7, "Work with Form Controls," covers the rest of the controls available within InfoPath, including how to insert different types of sections, create repeating tables, and utilize plain, numbered, and bulleted lists. You'll also learn how to use Picture controls to capture graphics on a form, insert hyperlinks into a form, and create expressions using XPath.

With all of those controls on a form, how about some formatting? Chapter 8, "Form Formatting," starts our discussion about formatting a form, including the use of layout tables. We also look at how to create and manage form views, and finish them off with borders and shading. How to conditionally format objects is another topic covered in Chapter 8.

If you are worried about the quality of the data that is entered using an InfoPath form, Chapter 9, "Validate Form Data," should help you resolve those issues. The chapter takes a look at how to eliminate blank fields, create validation rules, and use validation operators. You'll learn to create alerts inline and with dialog boxes.

For adding extra functionality to a form, Chapter 10, "Extend InfoPath," has it all. Here, you'll learn how to add scripting to a form, create custom task panes, and use secondary data sources to add additional lookups to your form.

How do you actually get the forms out to users? Chapter 11, "Publishing Overview," answers this question and sets the scene for the chapters that follow. In Chapter 11, you'll learn how to save your form and extract form files. You'll also get an overview of the form publishing process that should help you decide on a publishing method.

Chapter 12, "Work with Form Libraries," covers the first of the publishing methods: publishing forms to a SharePoint Form Library. The chapter will teach you how to use form libraries, create your own form libraries, and how to publish forms to a library. We'll also be looking at how to access form data from within SharePoint and the techniques you can use to analyze form data from within SharePoint.

If you prefer to install forms on user's local machines, you will need to read Chapter 13, "Install Custom Forms." Here, you'll create trusted forms using the RegForm utility, and create a script or MSI to install a form, as well as install a form on a user's PC.

If you have something else in in mind, Chapter 14, "Other Publishing Methods," covers several form publishing methods, including how to publish forms to a web server or shared location, send forms via e-mail, export a form to HTML, or view a form template using Internet Explorer and a style sheet.

Appendix A, "Sample Forms," provides an in-depth look at the sample forms that ship with InfoPath and that you can customize for your own use. In addition to a summary of each form, there is also information on how to view the underlying XML schema for your form.

Just getting started with JScript? Appendix B, "JScript Reference" provides a reference on all things JScript, including declaring variables, using functions, reserved words, and the like.

If you run into problems when working with scripting (or any other InfoPath feature), you just may find the answer in Appendix C, "Troubleshooting." This appendix covers common problems, troubleshooting resources, and more.

Finally, what is a form? What does it look like? What does the underlying schema look like? You can take a peek at underlying XML schema behind an InfoPath form in Appendix D, "InfoPath Form Template XML Schema."

So, without further ado, let's get into it! I sincerely hope you enjoy the book and working with InfoPath as much as I do.

Part I

Get Started with InfoPath

Chapter 1

Introducing InfoPath

How to...

- Understand the components of an XML document

- Understand how InfoPath is used

- Install InfoPath on your computer

InfoPath 2003 is the newest member of the Microsoft Office System and has been designed to capture and consolidate information traditionally gathered using paper-based forms or other electronic documents such as Excel spreadsheets, Word documents, and so on. Using InfoPath, you can create feature-rich electronic forms that can be used to gather information from users. InfoPath then enables you to reuse that information in a wide variety of systems and applications.

So, what does an InfoPath form look like? Figure 1-1 shows a typical InfoPath form that is designed to gather employee time-card information.

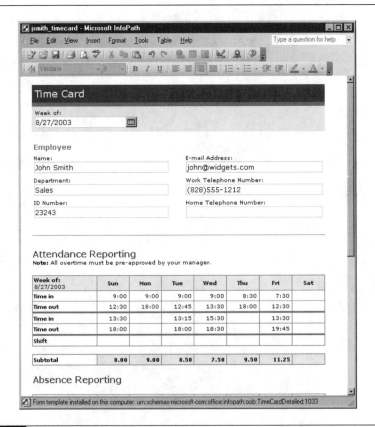

FIGURE 1-1   An employee time-card form

1

Like traditional paper-based or electronic documents, InfoPath forms can be designed to capture any information you require. The difference is that the information entered in an InfoPath form can be tied to a back-end system or database, thereby eliminating the need to retype information into disparate systems through extensive use of XML, XML Web Services, and direct database connections. The following sections look at some of the different ways that you can use InfoPath and introduce you to some of the key components and technologies that make InfoPath work.

What Is InfoPath?

InfoPath is a desktop application that is installed locally and can be used to design or fill out electronic forms. When InfoPath is installed, a number of sample forms are also installed with the product, including forms for timesheets, expense reports, leave requests, and so on. Often, organizations use these forms as-is or as a starting point for their own custom form development; the following section looks at InfoPath from the perspective of the developers who actually create or customize forms. Following that is a discussion of how end users use InfoPath to fill out those forms.

How Developers Use InfoPath

Developers use InfoPath as a feature-rich form designer to customize the sample forms that are a part of InfoPath, or to design their own forms from scratch. And it is not only application developers who can create forms within InfoPath—there are probably a number of "power users" within your organization who already create forms or gather information using spreadsheets, their own databases, and so on. These users can also learn to use InfoPath to create and publish feature-rich forms like the one shown in Figure 1-2.

 In the following sections that describe some of the InfoPath features that are applicable to both developers and power users, "developers" refers to both groups, because both will be developing InfoPath forms.

Data Integration

For developers who are familiar with developing web-based applications using other tools or platforms or for power users who create their own forms using other software tools, InfoPath provides an easy transition to learning how to quickly create feature-rich electronic forms. Using InfoPath, a developer can create a form that is tied into back-end systems or processes so that after the users fill out the

FIGURE 1-2 A typical InfoPath form

required information and submit the form, this information flows through to those systems. This is accomplished using one of three methods:

■ **XML file** When an InfoPath form is saved, the data within the form is saved in an XML file. XML is considered a "universal" file format and can be read and imported by a number of different systems or databases. In addition, InfoPath also includes the capability to consolidate XML files created from the same form, allowing you to create summary documents.

■ **Database** Developers can also create forms that submit information directly back to a SQL Server or Access database.

- **Web service**   To interface InfoPath to other applications, systems, and databases, developers can also use InfoPath to submit information to an XML Web Service.

> TIP   *For a primer on XML, check out Chapter 2. For more information on developing forms that interface to a database or web service, check out Chapter 5 and following chapters.*

For developers, one of the first choices when designing a form is where to store the form data. With that decision out of the way, they can then get down to creating the form itself.

Form Design

Designing a form using InfoPath is quick, thanks to the robust set of tools that are purpose-built for creating electronic forms. For the most basic forms, like the one shown in Figure 1-3, developers add fields, boxes, and tables for users to fill out; these objects correspond to the underlying data that the developers want to capture.

But InfoPath goes beyond just creating simple forms—using the tools and controls that are provided, developers can create complex forms that capture information using both plain and richly formatted text, like the form shown in Figure 1-4.

Scripting

To extend InfoPath forms, InfoPath also offers the capability to use VBScript or JScript within a form using the Microsoft Script Editor (shown in Figure 1-5),

FIGURE 1-3   A simple InfoPath form

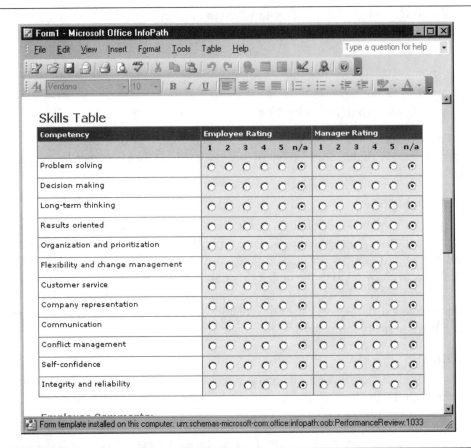

FIGURE 1-4   A more complex InfoPath form

enabling developers to create complex applications of InfoPath technology. This type of scripting can be used within InfoPath to validate data, make calculations, handle errors, and respond to events. In addition, you can use scripting to access external data for lookup lists and allow integration with other applications.

This would enable you, for example, to populate a drop-down list on your form from another database or system. Or you could pull information from a database that held shipping rates for different locations to help calculate the shipping rate on an order form.

SharePoint Portal Server

Finally, for publishing forms, InfoPath is integrated with SharePoint Portal Server, allowing developers to publish InfoPath forms to be distributed and used throughout

Did you know?

Adding Validation

Another handy feature of InfoPath is the capability to add validation to your forms. *Validation* is the process of checking the data that has been entered against some set criteria. In an expense report example, for example, an InfoPath developer could have specified that only expenses under $100 could be entered on the form. If a user tried to enter an expense line item for more than $100, a warning message could be generated or the field could be highlighted, and so on. This validation is performed in real time and allows developers to guide the user's data entry to ensure that the correct information is being entered and processed.

an organization. This integrated approach means that users won't have to hunt around for the forms they need—they all can be consolidated into one convenient place that can be accessed by multiple users.

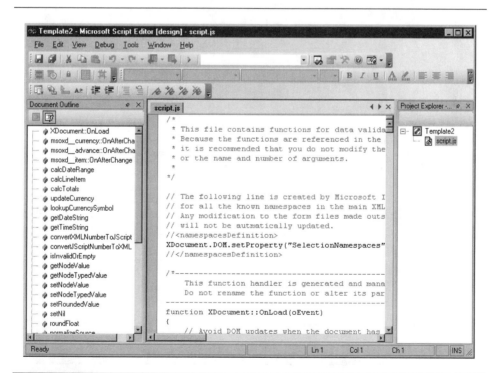

FIGURE 1-5   Microsoft Script Editor

For more information on how InfoPath works with SharePoint Portal Server, check out Chapter 11.

How End Users Use InfoPath

While developers may use InfoPath to design forms, the majority of people who use InfoPath are end users who use the tool to fill out forms. The following sections look at some InfoPath features that are specific to these users.

User Interface

When working with an InfoPath form, users can work in a feature-rich environment that allows the entry of formatted text (see Figure 1-6) and images, and includes a spell-checker, find-and-replace functionality, and other features found in word processing applications.

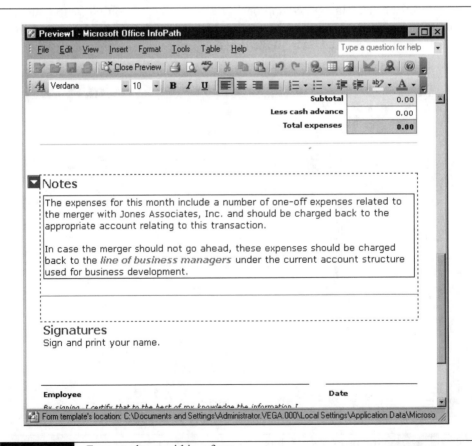

FIGURE 1-6   Formatted text within a form

1

The inclusion of this familiar set of intuitive tools and capabilities means that users with basic Windows skills should be able to fill out InfoPath forms with little or no training required.

In addition, users can use InfoPath forms as they would traditional paper-based or electronic forms created using other tools—for example, you can print InfoPath forms just like you would print any other document, as shown in Figure 1-7.

Office Integration

With integration into other Microsoft Office System applications, including Excel and Outlook, InfoPath can quickly share information between users and applications. This flexibility includes the capability to send an InfoPath form via e-mail, as shown in Figure 1-8.

This integration enables users to create simple workflow applications without having to rely on custom coding or other technologies. For example, you could fill out an expense form in InfoPath and then send it to your manager via e-mail for approval and any corrections that need to be made. Your manager could in turn make the corrections on the form and send the e-mail back to you with their

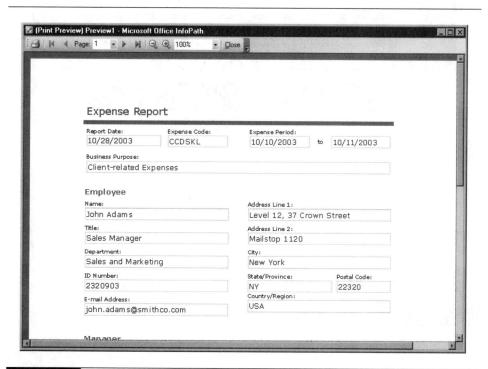

FIGURE 1-7   The print view of an InfoPath form

approval and copy it to the accounting department for processing. From that point, the accounting department could import the XML directly into the accounting system, eliminating the need to retype it. This type of simple workflow application is a popular use of InfoPath and adds an immediate return on your investment in electronic forms.

NOTE *For users who require more complex workflow or tracking applications, InfoPath can also work with Microsoft's BizTalk Server. For more information on BizTalk, visit www.microsoft.com/biztalk.*

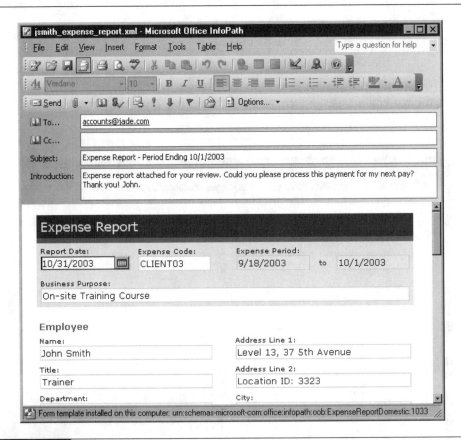

FIGURE 1-8   Sending an InfoPath form via e-mail

InfoPath also leverages the Microsoft Office System and is tightly integrated with Outlook, allowing users to send forms via e-mail directly from within InfoPath. To analyze data collected using InfoPath, data from an InfoPath form can also be exported to an Excel spreadsheet, like the one shown in Figure 1-9, allowing users to further analyze the information collected by the form.

When working with forms, users can also consolidate information held within multiple forms, which provides another way to collect, consolidate, and analyze data. For example, you could create an InfoPath form to survey employees on potential benefits they would like to see. When the forms are returned, you can use InfoPath to consolidate and merge the data and then export it to Excel for analysis and create graphs and pivot tables without having to do any manual data entry.

Now that you have had a peek at some of the features that InfoPath provides, you need to install it so that you can actually open the product and see some of these features for yourself!

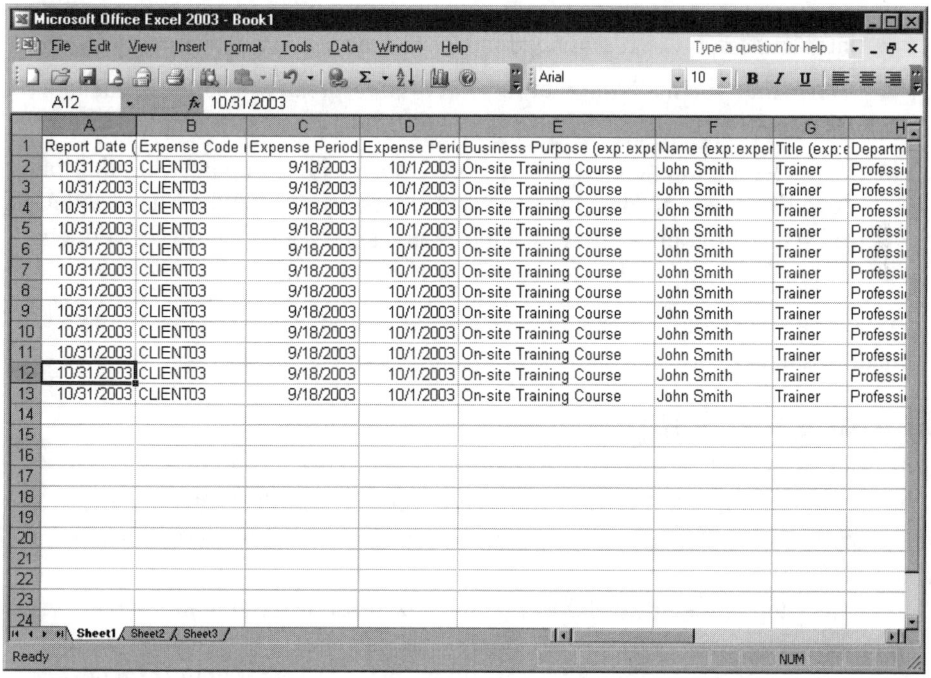

	A	B	C	D	E	F	G	H
1	Report Date (	Expense Code (	Expense Period	Expense Peri(	Business Purpose (exp:expe	Name (exp:exper	Title (exp:e	Departm
2	10/31/2003	CLIENT03	9/18/2003	10/1/2003	On-site Training Course	John Smith	Trainer	Professi
3	10/31/2003	CLIENT03	9/18/2003	10/1/2003	On-site Training Course	John Smith	Trainer	Professi
4	10/31/2003	CLIENT03	9/18/2003	10/1/2003	On-site Training Course	John Smith	Trainer	Professi
5	10/31/2003	CLIENT03	9/18/2003	10/1/2003	On-site Training Course	John Smith	Trainer	Professi
6	10/31/2003	CLIENT03	9/18/2003	10/1/2003	On-site Training Course	John Smith	Trainer	Professi
7	10/31/2003	CLIENT03	9/18/2003	10/1/2003	On-site Training Course	John Smith	Trainer	Professi
8	10/31/2003	CLIENT03	9/18/2003	10/1/2003	On-site Training Course	John Smith	Trainer	Professi
9	10/31/2003	CLIENT03	9/18/2003	10/1/2003	On-site Training Course	John Smith	Trainer	Professi
10	10/31/2003	CLIENT03	9/18/2003	10/1/2003	On-site Training Course	John Smith	Trainer	Professi
11	10/31/2003	CLIENT03	9/18/2003	10/1/2003	On-site Training Course	John Smith	Trainer	Professi
12	10/31/2003	CLIENT03	9/18/2003	10/1/2003	On-site Training Course	John Smith	Trainer	Professi
13	10/31/2003	CLIENT03	9/18/2003	10/1/2003	On-site Training Course	John Smith	Trainer	Professi

FIGURE 1-9 An InfoPath form exported to Excel

Installing InfoPath

InfoPath is easy to install and is available either as part of the Microsoft Office System Enterprise Edition or as a stand-alone product. Before you get started installing InfoPath, you need to look at a few guidelines:

- Close all other programs that are running on your machine.

- Have your Microsoft Office InfoPath license handy—the setup program will prompt you for this key and you will need to enter it before you can continue.

- Verify that you are running Windows 2000 Service Pack 3, Windows XP, or a later operating system.

- Make sure that your PC is a Pentium 233 MHz or greater with at least 100MB of hard disk space and 128MB of RAM. For installation requirements, plan to have at least 300MB of disk space available during the installation. A small amount of this space will be taken up by files that you can use for maintenance or updates that are left on the drive. If you don't want to keep these files, you will be prompted to delete these files later and can do so if you need the extra space.

- Verify that you have Internet Explorer 6.0 or greater installed—this is required by InfoPath.

- If you would like to check the Office Update site for updates or additional downloads, you need an Internet connection. Near the end of the installation, the setup program will ask whether you want to open a browser window and look for any updated files after setup is complete.

If you have met all the preceding criteria, you can now proceed with the InfoPath installation.

Running the Setup

InfoPath is provided on a product CD-ROM. To start the installation, place the CD-ROM in your CD-ROM drive. If the installation doesn't start automatically, select Start | Run and then type **D:\setup** (where D: is the drive letter assigned to your CD-ROM drive).

The first step of the InfoPath Installation Wizard, shown in Figure 1-10, assesses your system setup and copies any temporary files the wizard needs to get started.

Once this process is completed, you are prompted to enter your InfoPath Product Key using the dialog box shown in Figure 1-11. This 25-character key is usually found on the back of your CD-ROM case or cover.

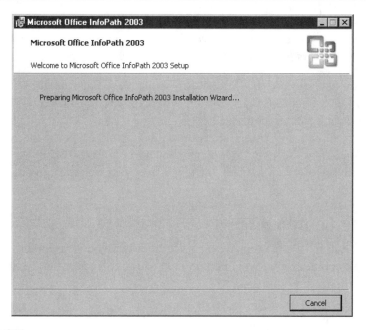

FIGURE 1-10   Getting ready to install

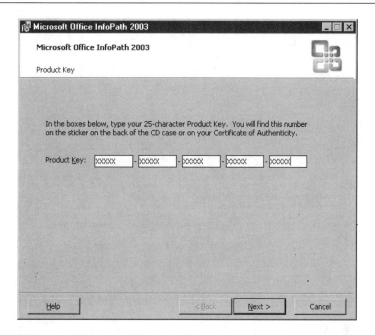

FIGURE 1-11   InfoPath Product Key

If you are unsure of where to find the Product Key for your product or if you have questions about licensing InfoPath, check with a system administrator or the person within your organization who looks after Microsoft licensing options.

After you have entered the Product Key, click Next and you will be prompted for your name, initials, and organization. When you are finished entering this information, click Next to continue.

You need to read and familiarize yourself with, and accept the terms of the Microsoft End-User License Agreement, shown in Figure 1-12, before you can proceed with the installation. Click the check box to accept the agreement and then click Next to proceed.

Selecting Components

When installing InfoPath, you have a choice of either using the default installation options or selecting exactly which components to install and where, using the dialog box shown in Figure 1-13.

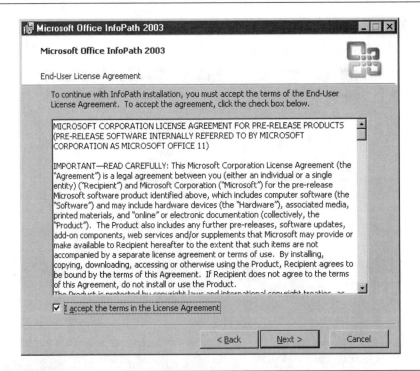

FIGURE 1-12 Microsoft InfoPath End-User License Agreement

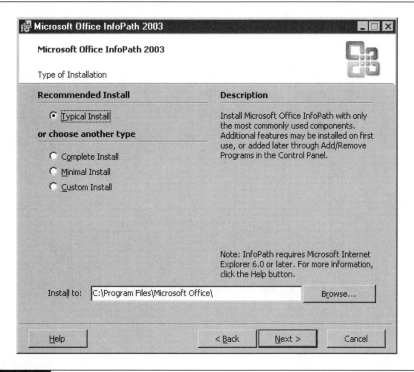

Installation type selection

At the bottom of the dialog box, you can select a location in which to install InfoPath, either by typing a path into the text box provided or by using the Browse button to locate a folder where you want to install the product.

At the top of the dialog box are a number of choices to specify which InfoPath components to install on your computer. If you select the option for a Typical Install, the most commonly used tools and features will be installed on your computer. You can also perform a Complete Install to install all the available tools and utilities. Or, if you are short on space, you can use the Minimal Install option to install only the files required to run InfoPath, with none of the extras.

If you are unsure about what will be installed with these options or if you would like to select which components are to be installed, you can use the Custom Install option for complete control over the installation. Selecting Custom Install and then clicking Next opens the Advanced Customization options, shown in Figure 1-14.

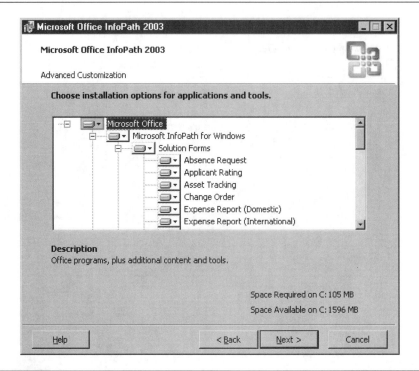

Advanced Customization options

You can select from the different InfoPath components that are available and mark them to be one of the following:

- Run from My Computer
- Run all from My Computer
- Installed on First Use
- Not Available

If you think you may need a particular component or feature in the future, it is always a good call to mark them as Run from My Computer as opposed to Installed on First Use. Selecting the Installed on First Use option could require that you have the installation CD-ROM or files handy to use a particular feature.

Some of the components listed in the Advanced Customization options are actually included with other Office programs and some are completely optional. If you are unsure of what a particular component is used for, use the Help button in the lower-left corner to do a little research on how the component is used.

Completing the Setup

When you are finished selecting the components you wish to install, click Next, which opens the Summary page, shown in Figure 1-15.

The file installation then begins, with a progress indicator displayed like the one shown in Figure 1-16, indicating the progress of the installation as it copies and registers files on your computer. If there are files that the setup program needs to update or change that are currently "locked" or in use by another program, you will be prompted to retry or ignore these errors during this step of the installation. If you do encounter errors, you may want to reboot without opening any additional applications and try the setup again.

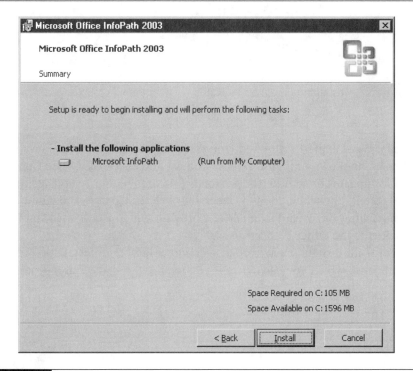

FIGURE 1-15   Installation Summary page

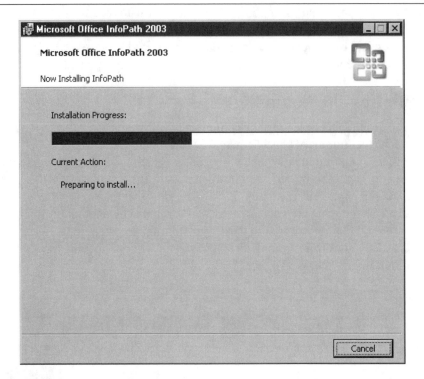

FIGURE 1-16   Installation progress indicator

When the installation is finished, you are prompted for a few final installation-related tasks, as shown in Figure 1-17. If you want to check the Office Update web site for updates or additional downloads (including security updates, sample files, and so on), click the option to Check the Web for Updates and Additional Downloads. After the wizard is finished, a browser window will open and you will be taken to the Office web site.

The InfoPath Installation Wizard also copies a number of installation files to your local drive, which you can delete if you require the space that they take up.

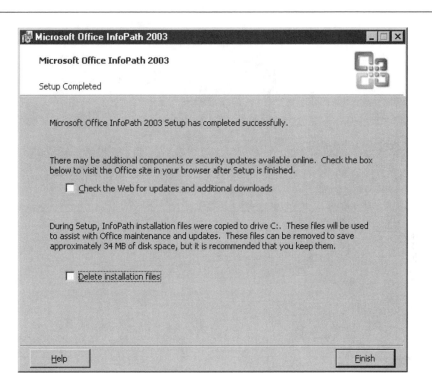

FIGURE 1-17   Updates and file deletion

The dialog box shows the size of these files and allows you to select the option to Delete Installation Files. If you have enough room on your hard drive, it is always a good idea to keep these files, because they can be useful when performing maintenance on your InfoPath installation. Click the Finish button to complete your setup and exit the InfoPath Installation Wizard.

You should now be able to open InfoPath from your Start menu or from the Microsoft Office Program Group, as shown in Figure 1-18.

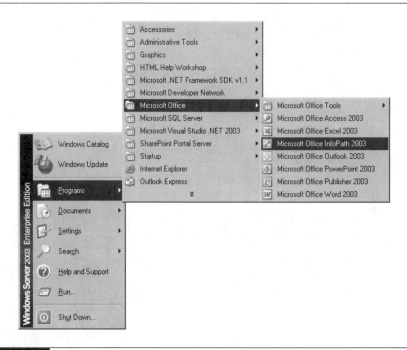

FIGURE 1-18   Starting InfoPath 2003

Summary

By now, you should have a good idea of some of the things that InfoPath can be
used for. As you go through the rest of the book, you will discover other ways that
you can use the product and look at some real-world forms and projects that you
can use in your own organization. But before you get too far, you need to have a
look at XML, which is one of the core underlying technologies in InfoPath and is
covered in the next chapter.

Chapter 2

XML Primer

How to...

- Recognize the components of an XML document
- Work with XML files and schemas
- Understand how InfoPath uses XML

Before you can go much further in your study of InfoPath, you need to take a look at the Extensible Markup Language (XML), the closest thing to a "universal" format for data. XML is one of the core underlying technologies within InfoPath, and this chapter provides the background information that you'll need a little later when you start to work with, and design, your own forms.

Introducing XML

Most of us look at web pages and don't think about how the page was designed or the complexity of the Hypertext Markup Language (HTML) behind the scenes. HTML is one of the core technologies behind web pages that you may have viewed on the Internet and it provides a good starting point for this discussion of XML.

If you navigate to a web page within Internet Explorer and then select View | Source, you can see the HTML markup that was used to create that page. A web browser takes this HTML markup and uses it to display the page, using the content and formatting settings that are present in the HTML. A sample HTML page is shown in Figure 2-1.

For example, you may have noticed that when you navigate to certain pages, the title of your web browser window changes to describe the page you are visiting. This doesn't happen automatically; within the HTML document is a special set of "tags," enclosed in angle brackets, that determines which text is the title of the page, as shown here:

```
<title>Product Listing Page</title>
```

When your browser reads this set of tags, it knows that the information within the tags contains the title of the page, "Product Listing Page," and that it can display that title at the top of the browser window, as shown here.

2

```
1  <html>
2  <head>
3  <title>Product Listing Page</title>
4  <meta http-equiv="Content-Type" content="text/html; charset=iso-8859-1">
5  </head>
6
7  <body bgcolor="#FFFFFF" text="#000000" leftmargin="30" topmargin="30" marginwidth="30" margi
8  <table width="85%" border="0" cellspacing="4" cellpadding="2" bgcolor="#0099FF">
9    <tr>
10     <td height="20">Product
11       Listing</td>
12   </tr>
13 </table>
14 <p><b>Xtreme Mountain
15   Bike</b><br>
16   Crazy Cycles<br>
17   $299.99<br>
18   Mountain Bike</p>
19 <ul>
20   <li>rust-free alloy
21     frame</li>
22   <li>metallic paint
23     finish</li>
24   <li>comfort-grip handlebars</li>
25   <li> cushioned saddle
26     seat<br>
27     </li>
28 </ul>
29 <p><b>Endorphin Racing
30   Bike</b><br>
31   Crazy Cycles<br>
32   $699.99<br>
33   Racing Bike<br>
34   </p>
35 <ul>
```

FIGURE 2-1   A sample HTML page

Originally, the Web worked entirely through HTML pages that contained different tags to display text and other objects, control formatting, and so on. The majority of web pages are still written using HTML in this manner. However, while HTML provides a standard method for developing web pages, it is limited in how it can be used.

XML, on the other hand, is a much more flexible markup format and can suit a wide range of uses, from creating web pages and sites to creating data and document exchange formats and files. This flexibility comes from the fact that XML is designed to be used in a number of different ways and is "self-describing," meaning that XML can communicate both the content and the content's structure or format.

To see this in action, first consider the web page produced by the HTML shown in Figure 2-1. You can see in Figure 2-2 that the page has a list of products that are available for sale.

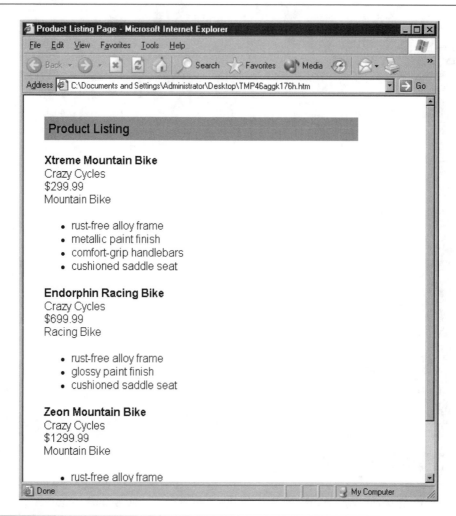

FIGURE 2-2 A typical product listing page

If you were to view part of the HTML behind this page, it might look something like this:

```
</table>
<p><b>Xtreme Mountain
  Bike</b><br>
  Crazy Cycles<br>
```

2

```
    $299.99<br>
    Mountain Bike</p>
<ul>
    <li>rust-free alloy
      frame</li>
    <li>metallic paint
      finish</li>
    <li>comfort-grip handlebars</li>
    <li> cushioned saddle
      seat<br>
      </li>
</ul>
<p><b>Endorphin Racing
    Bike</b><br>
    Crazy Cycles<br>
    $699.99<br>
    Racing Bike<br>
    </p>
<ul>
    <li> rust-free alloy
      frame</li>
    <li>glossy paint finish</li>
    <li>cushioned saddle
      seat<br>
      </li>
</ul>
```

While this provides all the information required to display the list of products in your browser, it really doesn't tell you anything about them. For example, if you were to send this information to someone else, how would they know what the numbers and description mean? Are the numbers the price of the product? Or the manufacturer's cost? Likewise, is the text the actual product name or just a description of the product?

XML allows you to specify all of these attributes in a well-structured file format that can easily be understood and interpreted by a wide variety of systems. ("Well-structured" means that the file has all the required start and end tags, as well as all the other elements that make up a basic XML file.) If you were to take the product information from the web page in Figure 2-3 and put it into an XML file, it might look something like this:

```
<?xml version="1.0" encoding="UTF-8"?>
<Products>
```

```
<Product name="Xtreme Mountain Bike">
 <manufacturer>Crazy Cycles</manufacturer>
 <type usage="mountain"/>
    <features>
         <Item>rust-free alloy frame</Item>
         <Item>metallic paint finish</Item>
         <Item>comfort-grip handlebars</Item>
         <Item>cushioned saddle seat</Item>
    </features>
 </Product>
</Products>
```

Before you get too far into the XML shown here, you need to understand some terms. XML documents are primarily made up of different *elements*. An element has a *start tag* and *end tag*, marked with angle brackets, and within the tags is some content. In the preceding example, there is a manufacturer element, and the content within the element is Crazy Cycles (the company that manufacturers the bike).

```
<manufacturer>Crazy Cycles</manufacturer>
```

If you look at the previous example XML document a little closer, you see that it is made up of a number of these elements. And just like an XML document is made up of different data elements, each of those elements can also have attributes—an *attribute* is a property that is associated with an element and describes the element content. For example, you might have an attribute associated with a Name element of the product that defines the SKU (or product number) for that particular product, like the attribute shown here:

```
<?xml version="1.0" encoding="UTF-8"?>
<Products>
    <Product>
        <name SKU="22122">Xtreme Mountain Bike</name>
        <manufacturer>Crazy Cycles</manufacturer>
        <price>299.99</price>
        <type>mountain</type>
        <features>
            <Item>rust-free alloy frame</Item>
            <Item>metallic paint finish</Item>
            <Item>comfort-grip handlebars</Item>
            <Item>cushioned saddle seat</Item>
        </features>
    </Product>
```

How do you know what data is contained within an XML file? Well, you could always look at the XML file and try to work out the structure. But XML can also be used to create a *schema* that defines both the structure and the type of data that is contained within an XML document.

The preceding example doesn't actually have a proper schema defined. But if it did, you could use it to describe how the product information is stored in the XML file, including the type of data that would be included in each element (string, integer, float, and so forth). The following code is actually part of a separate schema file for the example Products XML file:

```
<xsd:schema
xmlns:xsd="http://osborne.com/HTDEInfoPath/ProductsXMLSchema">
     <xsd:element name="products">
          <xsd:complexType>
               <xsd:sequence maxOccurs="unbounded">
                    <xsd:element ref="product"/>
               </xsd:sequence>
          </xsd:complexType>
     </xsd:element>
     <xsd:element name="product">
          <xsd:complexType>
               <xsd:sequence>
                    <xsd:element ref="name"/>
                    <xsd:element ref="price"/>
                    <xsd:element ref="manufacturer"/>
               </xsd:sequence>
               <xsd:attribute name="sku" type="xsd:string"/>
          </xsd:complexType>
     </xsd:element>
     <xsd:element name="name" type="xsd:string"/>
     <xsd:element name="price" type="xsd:float"/>
     <xsd:element name="manufacturer" type="xsd:string"/>
     <xsd:element name="type">
```

In addition to describing the different elements that can be used, this schema file also defines what type of data is associated with the element (for example, "float" for numbers, "string" for text, and so on), so when it comes time to use this field in a form, InfoPath will know exactly what type of data can be entered into a particular field.

How InfoPath Uses XML

You must be asking "What does this have to do with InfoPath?" If you were to skip ahead to the next chapter, which looks at filling out InfoPath forms, you would discover that when you fill out and save a form within InfoPath, the data can either be saved within an XML file or submitted to a back-end database or web service. And when working with a form, there is an XML schema behind the scenes that describes what values are acceptable to the form and are used for validating data.

When you are developing InfoPath forms, you can also use XML files and schemas as data sources. And when you save your form, the form definition file (which has an .xsf extension) is saved using XML, with a number of other supporting files that make up your form template.

The following sections look at all of these different uses of XML in detail, starting with using an XML file as the data source for your form.

XML Data Sources

When you are creating a form to collect information from a user, you have a number of different ways to get started, one of the easiest of which is to use an existing XML file as the data source for your form. Since XML is "self-describing" (meaning that the definition of the field is contained within the file itself) it is the perfect file format to use when creating a form template.

NOTE *You can also create forms based on other data sources, including Microsoft SQL Server and Microsoft Access databases, web services, and so on. These methods are covered in detail in Chapter 5, which describes how to work with data sources.*

Why would you use an XML file as a starting point for your form? To begin with, you may have an existing XML file or schema that you want to use. InfoPath can connect directly to Microsoft SQL Server or Access databases and web services to "push" form data back into a database. But if you are working with another database format, XML also makes it easy to exchange information.

For example, suppose that your organization uses a General Ledger application that runs on Oracle and you need to create a form to collect expense-related information. Your Oracle database administrator (DBA) could provide you with an XML file that matches the information that needs to be entered. You could then use this XML file as the data source for your form, ensuring that any data you collect with your form could be correctly imported into Oracle.

2

Most databases or applications released in the past few years can generate XML files, and there are many third-party tools available to transform data from various formats to XML. If you do have some experience with XML, you can create your own XML file as a starting point for your form—just make sure that it is a valid XML file before you start; otherwise, you may run into problems! If you aren't that handy with XML, you can create your data source on-the-fly by simply working with a blank form—as you add data entry controls, text boxes, and so forth, InfoPath will build the data source for you.

Form Templates

When you create your first form, you'll save the form to an XSN file format, which is unique to InfoPath. If you were to look at the structure of an XSN file, you would see that it is actually a compressed CAB file consisting of a number of other files that make up an InfoPath form, as shown in Figure 2-3.

NOTE   *CAB files are compressed files that are used to distribute software applications and data, similar to Zip files.*

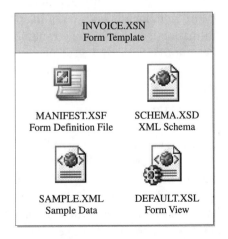

FIGURE 2-3   Structure of an XSN file

As you design forms like this one, InfoPath is creating all of these underlying files behind the scenes to correspond to different parts of your form's design, and all of these files are based on XML.

The filenames shown in the diagram in Figure 2-3 are from one of the sample invoice forms that ship with InfoPath. To see all the files that make up this InfoPath form, you can open the Invoice (Single Tax Rate) form in design mode (which is introduced in Chapter 4) and then select File | Extract Form Files.

A number of other types of files can make up a form template, but this chapter is concentrating on XML, so the other files aren't shown in this diagram.

The following sections look at the different types of XML files that are used in an InfoPath form, as well as what each type is used for, using the Invoice form as an example.

XML Schema

An XML schema file is used to describe the form definition file (which has an .xsf extension) and also provides the structure for the XML that will be generated when the user fills out and saves the form. In the example Invoice form, the XML schema describes all the fields that you would normally find on an invoice and includes information about the type of field, length, and so on. In addition to the other uses previously listed, this information is also used for simple form validation (you wouldn't be able to enter text into a field marked as numeric, for example).

Form Definition File

A form definition file (.xsf file extension) describes the form and layout, identifies any XML schemas that are in use, and contains information about other files related to the form and deployment settings. Form definition files are automatically created by InfoPath when you are working with the design of your form, and may contain information about how the form is deployed as well.

In the example Invoice form, this file is named manifest.xsf, which is a fairly accurate description of its function—it is a manifest of all the related files and includes information about how the form is deployed and the processing instructions that will be carried out when the form is saved or submitted.

2

XML Sample Data

When you are designing forms, another key area where XML is used is sample data. Often, forms do not make sense to users until they see some data entered into the form—sample data can be used to demonstrate what values should be entered into a particular field or section. In the example Invoice form, the sample.xml file is used to store sample values that may appear on the form.

Form Views

Another use of XML technology within InfoPath can be found in form views. A view within a form is used to organize form data. A form can have multiple views to display different controls or data entry objects. An easy way to think of views is to imagine your form as a multipage document—each one of those pages is a view. InfoPath uses a standard Extensible Stylesheet Language Transformations (XSLT) form to describe these views. The example Invoice form has a single default view; if you were to look in the associated XSL file, you would see all the formatting for this view, including fonts, colors, and other items.

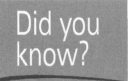

InfoPath Supports XPath

To create expressions or simple calculations within a form, InfoPath supports XPath, which is a language that was designed to reference parts of an XML document. In addition to enabling you to precisely reference part of an XML document, XPath also provides a number of operators and functions that you can use to perform simple arithmetic calculations, summaries, string manipulations, and more.

 *For more information about creating XPath expressions, check out Chapter 7.*

Form Data Files

With all of that XML technology behind the scenes, it is no wonder that the file format for any forms that you fill out is XML. In the next chapter, you will look at the most basic type of InfoPath implementation, where a form is created and used to save the results to an XML file. You can then use this file to import data into other applications or systems, and InfoPath provides the capability to merge multiple form data files into a single file for further analysis or use.

Summary

InfoPath relies heavily on XML which provides the flexibility that enables InfoPath to be able to work with a number of systems and database formats, as most will support XML. This chapter introduced you to some basic XML terms and concepts that you will need when getting started with InfoPath, but if you want to know more about XML or how it can be used with your existing applications, there are a number of good books on XML, including *Beginner's Guide to XML* (Dave Mercer, McGraw-Hill/ Osborne, 2001) and *Learning XML* (Erik T. Ray, O'Reilly and Associates, 2001). This chapter also covered how XML is used throughout InfoPath, and the rest of the book will be reinforcing these concepts.

For now, you need to move on to the starting point for all InfoPath users and developers: the InfoPath environment and filling out forms, the subject of the next chapter.

Chapter 3

Work with InfoPath Forms

How to...

- Understand the user interface
- Fill out InfoPath forms
- Print, save, and distribute InfoPath forms

InfoPath provides two "modes" of operation, depending on whether you are a developer or an end user. For developers, InfoPath provides a powerful environment in which to develop data-based forms, called "design" mode. In any organization that uses InfoPath, however, the number of people who actually design InfoPath forms is relatively small—the rest of the users use a "data entry" mode to fill out the forms that have been created for them.

This chapter focuses on what these end users will experience when they use this mode to enter data into existing forms. This chapter provides most of the information end users need to work with InfoPath and it also provides a good introduction for any developers or "power users" who may want to create their own forms.

Throughout the chapter, you will be looking at some of the sample forms that ship with InfoPath. In addition to providing an "out of the box" solution, you can also use these forms as a starting point for your own form design, which is covered in the next chapter. But for now, you are going to dive into the InfoPath user interface and learn how to work with forms from the end user's perspective. Whether you are an InfoPath user or developer, it all starts here.

First Looks...

The InfoPath user interface is broken down into two main sections and a number of toolbars and menus, as shown in Figure 3-1.

The following sections look at each of the areas labeled in Figure 3-1, starting with the Main View.

Main View

The Main View takes up the most real estate within the InfoPath window and is used to display and design forms. This area is empty when you first open InfoPath until you select whether to fill out or design a form. The Main View is used to display the form content, including the fields, tables, and so forth that are part of your form.

Menu bar   Toolbars

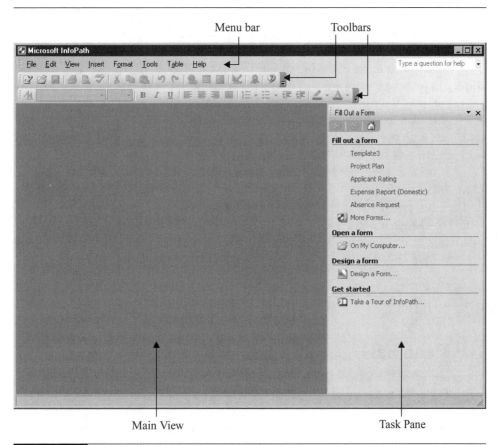

Main View   Task Pane

FIGURE 3-1   The InfoPath user interface

The Task Pane

The Task Pane is a dockable menu that contains shortcuts to commonly performed tasks. This area is called a "pane" because it contains a window that changes depending on the task you have selected. For example, if you are designing a form, this pane could contain all the tasks and tools related to form design. Likewise, when you are actually filling out a form, the pane shows tasks and tools relating to data entry.

The drop-down list at the top of the Task Pane controls the task view. There are different views for designing forms, filling out forms, and so on. You can change the view within the Task Pane by using the drop-down menu. Click the down arrow to open a list of available views, like the one shown here.

There are also icons at the top of the Task Pane that allow you to move backward and forward through any pages you may have opened in the Task Pane, as well as a Home icon to take you back to the original page associated with the view you have selected. These icons work in a similar fashion to the Back, Forward, and Home buttons in your web browser and make navigation a little bit easier.

For example, if you had selected to view the tasks related to Design a Form and then clicked New Blank Form and then Layout, you could use the icons to navigate backward or forward within these three pages or click the Home icon to take you back to your starting page (Design a Form).

You can show the Task Pane by selecting View | Task Pane or by selecting CTRL-F1.

The Menu Bar

The menu bar at the top of the InfoPath window contains all the common Windows menus (File, Edit, and so on). Most of the features and functionality used when working with InfoPath can be found in those menus. Table 3-1 lists the various menus within InfoPath and describes the functionality of the commands they include.

Menu	Related Tasks
File	Design, fill out, save, print, merge, submit and export forms
Edit	Cut, copy, paste, select all items, undo, redo, find and replace objects
View	Control the Task Pane, toolbars, and other tools
Insert	Insert tables, lines, pictures, hyperlinks, and sections

TABLE 3-1 InfoPath 2003 Menus

Menu	Related Tasks
Format	Format fonts, bullets, numbering, borders, shading and objects
Tools	Check spelling, change language settings, show error messages, use digital signatures, program customization and options
Table	Insert and format tables
Help	Invoke help, Internet links, product activation, customer feedback, detect and repair

TABLE 3-1   InfoPath 2003 Menus

Toolbars

To make working with InfoPath a little easier, commonly used features have been organized into icons that appear on various toolbars.

> **NOTE** *The toolbars are also dockable so that you can move them around the InfoPath window by dragging and dropping them in place using the handle that appears on the left side of the toolbar.*

There are four toolbars available (Standard, Tables, Formatting, Task Pane) and you can control which toolbars appear by right-clicking in the menu bar and selecting the menu you want to see. Menus with a check mark are visible—those without are hidden.

> **NOTE** *Since this chapter focuses on filling out forms, it looks only at the Standard and Formatting toolbars. The chapters in which you actually design forms will discuss the features and functionalities contained in the other two toolbars.*

The Standard toolbar contains shortcuts to some of the most commonly used InfoPath features. Table 3-2 lists the different icons on this toolbar and what each is used for.

The Formatting toolbar is used to format the data you enter on a form—if you have used Microsoft Word and are familiar with formatting text, the formatting options are similar here. Table 3-3 lists all the icons in the Formatting toolbar and their use with Rich Text fields.

Button	Name	Description
	Fill Out a Form	Displays the Fill Out a Form view in the Task Pane, which allows you to select a form to complete
	Open	Displays the Open dialog form and allows you to open an InfoPath form from the file system or SharePoint server
	Save	Saves the current form
	Print	Prints the current form
	Print Preview	Displays a WYSIWYG preview of how the form will look when printed
	Spelling	Verifies the spelling of the data you have entered into a form
	Cut	Removes the selection to the Clipboard
	Copy	Duplicates the selection to the Clipboard
	Paste	Copies the content of the Clipboard
	Undo	Reverts to the state before you performed the last action
	Redo	Performs the last action again
	Insert Hyperlink	Adds hyperlinks to Rich Text Format (RTF) fields on your form
	Insert Table	Adds tables to Rich Text fields on your form
	Insert Picture	Adds pictures to Rich Text fields on your form
	Design This Form	Changes the "mode" to show the design of the form
	Digital Signatures	Adds digital signatures to your InfoPath forms
	Microsoft Office InfoPath Help	Opens the InfoPath Help in the Task Pane

TABLE 3-2 InfoPath 2003 Standard Toolbar Buttons

Button	Name	Description
	Font	Opens the Font view in the Task Pane
Verdana	Font Name	Changes the font name of the selected text
10	Font Size	Changes the font size of the selected text
B	Bold	Applies emphasis to the selected text
I	Italic	Italicizes the selected text
U	Underline	Underlines the selected text
	Align Left	Aligns the selected text block to the left
	Align Middle	Aligns the selected text block to the middle
	Align Right	Aligns the selected text block to the right
	Justify	Spreads the alignment of the selected text block evenly across the selected area
	Numbering	Creates a numbered list from the selected text
	Bullets	Creates a bulleted list from the selected text
	Decrease Indent	Removes space immediately preceding the selected text
	Increase Indent	Adds space immediately preceding the selected text
	Highlight	Changes the background color of the selected text
A	Font Color	Changes the color of the selected text

TABLE 3-3   InfoPath 2003 Formatting Toolbar Buttons

Opening InfoPath Forms

To open a blank InfoPath form for data entry, select File | Fill Out a Form, which changes the contents of the Task Pane to appear as shown here.

From the Task Pane, you are presented with a list of recently opened InfoPath forms from which you can pick, or you can select from the options immediately below this list to open an installed form or a form from your local drive or SharePoint server.

To open a blank InfoPath form, you can also select Fill Out a Form in the drop-down menu of the Task Pane or click the Fill Out a Form button on the Standard toolbar.

Opening an Installed Form

To open a form that has been installed on your computer (when InfoPath was installed or that was subsequently installed by an administrator), click the More Forms folder, which opens the dialog box shown in Figure 3-2.

Forms installed locally appear in this dialog box either under Custom Installed Forms, which is a listing of all the forms that have been installed on your machine, or Sample Forms, which lists the sample forms that ship with InfoPath 2003.

3

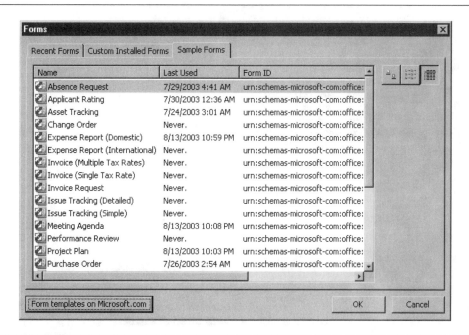

FIGURE 3-2   Opening an existing form

 The examples in this chapter show you how to fill out one of the sample forms that ships with InfoPath. If you want to follow the walk-throughs in the chapter, open the Expense Report (Domestic) sample form.

InfoPath includes a number of sample forms that you can use within your own organization or as a starting point for your own form design. For a complete list of all the sample forms that ship with InfoPath 2003, refer to Appendix A.

Opening a Form Saved Locally

To open a form that has been saved locally or is on a network drive, click the On My Computer icon that appears immediately below the Open a Form heading in the Task Pane. This opens a standard Open dialog box, as shown in Figure 3-3, which allows you to browse for the InfoPath form you would like to open. You can use the drop-down list to select the type of form you want to open.

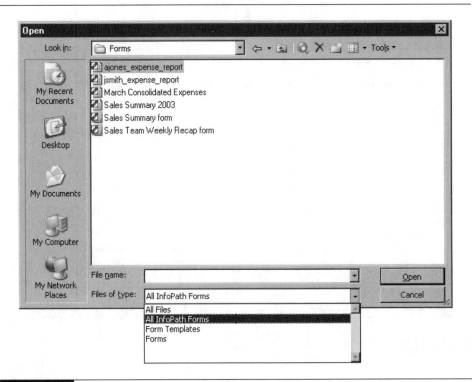

FIGURE 3-3   You can open both InfoPath form templates and forms with data.

To open an InfoPath form template, look for files with an .xsn file extension; to open a form that has data associated with it, look for an .xml file extension.

Opening a Form from SharePoint

Finally, if your organization uses SharePoint Portal Server to manage your InfoPath forms, you can open InfoPath forms directly from your SharePoint server by using the same Open dialog box. Click My Network Places in the lower-left corner and navigate to your SharePoint server location.

If you haven't configured a connection to your server, you need to use the Add a Network Place Wizard to specify the URL or your server, as well as a name for the connection. After you select your SharePoint server, you see a dialog box similar to the one shown in Figure 3-4 that allows you to navigate through the document libraries on your SharePoint server to locate the form you want to open.

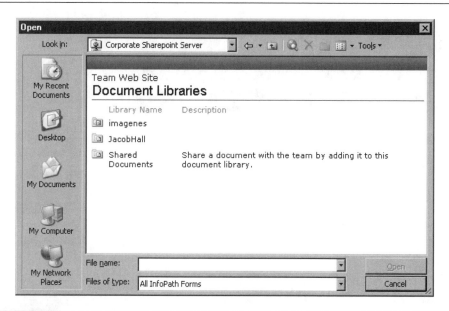

3

Navigate through your SharePoint server document libraries to find the form you want to use.

Filling Out InfoPath Forms

Invariably, every InfoPath form you fill out is going to be different, depending on how the form was created. In the following sections, you are going to be working with an Expense Report form, but the techniques you learn can be applied to any form you are working with.

When you first open a form in InfoPath, the form appears in the Main View and the Task Pane is hidden, as shown in Figure 3-5.

Entering Form Information

An InfoPath form can be made up of any number of different fields, including text boxes, drop-down boxes, date fields, and so on. The following sections describe how to work with these different types of fields and how to navigate between them.

Navigating Through the Form

You can navigate through the fields on an InfoPath form by using the TAB key to move sequentially from field to field or by using the arrow keys to navigate

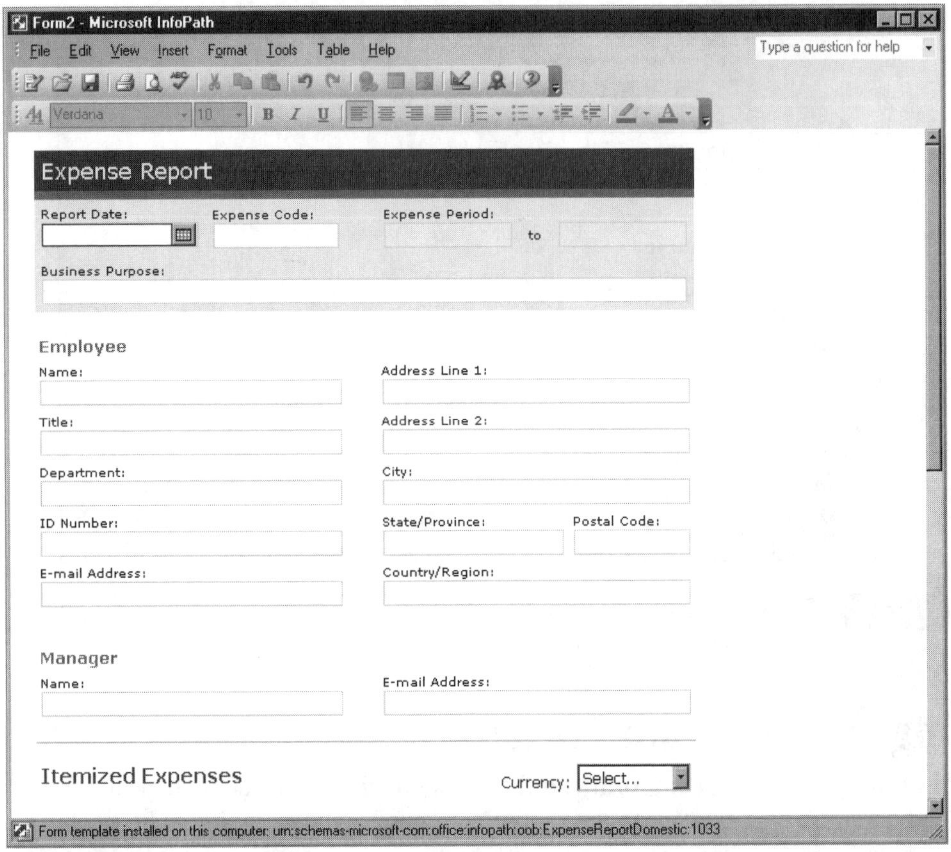

FIGURE 3-5 When you first open an InfoPath form to fill out, the Task Pane is hidden.

through the fields on your form. If you want to enter information in a specific field on the form and don't want to "hop" around using these methods, you can also just click directly in the field where you want to enter your data.

Changing Form Views

Forms within InfoPath can consist of any number of separate pages, which are called form views. When a developer creates an InfoPath form, they create these views to help organize fields, tables, and so on, into logical groupings.

When filling out a form, you can change the view you are working with by selecting the View menu. The different views that are available appear at the top of the menu, as shown in here.

In this example, there are three different views available: Main View, Comments, General Information, and Sales Data. To switch between the views, you can use the View menu, or some developers may also put a button on your form to change to a specific view. (In the form used in this chapter, there is only one view, so there is no option to select another view under the View menu.)

Entering Data

Entering text into InfoPath fields is easy—simply navigate to the field you want to use and use the keyboard to enter the information. All the standard Windows Clipboard shortcuts (Cut, Copy, Paste) and common work-processing features (like Find and Replace) work with InfoPath so that you can quickly move information around as required. If you do make a mistake, you can either correct it by editing the field you are working with or using the Undo functionality by selecting Edit | Undo.

> **NOTE** *You can also check the spelling of data that you enter into a form by selecting Tools | Spelling.*

There are some types of fields that have their own unique attributes. When a user clicks the calendar icon beside a date field, for example, it can display a pop-up calendar like the one shown here, which allows you to select a date instead of having to type it.

Similarly, some fields have drop-down lists that you can use to select information from a list. To open a drop-down list similar to the one shown in Figure 3-6, click the down arrow icon that appears to the right of the field. You can then click an item to select it.

Formatting Text

The majority of the fields you will work with on an InfoPath form are simple text boxes. Since text boxes are used for data entry, they don't have a lot of

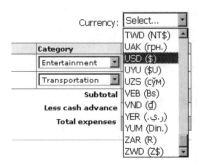

FIGURE 3-6   Drop-down lists provide a quick method of entering data.

formatting options. But your form may also include Rich Text boxes, which allow you to enter and format text, as shown here.

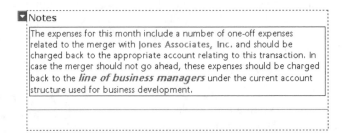

Working with Fonts

When working with a Rich Text box, you can control the fonts and formatting within the box by highlighting or selecting the text and using the options found in the Formatting toolbar to change the font name, size, and so on. You can also select Format | Font to open the Font view in the Task Pane, as shown in Figure 3-7.

You can format text by highlighting a section of text and changing individual properties or by applying one of the preformatted Styles to the text.

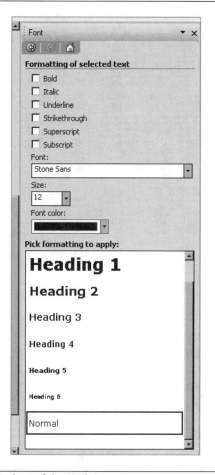

FIGURE 3-7 The Font view of the Task Pane

Using Bullets and Numbering

In addition to formatting the font, you can also format blocks of text by using bullets or numbering, similar to the formatting features that are available in Microsoft Word. To create a bulleted or numbered list, click within a Rich Text box and then select Format | Bullets and Numbering to open the Task Pane shown in Figure 3-8.

From the Task Pane, you can select a format by selecting one of the list styles, and then you can type in your Rich Text box as you normally would. To move to the next line (and number or bullet), press ENTER at the end of the line.

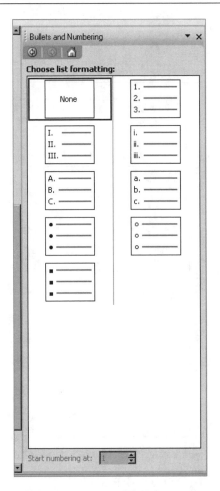

FIGURE 3-8   Select a format by clicking one of the list styles.

If you have an existing block of text within a Rich Text box that you would like to format, you can also highlight the text and use the same method to select the format you wish to apply.

Inserting Hyperlinks

You can also add hyperlinks to RTF boxes by placing your cursor where you want the hyperlink and then selecting Insert | Hyperlink to open the dialog box shown next.

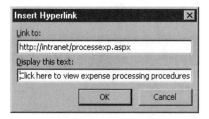

To create a hyperlink, enter the URL of the web site you want to link to (for example, www.microsoft.com), enter some text to be displayed (for example, "Click here to go to the Microsoft web site"), and then click OK. A hyperlink will be inserted into the text. When you click the link, the URL will be launched.

NOTE *To create a link to an e-mail address, use mailto:address@domain.com.*

Inserting Tables into Rich Text Boxes

Another way to organize text within a Rich Text box is to add a table and enter your text in the rows and columns. To insert a table, select Insert | Table and enter the number of rows and columns to be created. Once you have inserted a table into a Rich Text box, you can then format the table by right-clicking the table and selecting Table Properties from the right-click menu, as shown here.

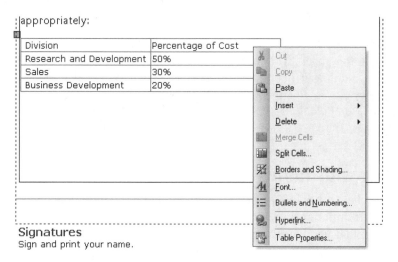

You can also use the right-click menu to insert and delete rows, merge and split cells, and set the borders and shading for your table.

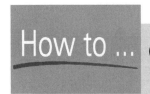 **Combine Text and Pictures**

You can add pictures or graphics to Rich Text boxes by selecting Insert | Picture and browsing for a graphic. InfoPath supports most of the standard graphic file formats, including WMF, BMP, GIF, PNG, TIF, EPS, and others.

To format pictures that you have inserted, right-click the picture and select Format Picture to open the dialog box shown here.

You can then select the alignment for your graphic, as well as the graphic size and any alternate text to be displayed. For better control over the placement of images and the surrounding text, consider placing your graphic into a table. This allows you to evenly space the images and text using the rows and columns provided.

Working with Tables

So far, this chapter has looked at entering data into individual fields on your form that have a 1:1 relationship with the form itself. For example, in the Expense Report form that you have been working with, the fields at the top of the form only appear once, as shown in Figure 3-9.

This is by design, because an expense report is usually submitted by an individual who has a single e-mail address, manager, and so forth. But what about fields that you want to repeat on a form? For example, in the Itemized Expense

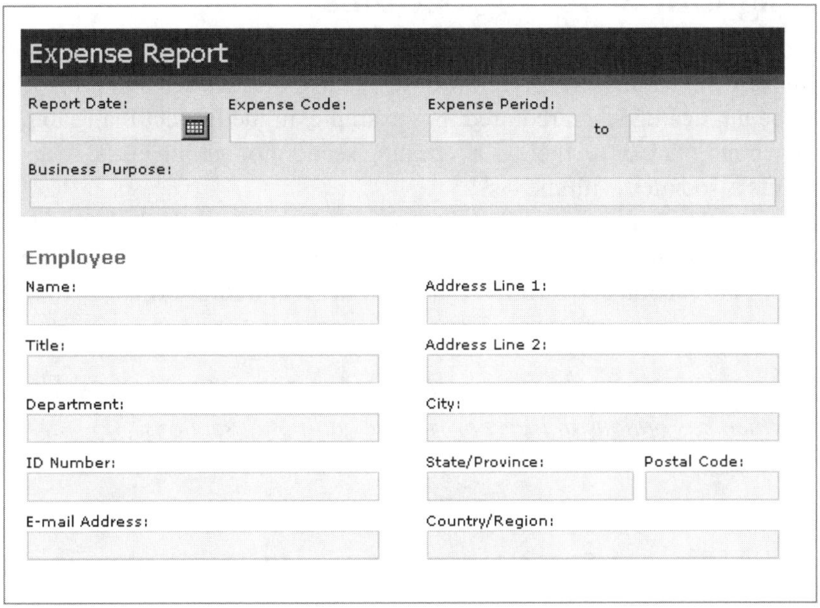

Expense Report

Report Date: Expense Code: Expense Period: to

Business Purpose:

Employee

Name: Address Line 1:

Title: Address Line 2:

Department: City:

ID Number: State/Province: Postal Code:

E-mail Address: Country/Region:

FIGURE 3-9   1 relationship with the form

section of the form, you would want to put all of your expenses—you may have
one expense item or 20. To help create flexible forms that can accommodate
multiple items, InfoPath developers sometimes create forms with repeating tables,
like the one shown here.

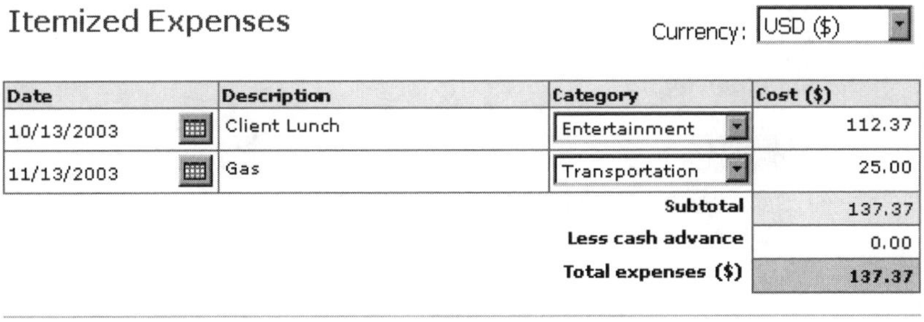

Itemized Expenses   Currency: USD ($)

Date	Description	Category	Cost ($)
10/13/2003	Client Lunch	Entertainment	112.37
11/13/2003	Gas	Transportation	25.00
		Subtotal	137.37
		Less cash advance	0.00
		Total expenses ($)	137.37

Most repeating tables have a drop-down menu that appears on the left side of
the form and allows you to add or delete rows to your table. This allows you to
enter additional lines as required.

Working with Repeating Sections

In addition to repeating tables, you can also have repeating sections within an InfoPath form. repeating sections allow developers to create a section of the form that can be duplicated when required. For example, in the Project Plan sample form shown in Figure 3-10, there is a repeating section for adding tasks, with a set of fields associated with the task.

To add another task, you can use the drop-down menu on the left to add another section immediately below the current task. The new section will repeat the fields in the section and allow you to enter the required information for the next task.

> **NOTE** *Like tables, you control repeating sections through the drop-down menu, which has options to insert or remove additional sections.*

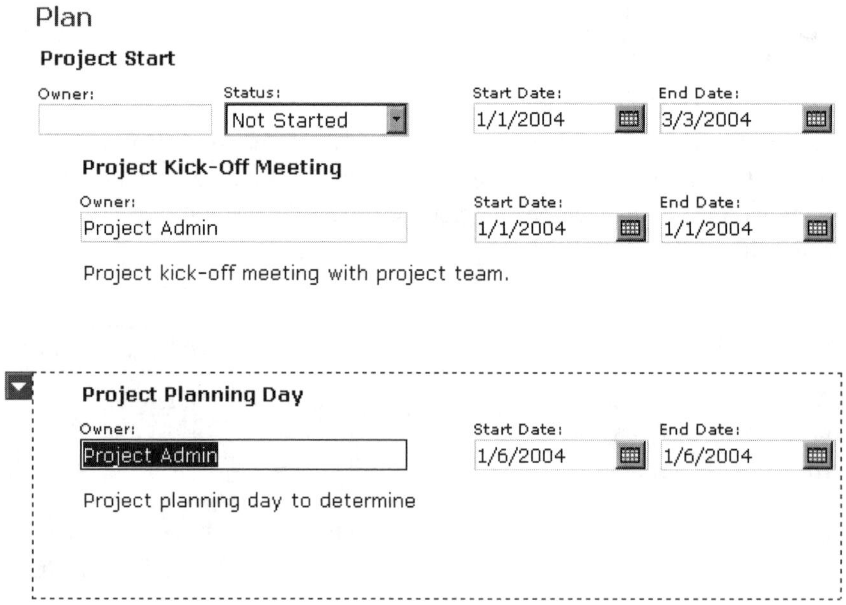

Plan
Project Start

Owner:	Status:	Start Date:	End Date:
	Not Started ▾	1/1/2004 ▦	3/3/2004 ▦

Project Kick-Off Meeting

Owner:	Start Date:	End Date:
Project Admin	1/1/2004 ▦	1/1/2004 ▦

Project kick-off meeting with project team.

▾ **Project Planning Day**

Owner:	Start Date:	End Date:
Project Admin	1/6/2004 ▦	1/6/2004 ▦

Project planning day to determine

FIGURE 3-10   A typical repeating section

Working with Optional Sections

Another InfoPath feature allows you to mark sections as optional when designing the form. This allows InfoPath developers to place additional sections in your form—when filling out the form, these sections appear collapsed as a single line with a small arrow icon, as shown here.

Involvement in various activities	○	○	○	○	○	◉
Effective time management	○	○	○	○	○	◉
Interest in continued learning	○	○	○	○	○	◉

Average rating

○ Click here to insert the Clerical Skills section

○ Click here to insert the Managerial Skills section

○ Click here to insert the Technical Skills section

If you want to complete the optional section, you can click the icon or line to open the section and enter data as you normally would, as shown here.

Involvement in various activities	○	○	○	○	○	◉
Effective time management	○	○	○	○	○	◉
Interest in continued learning	○	○	○	○	○	◉

Average rating

Clerical Skills	1	2	3	4	5	n/a
Typing and data entry	○	○	○	○	○	◉
10-Key calculator	○	○	○	○	○	◉
Shorthand	○	○	○	○	○	◉
Communication skills	○	○	○	○	○	◉
Computer skills	○	○	○	○	○	◉

Average rating

○ Click here to insert the Managerial Skills section

○ Click here to insert the Technical Skills section

Saving InfoPath Forms

Once you have completed the data entry on your form, you can save your InfoPath form with data by selecting File | Save. This creates an XML file that contains both the form and the data you have entered. You can then send the file to other users, import the data from your XML file into other systems, and so on.

> NOTE *InfoPath forms can also be directly tied into a data source or back-end process, which would allow you to submit the information directly to the database or process. You'll look at how to submit forms using these methods in Chapter 5.*

Printing InfoPath Forms

One of the strengths of InfoPath is that it can be used to create presentation-quality forms that can be printed and distributed. Going back to the sample Expense Report, there is a section at the bottom of the form for the employee and manager signature to authorize the expense. By printing this form, you could get the signatures required and still send the electronic copy of the file to the accounts department for processing.

> NOTE *Saving and sending InfoPath forms are discussed in upcoming sections.*

The following section details some of the printing options within InfoPath as well as how to preview and print your form.

Page Setup

To control the paper size, orientation, margins, and so on, used when you print your form, select File | Page Setup to open the dialog box shown in Figure 3-11. You can then use the drop-down lists to specify your choices.

By default, the margins are set to .75, and any settings changes that you make here will not affect the form's design—these options are for printing the form only.

Previewing a Form

To see what your form will look like when printed, select File | Print Preview, which opens the window shown in Figure 3-12.

3

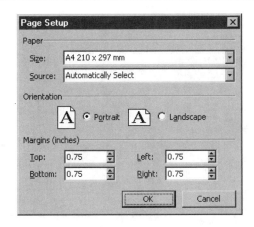

FIGURE 3-11   Page setup options

FIGURE 3-12   The Print Preview window

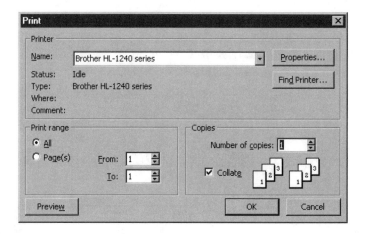

FIGURE 3-13 Print options

You can print your form directly from the Print Preview window, navigate through pages, zoom to sections of the form, and so on, by using the toolbar provided at the top of the window.

Printing a Form

You can also print your form without first previewing it by clicking the Print icon in the toolbar—this prints the form to your default printer. If you want to select a printer, which pages to print, collation options, and the number of copies, select File | Print to open the dialog box shown in Figure 3-13.

Distributing InfoPath Forms

Another way to distribute your InfoPath form is to export it to another file format. This option comes in very handy if you want to distribute information entered into a form to users who may not have InfoPath installed on their machine.

Exporting to a Web Page

InfoPath provides an HTML export facility to allow users to view your form and data in a web browser. To export your form, navigate to the Form View you would like to export and select File | Export To | Web to open the dialog box shown in Figure 3-14.

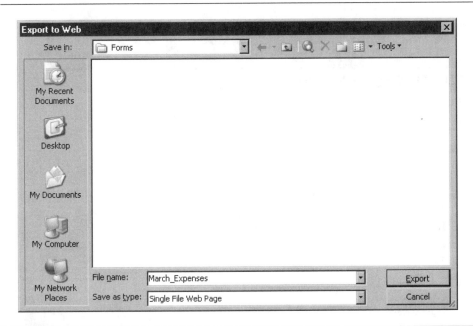

FIGURE 3-14   To export your form and data, enter a filename and location and click OK.

You need to specify a filename for your exported form, and when you click OK, your form will be exported to a single HTML file that you can then view in your web browser, as shown in Figure 3-15.

Exporting to Excel

In addition to HTML, you can also export the data from an InfoPath form to Excel for further analysis and consolidation.

This feature requires Excel 2003 or later to be installed.

To export to Excel, navigate to the Form View you want to export and select File | Export To | Microsoft Excel to open the Export to Excel Wizard, shown in Figure 3-16.

After you click Next, the first step of the wizard is used to determine what type of data you would like to export. You have two choices. If you select the option for Form Fields Only, the data held in fields on your InfoPath form will be exported

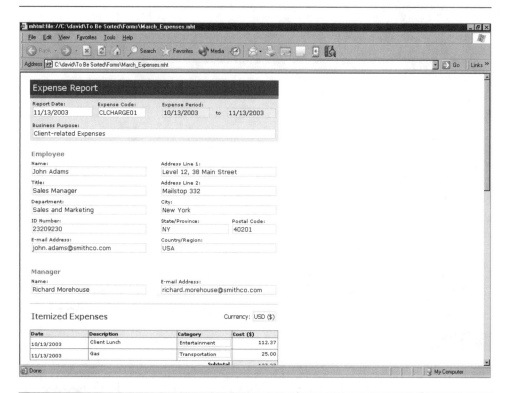

FIGURE 3-15 An InfoPath form exported to HTML

without any of the information held within tables or lists that may also appear on your form. For example, from the Expense Report form that you have been working with in this chapter, only the information at the top of the form (name, address, and so on) would be exported, and the expense information in the table below would not.

The second option, Form Fields and This Table or List, allows you to export the data held in fields, as well as from the table or list you have selected.

Once you have made your selection, click Next to proceed to the next step in the wizard, shown in Figure 3-17, where you select the fields to be exported.

Use the check boxes to select the fields to be exported and then click Next to continue. The last step of the Export to Excel Wizard is to select additional forms to be exported. By default, the Export to Excel Wizard exports data from the form you are working with, but you can specify additional forms, which allows the wizard to combine data from many different InfoPath forms into one Excel file.

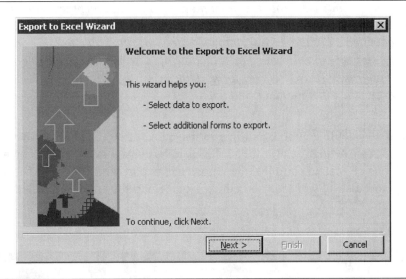

FIGURE 3-16   The Export to Excel Wizard

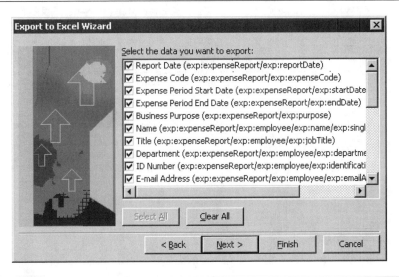

FIGURE 3-17   Select the fields you want to export.

NOTE *You can only combine data from the same InfoPath form template. For example, if you had Expense Reports from multiple employees, you could combine all of these forms into one Excel file, but you can't mix and match forms; for example, you can't combine data from an Expense Report with data from a Leave Request form. (Otherwise, InfoPath doesn't know where to put the different fields and data.)*

If you do want to combine multiple forms, click the Add and Remove buttons to add and remove additional InfoPath forms to be consolidated. When you are finished, click Finish to complete the wizard and export your data to Excel. The resulting spreadsheet will look something like the one shown in Figure 3-18.

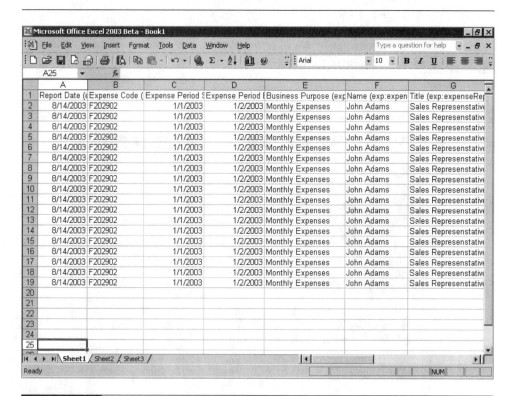

FIGURE 3-18 An InfoPath form exported to Excel

Sending an InfoPath Form via E-mail

For sending forms via e-mail, InfoPath features a tight integration with Outlook 2003 that allows you to send an InfoPath form as the body of an e-mail message with the InfoPath form file attached. The recipient can see the InfoPath form in the e-mail and, if they have InfoPath installed, can open and work with the attached form file.

To send your form, select File | Send to Mail Recipient to open the dialog box shown in Figure 3-19.

Enter the e-mail address or alias of the recipient as well as a subject for your e-mail message and introduction—the introduction can include instructions on what to do with the form (for example, "Please review and send back with comments") or notes that you want to pass along with the form. When you are finished entering this information, click the Send button to send your form.

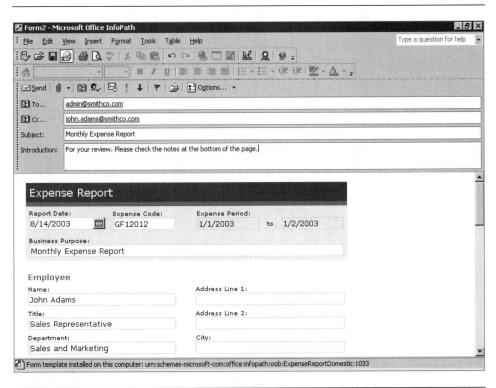

FIGURE 3-19   E-mail options dialog box

Summary

This chapter looked at forms from the end user's perspective, from filling out forms and working with different sections of a form all the way to saving and distributing your form. With the basics out of the way, you need to look at how to actually customize or create an InfoPath form, which is what you will start to look at in the next chapter.

Part II

Design Forms

Chapter 4

Get Started with Forms

How to...

■ Design a form

■ Create a simple form using InfoPath

■ Format forms you have created

■ Preview and save forms

Now that you have seen what the end user will experience when using InfoPath, it's time to get your hands dirty and start creating some InfoPath forms of your own. This chapter first looks at the form design process. It then moves on to show how to create a simple InfoPath form that can be used to save the data entered into an XML file. This chapter provides you with the opportunity to look at some of the commonly used features and formatting techniques, and sets the stage for later chapters that delve deeper into specific areas within InfoPath.

As you go through this chapter, you are going to walk through the process of creating an Employee Information form that can be used to collect information such as the employee's name, address, e-mail, and so on. By the time you reach the end of the chapter, you should have the basic skills needed to create and distribute your own InfoPath forms.

Form Design Overview

To create forms that integrate with your existing systems and databases and meet end-user requirements (and before you actually sit down in front of the computer and start designing forms with InfoPath), you need to design your form and have some idea of what the finished product will look like. The form design process has the following six basic phases, each of which is described in turn in the sections that follow:

1. Defining the concept

2. Determining the processing model

3. Sourcing the data

4. Creating the design

5. Developing and testing the design

6. Deploying and operating the form

Defining the Concept

Because InfoPath is a relatively new software application, many developers and users are unsure of how it will be used within their own organization. That's why the first step in the form design process is critical—if you can define the concept of what information the form will collect and then can extend that to how the information will be used, users will have a better understanding of how InfoPath fits into your organization and developers will have a concept to work toward when creating their own forms.

How do you define the concept for a form? How is InfoPath used? How *can* it be used? A good starting point for these types of discussions is with the sample forms that ship with InfoPath. The sample forms can be viewed by selecting File | Fill Out a Form and then clicking the More Forms option in the Fill Out a Form view in the Task Pane. This opens a list of installed and sample forms, as shown in Figure 4-1.

The sample forms are provided within InfoPath to give you some idea of the types of applications that InfoPath can be used for and to give you a starting point for your own development. Before you continue with the design process, take time to look through these samples. Perhaps a sample will give you an idea of where

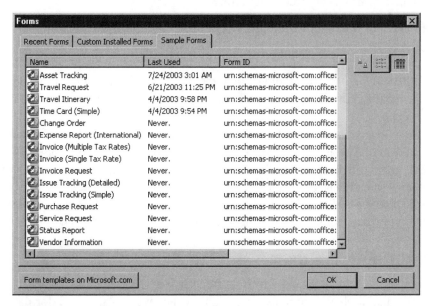

you could apply a similar concept or perhaps you will find forms you can use with your own systems or databases.

Once you have a good understanding of the capabilities within InfoPath, you can then tackle your first form. It may be a form you need to create for your own use or a form requested by another user.

To ensure that you understand other users' form requests, spend some time interviewing them to find out what information they would like to gather using the form. A good way to get them thinking about what their form could look like is to bring along printed copies of the sample or existing forms currently in use. This could be forms that were previously completed in hard copy, electronic forms, or forms in existing systems or applications that are used to enter or gather information.

When you are interviewing users for their requirements, there is no group of questions set in stone that you should ask every time, but the following list should help you to gather the information you need to complete your form design:

- Who will use this form?

- What is the purpose of the form? (To gather information, consolidate, and so forth.)

- Will this form replace an existing form or process? If so, what does that form or process currently look like?

- What information would you like to see in the form?

- What is the title of the form?

- What type of form should be generated? (A simple field-based form, repeating rows or columns, a multipage form, and so on.)

After you have interviewed the users and understand what they would like to see in a form, the easiest way to develop and communicate this concept is to create a prototype, or mock-up, of the form that you wish to create. You can use a word processor, a spreadsheet, or the low-tech option of pen and paper, but you should try to make the prototype of your form as complete as possible. This will help you later when you are trying to determine whether the form that you wish to create is feasible.

Determining the Processing Model

After you have met with the users who will actually be using the form and understand what information they want to capture and how they want to use the information entered, the next step is to select a processing model for how the form will be processed. There are a number of different ways you can deploy InfoPath forms depending on your own needs. The following is a list of some of the most popular methods of processing InfoPath forms:

- **XML file**   Using this method, you can create forms that can be saved to an XML file and used with a variety of systems and databases.

- **Consolidated XML file**   Using this method, users would consolidate the data from multiple InfoPath forms into a single XML file.

- **Database integration**   You can also create forms that submit the information entered directly into a database, eliminating the need to save and process an XML file.

- **Web Service**   Using this method, you could create a web service that could be used to capture information entered into a form or return data to a form.

Keep in mind that this section only lists a few of the ways that InfoPath can be used—there is also broad scope for creating workflow applications and integrating InfoPath with SharePoint, BizTalk Server, and other applications or systems.

Did you know?

The "silo" approach

Out of the four popular processing methods listed, the two for working with XML files and consolidated XML files are the easiest and don't require any additional work on the database, nor any need to develop a web service to collect and aggregate information. Users can use this information in other systems or export it to Excel for their own analysis. This "silo" approach to InfoPath could mean that you have a number of disparate forms in use around the organization, so if you do have the support to create and maintain an Access or SQL Server database, it is probably a good idea to have your InfoPath forms submit the data directly into the database.

If you do have developers within your organization who are experienced working with Web Services or if you want to push information directly into other database systems or applications (for example, Oracle, DB2, and so on), the web service method might be the best.

For more information on working with SharePoint, check out Chapter 11.

Sourcing the Data

After you have decided how your InfoPath form will be processed, it is time to look at where the data for your form resides. You don't necessarily need to have an existing XML file or data source to create an InfoPath form (as you will see in this chapter), but if you are planning to create a form that pushes information directly into a database, you probably want to have a look at the database schema to determine which tables will be used in your form and how the data will be submitted to the database. Some developers prefer to have InfoPath write data to a specific set of tables that are separate from their core systems and then run an import process to update the correct database tables, whereas other developers may allow InfoPath forms to directly update core tables. At this point, you need to sit down with your database or systems administrator and talk about where the data from this form will reside and how it will be handled once it has been submitted to the database.

Also, if you want to push data into another database format besides Access or SQL Server, you need to work out who will create the web service that will accept your data and find out what input they are expecting from you.

NOTE *Microsoft has provided a number of Visual Studio .NET samples for InfoPath that will help developers who are familiar with web services to get started designing applications to interface to InfoPath forms. You can find these technical resources at www.microsoft.com/infopath.*

Creating the Design

After you create a prototype and determine your data source, the next step is to design the form. You must be asking yourself at this point whether this is where you get to use InfoPath. The answer is "No." The best form design is one that is completed first on paper and then re-created using InfoPath. During the design phase, you want to revisit your prototype form and, given what you now know about the database, indicate which of the fields on your form are going to come from the database, which are going to need to be validated, and what criteria are to be used in those validations.

You should also have a good idea about how the data is organized and be able to determine what grouping and sorting is required, as well as which records to select to get the results you need.

Developing and Testing the Design

With the design completed on paper, it is time to open InfoPath and get down to business. After you have laid the groundwork, the actual form design process should be quick and simple, after you learn the skills in the upcoming chapters. After the initial form development is complete, you should test your form on a number of different computers or operating systems. Note any performance issues and revisit your form design to see if you can make any performance enhancements.

If you have created a form that validates user input, try entering bad dates, the same date, incorrect text, and so on to view the error messages that will appear. You need to be prepared to handle any situation that a user may encounter.

Deploying and Operating the Form

As the final step in the form design process, consider how your form is going to be used. Will users access the form locally? How does the data captured in the form translate when you export to Microsoft Excel or HTML? Try to export the form yourself. You may need to revisit your form design based on the results of your exporting attempts.

Will users be able to modify the form? Have you locked the form design for changes? Again, you may need to modify the form design based on these answers.

Finally, when the form is in production, you need to monitor the operation of the form to ensure that it performs as expected and that the form is still relevant. Many organizations think that creating a form stops when the form is handed to its user. To the contrary, the form design process should be ongoing throughout the life cycle of the form and should continually analyze ways to enhance the information captured and to add additional value to the data.

An easy way to learn how to develop a form prototype is to jump right in and tackle an existing form request. If you are creating the form on behalf of someone else, there may be a little extra work spent interviewing the user and making sure the form prototype meets their needs, but it is definitely time well spent. If you ensure that the user is happy with the form's design before you begin, there will be no surprises when you deliver the final product.

Creating a New Blank Form

To create a new InfoPath form, select File | Design a Form to open the Design
a Form view in the Task Pane, as shown in Figure 4-2.

In this chapter, you are concentrating on basic form-building skills, so select
the option for New Blank Form, which opens a blank form within the InfoPath
designer, as shown in Figure 4-3.

This method of creating a form does not rely on an underlying data source—
you are actually going to build the required fields and structure for the data entered
as you go along.

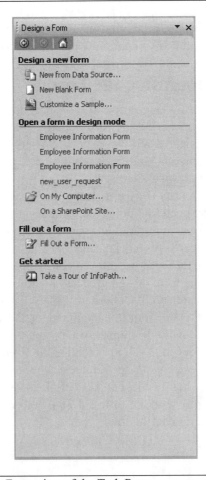

FIGURE 4-2   Design a Form view of the Task Pane

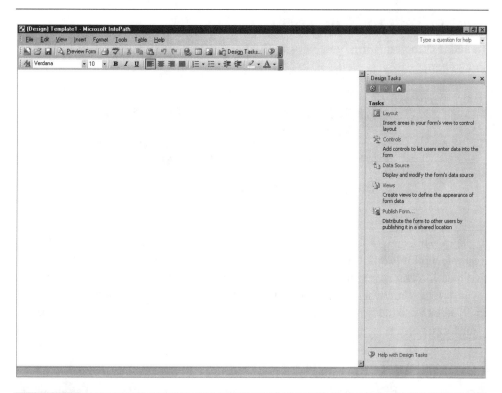

FIGURE 4-3   A new blank form

TIP   *If you are planning to build forms to populate data into a database (Access, SQL Server, and so on) from an existing XML file or schema or through a web service, don't worry—both of these methods are covered in Chapter 5.*

Working with the InfoPath Designer

If you have ever worked with a WYSIWYG web development tool, the InfoPath designer will seem familiar. When working with a form, you can type directly on the form and add text, controls, pictures, horizontal lines, tables, and more. In addition to these features, InfoPath also makes extensive use of layout tables to organize content and control the positioning of objects on your form. Even if you don't have any experience working with other web development tools, you should be able to create forms quickly and easily with the skills you'll pick up in the following sections.

Adding Text to Your Form

To add text to your form, you can simply type the text directly onto your form, as shown here.

For your example form, you need to add a title for the form; for purposes of this example, call it Employee Information Form. InfoPath will automatically wrap the text that you enter, or you can press ENTER to move to the next line. You can use all the standard Windows shortcuts (Cut, Copy, Paste, and so forth) within InfoPath, and you can use the Find and Replace functionality to quickly replace text within your form.

Formatting Text

To format text on your InfoPath form, you can use the Formatting toolbar shown in the following illustration to select the formatting attributes you would like to apply to your text.

In addition to the options on the toolbar, you can also highlight a selection of text, right-click your selection, and select the Font option. This opens the Font pane on the right side of the window, allowing you to select the font name, size, color, and so on for the text you have entered.

In your example form, highlight the title and make the font Arial at a size of 18 points so that your form looks something like the form shown in Figure 4-4.

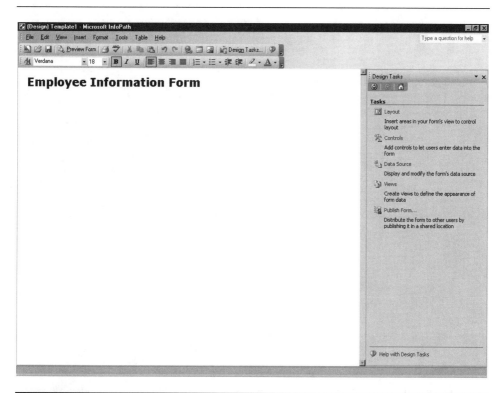

FIGURE 4-4   The example form with the formatted title

Adding Controls to Your Form

The majority of the content of your form is going to be taken up with fields that will be used for data entry, similar to the finished form shown in Figure 4-5. In this section, you are going to discover how to add these fields to your form and work with them.

The form shown in Figure 4-7 has a number of fields that have been added to capture information about the employee, including the employee's name, address, and so forth. The majority of this information is entered using a simple text box, but you can develop InfoPath forms that use several of different types of fields. In InfoPath, these fields are called *controls*.

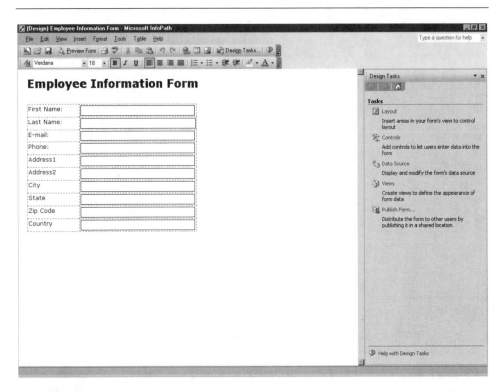

FIGURE 4-5 The finished form

> TIP
>
> *This chapter looks at only a few basic types of controls. More advanced techniques for working with controls are presented in Chapter 7.*

To add controls to a form, select Insert | More Controls to open the Controls view of the Task Pane, shown in Figure 4-6.

To insert a control onto your form, simply click within your document where you would like to place the control and then click the name of the control in the list that appears in the Task Pane. Alternately, you could also drag a control from the list and drop it into position on your form.

> TIP
>
> *If you want to add some extra space in between fields, use the ENTER key to move down a line.*

Controls view of the Task Pane

Because you are creating an example form to capture employee details, you want to add controls (or fields) to capture the employee's first name, last name, address, and other information. But before you get into that, you need to look at the design of your form. If you were to start typing labels for all the fields that you want to use and then adding the controls to your form in "free-form" fashion, it wouldn't look very organized, as shown in Figure 4-7.

Fortunately, InfoPath enables you to use some of the same tricks that are available in web development tools to help you organize your form layout. Most InfoPath forms use a feature called a layout table to help organize headings, controls,

FIGURE 4-7   A form created with "free-form" placement

and so on, and to give the forms a more uniform, well-spaced layout. A layout table is an invisible table within your form that is used to position objects within the form, as shown in Figure 4-8.

You'll actually take an in-depth look at working with tables in Chapter 8, but for now you are going to insert a simple layout table to keep your first form looking good. To insert a layout table, select Insert | Layout Table to open the dialog box shown here.

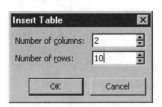

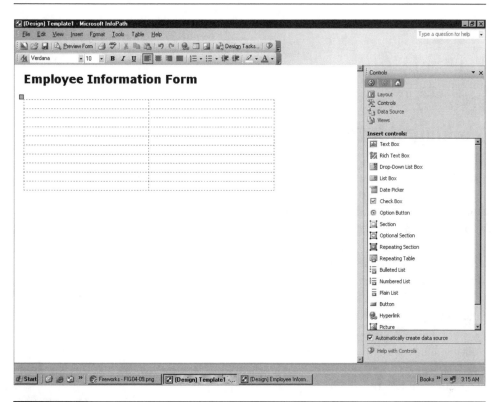

FIGURE 4-8   An example of a layout table

Since you are going to create a form that has ten fields of data to enter, create a table that has two columns and ten rows. One of the columns will be for the field label and the other column will be for the field object itself. Once you have created a layout table, you can then start entering the text labels in the first column and place text box objects in the second column. You should add the following labels and corresponding text boxes:

- First Name
- Last Name
- Address1
- Address2

- City
- State
- ZIP Code
- Country

Working with Control Properties

Now that you have added all the labels and text box controls to your form, you
need to look at how to work with these objects. You may have noticed that as you
added text boxes to your form, InfoPath automatically numbered and named these
boxes (such as field1, field2). If you were to leave these fields with their current
naming convention, these names would be used to describe the data that was entered
on the form. Clearly, you need to change these names to reflect the data that is being
entered. To change the name and set other field properties, right-click a field
directly and select Text Box Properties to open the dialog box shown in Figure 4-9.

When working with text boxes or other objects, you can enter a field name and
select the data type and any default values for the field. The field name itself should
be something descriptive (for example, first_name) and should not include spaces or
special characters. You can use the Data Type drop-down list shown in Figure 4-9 to
select a data type for your field; for your example form, you are going to select Text
for all of your text boxes.

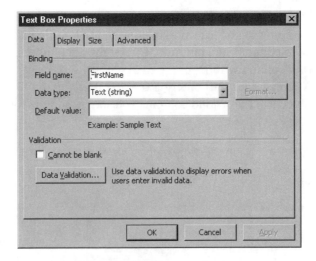

FIGURE 4-9   Text Box Properties dialog box

TIP   *If you are interested in learning about the other types of fields and how they are used, flip ahead to Chapter 7.*

You can also enter in the Default Value text box a default value that will appear in the field when the form is filled out. You can use the check box at the bottom of the dialog box to require this field to be completed.

You could use this method to rename and set the options for all of your fields, but there is also an easier method that you can use to quickly change multiple fields. To see the fields that you have created when creating your form, select View | Data Source to open the Data Source view of the Task Pane, shown in Figure 4-10.

4

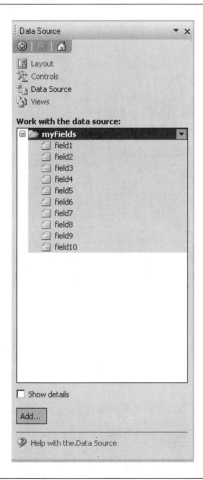

FIGURE 4-10   Data Source view of the Task Pane

You can use the Data Source view to quickly select and rename fields that appear on your form. By default, these fields have been placed into a group called myFields, so you probably want to rename the group as well to something more descriptive (for instance, Employee_Information). When you are finished updating your fields, the Data Sources view should look something like Figure 4-11.

Now when a user saves or exports the form data, it will be labeled correctly and the fields can be mapped to other database formats or systems for import. With the basic form design out of the way, you need to look at how to preview your form.

 *You can also validate information that is entered into forms, which is covered in Chapter 9.*

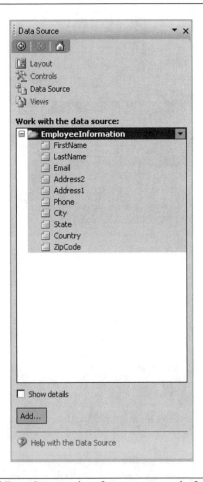

FIGURE 4-11   Updated Data Source view for your example form

Previewing a Form

Previewing is an important part of the form design process, because it enables you to see the form as the user will see it when filling out the form. To preview your form, select File | Preview Form | Default, which opens a separate window like the one shown in Figure 4-12.

    This preview is exactly what the end user will see, and you can fill out the form in the preview to see exactly how the form will be used.

Previewing a Blank Form

By default, when you preview your form, it will be shown as a blank form, with no data in any of the fields. This can be helpful during the design process, because it allows you to enter information and test any validation criteria you may have added to fields and test buttons, hyperlinks, scripting, and so on.

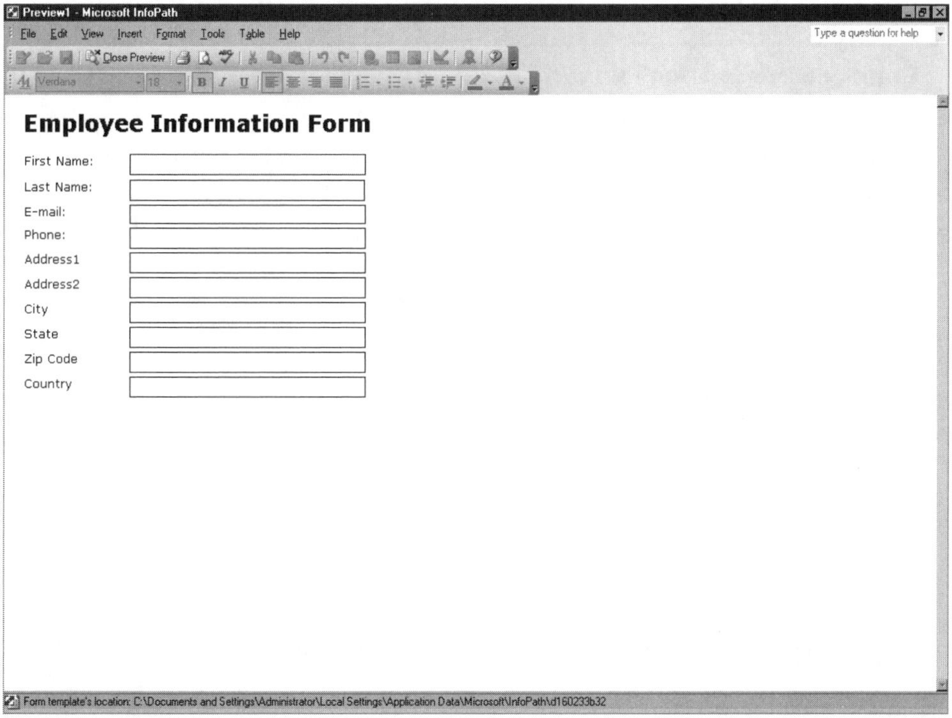

FIGURE 4-12   A preview of your example form

Previewing a Form with Data

If you would like to see what the form looks like with data (and you don't want to enter the data yourself), InfoPath also has the option to preview the form using some sample data. To set up this feature, save your form using File | Save and then open the form and enter any data you would like to use for your sample data. Next, select File | Save to save your form data. For this example, call this file **sample_employee.xml**.

To preview using this data file, select File | Preview | With Data File, which opens the dialog box shown in Figure 4-13 and allows you to select the file you just created with your sample form data.

Your form will then be previewed using the data contained within this file, allowing you to see what the form will look like when filled out, without having to enter the data every time yourself.

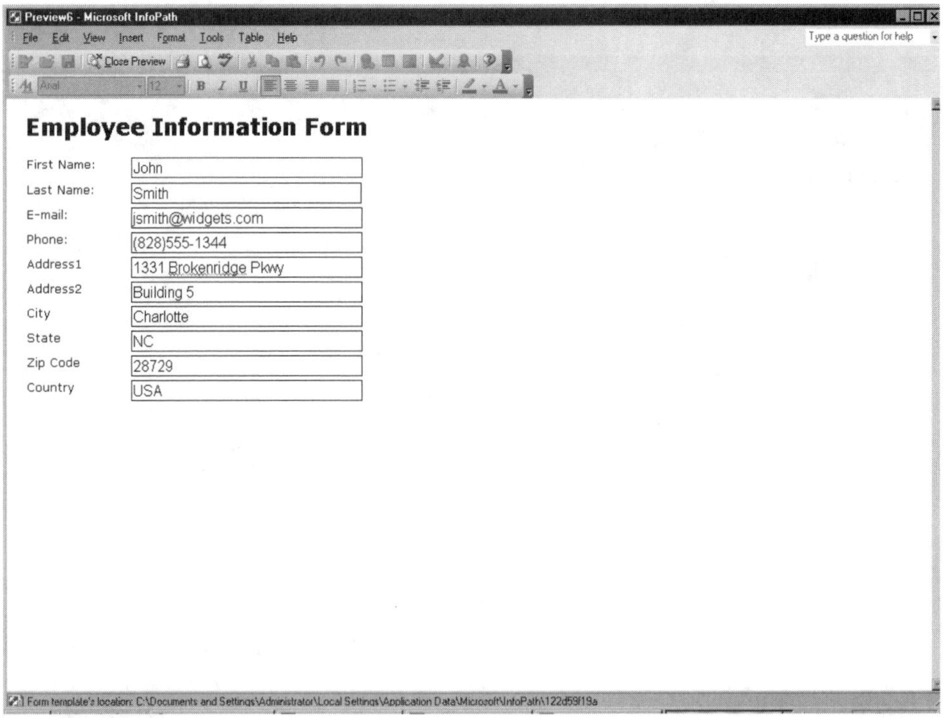

FIGURE 4-13   A preview with data

You can run into errors using this functionality if you are continually updating your form. Each time you make a change to the form's structure, fields, and so on, you need to save a new sample data file. Otherwise, you will receive an error when you try to preview a form with a sample data file that doesn't match the current design.

Saving Your Form

If you are satisfied with your form design, it is time to save your form for distribution. To save the form you have been working on, select File | Save to open the dialog box shown here.

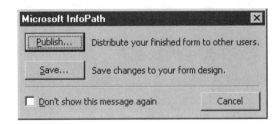

You have two choices at this point: You can either publish the form to be used by other users or save changes to your form design. Since you are creating a simple form that you will be not be sending to other users, select the option to Save, which opens a standard Save As dialog box like the one shown in Figure 4-14.

Use the Change Name button to enter a title for your form, and then enter a filename and location and click Save to save your form. The form will be saved as an InfoPath form template with an .XSN extension.

    For more information on other methods of publishing forms, check out Chapter 11.

Now you can distribute your finished form to other InfoPath users. They can use the techniques from the previous chapter to complete the form and save the form data as XML, export it to Excel or HTML, or consolidate data from multiple forms for analysis.

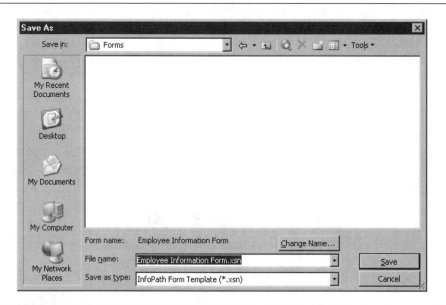

FIGURE 4-14   Saving options

Summary

Now that you have created your first form, you should have a better feel for how the InfoPath designer works and you should be ready to start gathering requirements from users and building your own simple forms. While the techniques covered in this chapter provide the basis for the rest of the tasks you'll be learning throughout the book, the example you walked through was very simple, resulting in a single XML file that contained the data that was entered. While this will be a popular way to use InfoPath, one of the product's strengths is the ability to push data into a database or other data source. That's what you will look at in the next chapter.

Chapter 5

Work with Data Sources

How to...

- Create forms from an existing XML schema or file

- Create forms from an existing SQL Server or Access databases

- Create forms from XML web services

Chapter 4 walked you through the process of creating your first InfoPath form—the method you used was to build the form on-the-fly, whereby you built the form based on your requirements, with no preexisting data source. While this provides an easy method to get started with InfoPath, the most common use of InfoPath is to populate an existing database or data source.

In this chapter, you are going to look at how to create InfoPath forms that can "push" data into different data sources, starting with forms created from an existing XML file, moving through to forms that submit data to Microsoft SQL Server or Access databases, and finishing off with forms that are submitted to a web service. At the end of the chapter, you should be able to create your own simple forms that can connect and submit data to these different types of data sources.

Creating Forms from Existing XML Schemas or Files

Most popular relational databases and applications can use XML files to import and export files. As you saw in Chapter 2, XML provides a nearly "universal" format for data exchange, combining the data itself with a descriptive tag language that can be used to define the data as well.

When working with InfoPath, you can use an existing XML schema or file as the source of your form. This functionality enables you to create forms that can be used with a wide variety of back-end systems. A common scenario might be one in which an application developer is working on a new system to process expenses within your organization and wants to use InfoPath to capture expense report information. In such a scenario, the application developer could provide to you an example XML schema or file that contains the structure and data that the developer is expecting to receive. You could then base your InfoPath form on the structure contained within the schema or file to ensure that your InfoPath form could collect the required information.

To see this in action, this section walks you through an example in which you build an InfoPath form from an existing XML file. The form that you are going to create will be used to collect employee details and is based off of employees.xml, which is one of the sample XML files that is available with the download file that accompanies this book, available from www.osborne.com.

To create your form from an existing XML file, open InfoPath and select File | Design a Form to open the Design a Form view in the Task Pane. From the options under Design a New Form, select New from Data Source to open the Data Source Setup Wizard, shown in Figure 5-1, which you use to create new InfoPath forms from existing data sources.

In this instance, you are using the wizard to create a form from an existing XML file, so select the XML Schema or XML Data File option and click Next to continue to the window shown in Figure 5-2.

Click the Browse button to locate the XML file you want to use as the basis of your form. In this example, you are creating a form from a sample XML file that is available with the download files for this chapter. Locate where you saved the files from this file and select the employees.xml file. After you have selected the file, click OK to return to the wizard and then click Finish to complete the wizard.

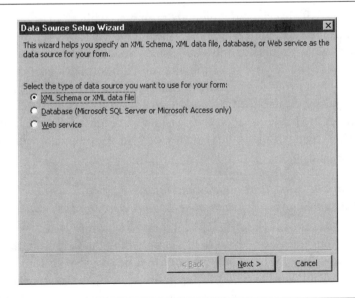

FIGURE 5-1   The Data Source Setup Wizard's opening page

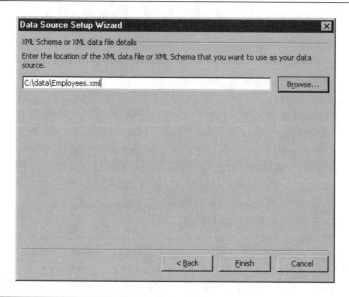

FIGURE 5-2 Identifying the XML data file to use as the data source

If your XML file has data in it, you are prompted with a dialog box asking if you want to use the data within the file as the default data for your form. Select Yes to preview your form using this data; select No to discard the data.

After you have made your selection, the InfoPath form designer opens and allows you to create your form as you normally would. Unlike your first form, in which you actually created the fields on-the-fly, with an existing XML schema or file, these fields are predefined for you, as shown in Figure 5-3. The Data Source view of the Task Pane displays the structure of your data source, including all the groups, fields, and so on.

TIP   *If you would like to see additional information related to each of the fields, select the Show Details option at the bottom of the Task Pane.*

To create your form from these fields, simply drag the field from the data source onto your form. When you drag your first field onto your form, you'll notice that InfoPath puts the field in a repeating section, as shown next.

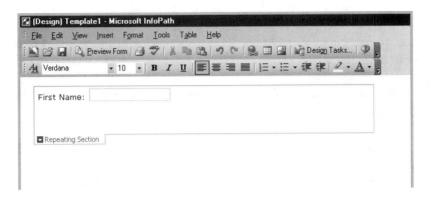

The sample XML file you started with includes a group called Employees that contains all the different fields that relate to each employee (name, address, and so forth), so InfoPath allows you to use one form to enter information for multiple

FIGURE 5-3   Fields from an existing XML file

employees. When you preview or fill out your form, this repeating section is used to allow you to enter multiple employees' information using this form, as shown in the finished form in Figure 5-4.

For more information on working with Repeating Sections, check out Chapter 7.

An easy way to visualize repeating sections is to think about paper forms. If you had a paper form that you were using to collect one employee's details, what would you do if you needed to use the form to collect another employee's details? You would probably make a copy of the form and fill it out for the second employee. With InfoPath, you can simply insert a repeated section to capture this information. With repeating sections, your form can be used to enter details from one employee or 100 employees.

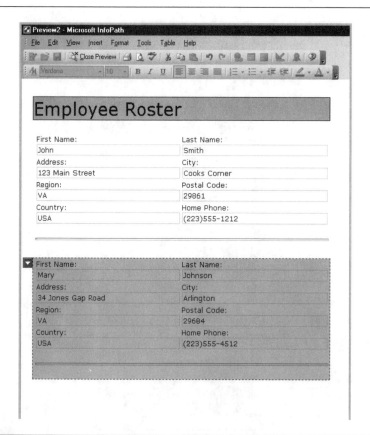

FIGURE 5-4   The finished form

When working with a form created from an existing XML file or schema, you can use all the same formatting tricks and techniques that you would use for any other form. You can then distribute this form to users for them to complete and instruct them to save the data that they entered to an XML file that is guaranteed to work with your source system.

Creating Forms from Existing SQL Server or Access Databases

One of the most popular features of InfoPath is its capability to push data back into existing SQL Server or Access databases. While XML provides a nearly universal standard for data exchange, Microsoft Access and SQL Server are the standard, respectively, for desktop and enterprise-class databases.

Using InfoPath, you can create forms that submit data directly back to a database hosted on either of these platforms. A typical scenario would be to use InfoPath forms to consolidate information from multiple users into a single database or table. You could then use this information for reporting purposes or to update other core systems.

In addition, this method also provides a flexible front end for simple data entry—while Access has its own method of creating forms for data entry, SQL Server has long relied on forms and applications created using Visual Studio and other programming tools to enter and maintain data. With the database features and functionality within InfoPath, you can quickly create InfoPath forms to replace these custom applications.

To start creating a form from an existing SQL Server or Access database, open InfoPath and select File | Design a Form to open the Design a Form view of the Task Pane. From the options under Design a New Form, select New from Data Source to open the Data Source Setup Wizard (refer to Figure 5-1). Select the Database option and click Next to continue to the next wizard page, shown in Figure 5-5, where you can select a SQL Server or Access database to use as the basis of your form. The steps that you follow next to create your form from an existing database vary depending on whether you want to use an Access database and connect directly to the database, use an ODBC connection to your Access database, or use a SQL Server database. The following sections describe how to connect to these different data sources.

Selecting a Data Source

Click the Select Database button to select your data source using the Select Data Source dialog box, shown in Figure 5-6.

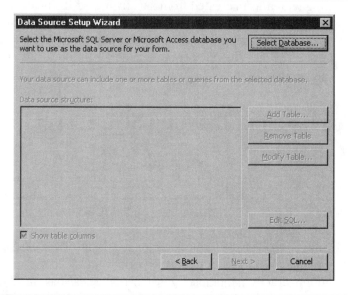

FIGURE 5-5   Selecting the database to use as the data source for your form

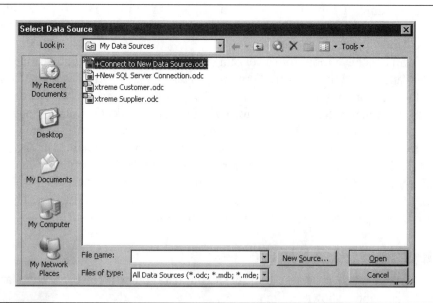

FIGURE 5-6   Selecting the data source to use for your form

If you want to work with an Access database and want to connect directly to the database, use the Select Data Source dialog box to browse and select your Access (MDB) database file. After you have selected the database file, a list of available tables appears, similar to the one shown in the following illustration, which allows you to select the tables you want to use as the basis of your form.

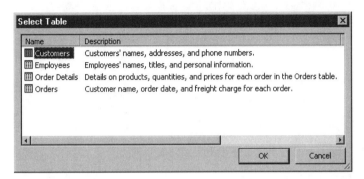

If you are using this method to connect directly to your Access database, you can skip ahead to the section marked "Working with Tables," as the next section details how to connect to an SQL Server.

If you are working with SQL Server or you want to use an ODBC connection to your Access database, you need to create an Office Data Connection (ODC) file for the data source.

Creating a New Data Connection

An ODC file contains information about the type of data source you are connecting to, its location, its username, and so on. To create a new ODC file, click the New Source button in the Select Data Source dialog box to open the Data Connection Wizard, shown in Figure 5-7.

The first thing you need to do is select the type of data source you want to connect to—while the list you are presented with may show other data sources (Oracle, and so forth), the only two data sources that are valid (that is, the only two you can use successfully) are Microsoft SQL Server and ODBC DSN.

If you select ODBC DSN, you need to select a data source name from the standard list of ODBC data sources configured on your computer, and the name you select must be pointing to a SQL Server or Access database. You will also be able to select the tables for your data source and then save your data connection file as described next.

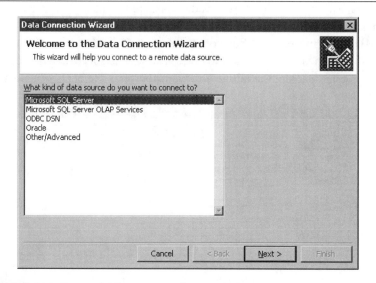

FIGURE 5-7   Data Connection Wizard Welcome page

In this example, select the Microsoft SQL Server option and click Next to continue to the next step of the wizard, shown in Figure 5-8, where you need to specify the name and credentials of the server you want to work with.

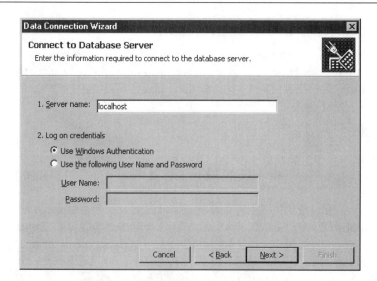

FIGURE 5-8   Providing logon information

Your database administrator should be able to provide you with the name of the server on which your SQL Server installation resides and tell you whether you are using Windows Authentication (meaning that your existing login and password from Windows will be used) or whether you need to enter a SQL Server–specific username and password. When you are finished entering your database details, click Next to continue to select the database and table that you want to work with, as shown in Figure 5-9.

Using the drop-down list at the top of the wizard page, select the database where your data resides. A list of associated tables will appear in the pane immediately below the drop-down list. You can click to select a specific table or, if you are unsure of which table you want to use, you can uncheck the Connect to Specific Table option to create a generic connection to this database. (You will be prompted later for the table you want to use for your InfoPath form.)

After you click Next, the final step of the Data Connection Wizard is to save your ODC file, as shown in Figure 5-10. You can enter a name for your ODC file, as well as a description and some search keywords. By default, InfoPath stores these ODC files in a folder called My Data Sources, which appears under the standard My Documents folder, but you can save the file anywhere you like.

TIP *In addition, you can also share ODC files with other users so that they don't have to go through the same setup to access data sources you have already created.*

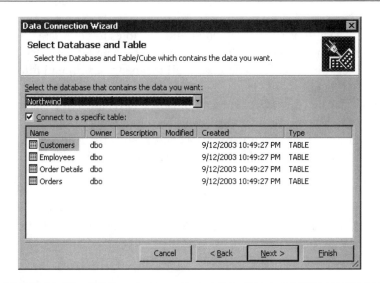

FIGURE 5-9   Database and table selection

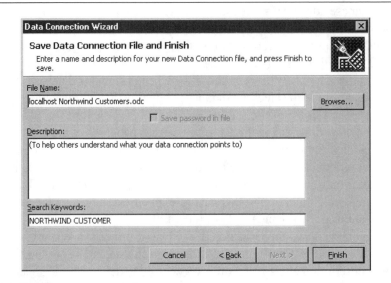

FIGURE 5-10   Saving your ODC file

Working with Tables

You are now ready to start working with the data source you have just created. The Data Source Setup Wizard should now appear again and show your database details at the top of the page, as shown in Figure 5-11, as well as any tables you may have selected earlier.

Using this wizard page, you can add multiple tables to your data source and specify the relationship between them. For example, in an Order Entry form, you could have a customer table that contains all the customer-related information, including name, address, and so on, and then you could have another "child" table for the orders for that customer. You could use the two tables to create a custom Order Entry form within InfoPath that would write directly back to these tables.

To add an additional table to your data source, click the Add Table button to open the Add Table or Query dialog box, shown in Figure 5-12, and select a table from the list. Then click Next.

The next step is to specify the relationship between the two tables (which is also sometimes called a "join type" because it details how the tables are joined back together). To add a relationship between two tables, click the Add Relationship button.

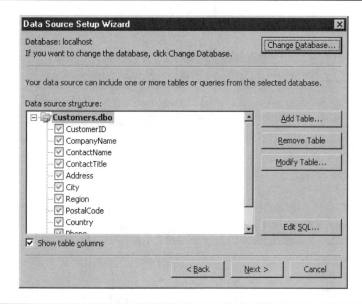

FIGURE 5-11   Selecting tables

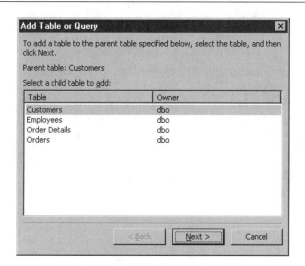

FIGURE 5-12   Adding a child table to your data source

This opens another dialog that allows you to select the field in each table that will be used to define the relationship, as shown here.

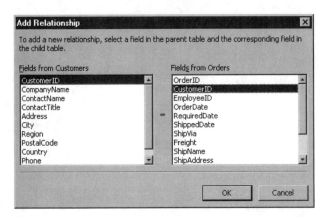

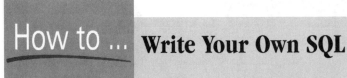 **Write Your Own SQL**

If you are familiar with SQL (Structured Query Language), you can write your own SQL statements to extract information from your database instead of selecting the tables where the information resides. You need to be fairly experienced with SQL to use this functionality, because you will have to enter an entire SQL statement without the benefit of a user interface or query tools. To enter a custom SQL statement, click the Edit SQL button in the Data Source Setup Wizard to open the dialog box shown here.

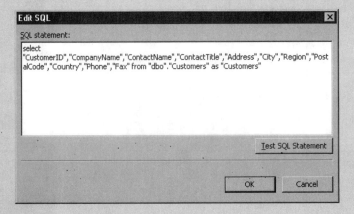

> Enter your SQL statement and use the Test SQL Statement button to check your SQL against the database. Although InfoPath won't be able to determine whether you are bringing back the correct data, it will be able to determine whether your SQL is well-formed and whether it will return a result set.
>
> Before you actually enter your SQL statement here, try it out first in a Microsoft Access query or in the Query Analyzer tool that is available for SQL Server.
>
> The fields that are present in the SELECT part of your SQL statement will be displayed as fields in your data set, and you can now use that result set as the basis of your InfoPath form.

For example, a Customer table and an Orders table could be used in one form—there would be a field in both of these tables called CustomerID that would specify the relationship between the two tables (for example, one customer has many orders). Using this dialog box, you would select the CustomerID field from both tables and click the OK button to add this join. You can specify multiple relationships based on fields within your tables or remove them using the Remove button. When you are finished, click Finish to return to the Data Source Setup Wizard.

TIP *You can also use the Remove and Modify buttons in the Data Source Setup Wizard to remove tables or modify the relationships between tables.*

The final step of the Data Source Setup Wizard is used to select which view of your new InfoPath form you want to work with first. The Query view, shown in Figure 5-13, is used to query your data source for a record to return.

For example, if you want to edit a certain customer's details, you could query or search for that customer and then use the form you create in the Data View of your InfoPath form to edit the customer's details, as shown in Figure 5-14.

TIP *You don't necessarily need to even create a Query view for your form—you could simply create a form that creates new database records each time it is submitted.*

Using the Design view, you can create your form just like you would any other InfoPath form, by adding fields, objects, and so on.

TIP *If you just can't wait to get started, flip ahead to the next chapter, which starts the coverage of some more advanced form design techniques.*

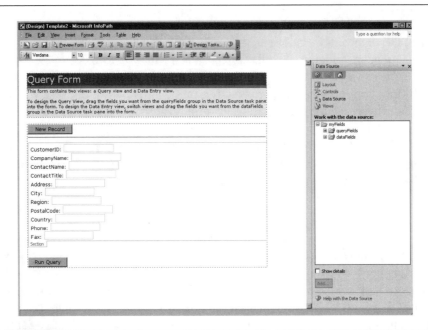

FIGURE 5-13   Query view of a form

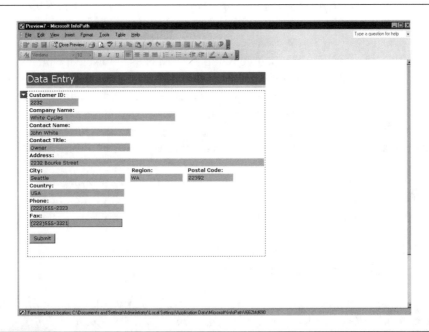

FIGURE 5-14   Data Entry view of a form

Creating Forms from XML Web Services

The last option for tying an InfoPath form to a back-end data source is through the use of an XML web service. A web service is a software component that is used to build applications and is based on an open standard, enabling organizations to share these services within their own organization and with external organizations as well.

InfoPath uses web services to submit information to disparate systems and applications. Web services can be created using a number of different languages and platforms and can be interfaced with just about any system or application. This makes web services an ideal back-end platform to be used with InfoPath forms.

Say, for example, you want to create a Travel Request form for your travel agent where you (the customer) could fill in the details of the trip that you want to take and the form would automatically be submitted to the travel agent's reservation and booking system, which runs on a Unix server and has its own proprietary database system. You could create an InfoPath form to collect the information required and then save an XML file and e-mail it to your travel agent, but then they would have to import it into their own systems using time-consuming manual processes that would have to be repeated for each request.

A much easier solution would be to ask your travel agent to expose this system using a web service. A developer within their organization could create a web service that would accept the information required and put this information directly into their reservation and booking systems. From that point, you could create an InfoPath form that submits the information directly to this web service, eliminating the need for all of the extra manual processes. InfoPath also supports receiving information from web services, meaning that you could display information from a web service on your form.

This has a number of advantages, in that this web service can now be used by other organizations to submit their own forms and have that information directly entered into the back-end systems.

In the following section we are going to look at how to create InfoPath forms that can retrieve and submit information directly back to web services. To walk through some of these examples, you need a web service to work with—Microsoft has provided a number of sample web services in the Software Developer's Kit (SDK) for InfoPath, but you need to install and configure these samples before you will be able to work through this section.

Getting Started

To start creating a form from a web service, open InfoPath and select File | Design a Form to open the Design a Form view of the Task Pane. From the options under Design a New Form, select New from Data Source to open the Data Source Setup

Wizard. Select the Web Service option and click Next to continue to the next wizard page, shown in Figure 5-15. The following sections describe your options after you reach this point.

Selecting Send/Receive Options

The first decision you need to make is whether your form is connecting to a web service that can send and receive data or do both. If you are using a web service that was created internally by a developer in your organization, you need to ask them which methods the web service supports—likewise, if you are working with a web service provided externally, you need to check to see how that web service is to be used.

Selecting a Web Service

If you know the name and URL of the web service you want to use, you can type it directly into the text box provided. If you don't know the exact name or if you want to search for a web service to use, click the Search UDDI button to open the dialog box shown here.

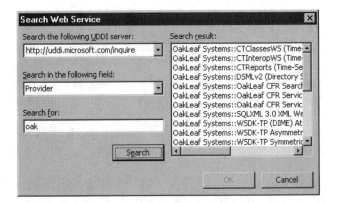

UDDI stands for Universal Description, Discovery, and Integration, which is a protocol that is used to define and find web services. By default, InfoPath shows the Microsoft UDDI Server and you can search by provider or service by entering a keyword in the Search For text box at the bottom of the dialog box. For example, if you know that one of your vendors offers an order-entry facility, you could specify Provider in the Search in the Following Field drop-down list and then enter the company's name in the Search For text box and click Search. If you don't know the name of the provider, you can also search based on the type of service that you want to find.

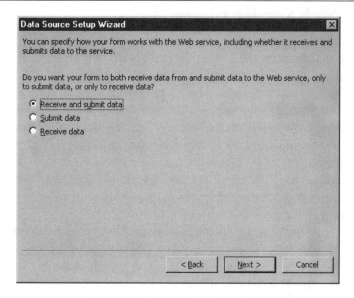

5

FIGURE 5-15 Specifying how your form works with the web service

Once the Search process has found a matching web service, you are presented with a list of web services that match your criteria. Highlight the web service you would like to connect to and click the OK button to return to the Data Source Setup Wizard.

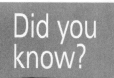

About XML Web Services

Not all XML web services can be used to retrieve and submit information through InfoPath forms. Make sure that you check with the developer who created the web service or other resource before you attempt to connect to the web service. If InfoPath is unable to utilize the web service as presented, you will receive an error message and will not be able to proceed with your connection.

Selecting Web Service Operations

Next, InfoPath looks at the web service you have selected and determines what operations are supported by the service. You are presented with a list similar to the one shown in Figure 5-16.

These operations could cover anything from retrieving data from a data source to submitting information to the same—each web service has its own operations that have been defined by whoever created the web service. Select the operation you would like to use for this form using the dialog shown in Figure 5-17 and click Next to continue.

Some operations require parameters, and if you have selected an operation that does require one or more parameters, you are presented with a dialog box similar to the one shown in Figure 5-18.

Highlight a parameter and click the Modify button to map a field on your form to the parameter required. For example, you could have a parameter called Order Date that is used to return a list of orders based on the date entered. You could then tie this parameter to a field on your form.

After you have finished setting up any parameters that are required by your web service, click Next to proceed to the last step in the Data Source Setup Wizard, which presents a confirmation of the selections you have made and allows you to select whether you want to start with the Data or Query view first. After you have

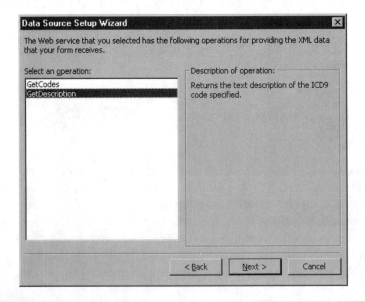

FIGURE 5-16   Web service operations

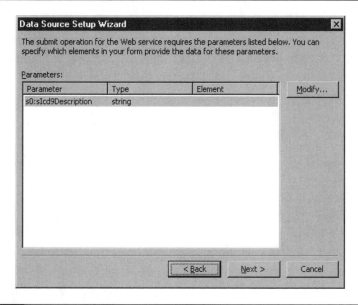

FIGURE 5-17   Web service parameters

made your selection, click Finish to return to the InfoPath form designer and start working with your form using some of the skills you learned in the last chapter.

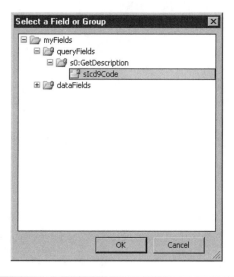

FIGURE 5-18   Setting web service parameters

Summary

Now that you can connect to your data, what's next? With the data side of things sorted out, you need to have a look at field objects, which are the basic building blocks you use to create your own forms. They're described in Chapter 6.

Chapter 6

Work with Data Entry Controls

How to...

- Work with the Form Designer
- Create and modify data entry controls
- Use plain and rich text boxes
- Create drop-down lists and list boxes
- Select dates using the Date Picker
- Use check and option boxes

Now that you have had a look at working with data sources within InfoPath, you need to drill down into working with forms. In Chapter 3, you worked to create your very first form using the InfoPath Form Designer. In that chapter, you looked at some of the basic features of the designer and how they can be used. Now that you have a good understanding of the form design process and how to connect to your own data source, you need to look in depth at the designer and how it's used.

Since the majority of content on any form will be held in data entry controls that are inserted onto the form, this chapter is also going to look specifically at the different types of data entry controls that are available for use within InfoPath and how each is used to enter and display data. This includes the controls for text boxes, rich text boxes, drop-down lists, list boxes, check boxes, and option buttons—at the end of this chapter, you should be able to add these controls to your forms and format them.

Working with the Form Designer

The InfoPath Form Designer is the tool you use to create and modify InfoPath forms. Recall from the example in Chapter 3 that you can open the designer itself simply by creating a new form.

If you have ever worked with another web development or word processing application, the concepts behind the Form Designer will be easy to pick up. Each InfoPath form is created as a "flowing" document, such that the contents of the form are not placed precisely on the page but are placed in relation to other objects on the form. For example, if you wanted to put the title of your form on the second line from the top, you could simply press the ENTER key to insert a new line, similar to how you would in a word processor.

Likewise, once you had entered your form title on the second line of the page, you could click in the first line of the document and add additional space at the top by pressing ENTER. The form title and everything below it would be moved in relation to the extra blank lines you have created.

There is a way to add more structure to your form design, through the use of layout tables, which are discussed in the next chapter.

Just like a word processor or WYSIWYG web development tool, you can type directly onto your InfoPath form and you use all the standard Windows shortcuts (Cut, Copy, Paste, and so on) on the text and other objects within your form design.

To format text or other objects that appear on your form, you can use the Formatting toolbar that appears at the top of the designer or you can highlight a selection of text or an object and then right-click the text or object directly to access the property pages and options relating to it.

To access the tools that you will need to create your form, click the Design Tasks button on the toolbar, which opens the Design Tasks view in the Task Pane to the right of the InfoPath workspace.

The Design Tasks button is like the Preview Form button—it only appears when you are in design mode working with a form design.

This Task Pane view contains links to most of the areas of the designer you will need to access while designing your forms.

Over the next few chapters, you are going to be working with the Form Designer itself and the various objects, controls, and techniques that you will need to use to create your own feature-rich forms, so this section is not complete by far. Sometimes the best way to learn how to do something is hands-on. To that end, you will continue working with the InfoPath Form Designer in the next section, which looks at the controls that are used to enter data on the forms you create.

Working with Data Entry Controls

Controls for data entry are an integral part of an InfoPath form, so this section focuses on how to insert and modify these data entry controls on your forms. You have already had a brief look at how to do this in Chapter 4 when you created your very first form, but the following sections describe this process in further detail— the properties you are going to look at are common to most controls that are used for data entry. Once you have had a look at the generic properties that these controls share, you can then look at specific formatting attributes and features associated with each control.

Adding New Controls

When working with an InfoPath form, you can quickly add new controls to your form by dragging and dropping a particular control type from the Controls view of the Task Pane. All controls on an InfoPath form are bound to fields within your form. You can see these fields by selecting Data Source from the drop-down menu at the top of the Task Pane, as shown in Figure 6-1.

If you are creating a form to push data into an existing data source, an intermediary dialog box opens when you attempt to place one of these data entry controls onto your form. This dialog box, shown in Figure 6-2, is used to specify to which field your control is bound.

In this example, a Text Box object is added to your form. When you submit this form to a database, the information entered into this object will be placed in the database field you have specified. This is one of the fundamental concepts of

FIGURE 6-1   InfoPath data source

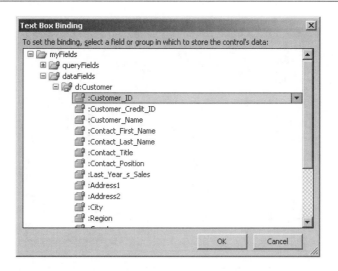

FIGURE 6-2 A typical binding dialog box

InfoPath—end users don't need to know the underlying database structure or XML schema. All they see are the form controls, with meaningful labels indicating what data should be entered, and your form design takes care of the behind-the-scenes matching of the data they enter to your data source or XML file.

If you were creating a form from scratch, without having a back-end database or XML schema or file, you would be able to drag this Text Box object directly on your form without having to bind it to a particular field. This on-the-fly method that you used in Chapter 2 actually creates the data source as you go along. For example, if you were to drag a Text Box object onto a blank form, InfoPath would automatically create a field called Field1 in your data source.

Working with Control Size

After you have added a control to a form, you can quickly resize the control by using the "handles" that appear on each side of the control when you click to select it. By dragging these handles, you can control the height and width of the object. If you would like more precise control over the size and appearance of the control, you can also use the property pages associated with the control to set the height, width, and other formatting options.

To set these options, right-click the object, select Properties from the right-click menu, and then click to select the Size property page, which should look similar to the dialog box shown in Figure 6-3.

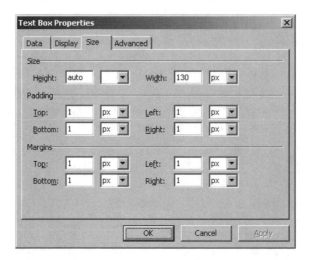

FIGURE 6-3 Size property page

About Padding and Margins

There are also two other measurements that you can set from this dialog box—the Padding and Margins settings. Padding refers to the buffer of space on the inside of the box, in between the perimeter of the object and the data that is entered. Increasing the Padding setting results in a white border that appears around the inside of your object, like the text box shown in the following illustration, where the Padding setting has been changed from 1 pixel to 10 pixels.

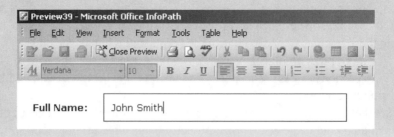

Padding can be useful to add some white space to your form and evenly space the text boxes and text that appear on your form.

Margins refer to the buffer of space on the outside of the box, between the perimeter of the object and any other objects that may appear on your form. The form shown in the following illustration has had multiple Text Box objects added to the form, each with a margin setting of 20 pixels all the way around.

By default, some objects (like Text Boxes) are set to an Auto height, where the height of the object is set in proportion to the text that is entered into the box. For example, if you enter five lines of text and have the wrapping option turned on, the height of the text box will be automatically stretched to five lines high. You can change this setting and the width of the field by entering a value in the field provided and selecting a unit of measure (cm, px, and so on).

Working with Advanced Properties

To set a number of unrelated options that are common to most objects, you use the Advanced property page, shown in Figure 6-4, as a "catch-all" for properties associated with a field that really didn't fit anywhere else.

Screen Tips are used to display text when your mouse moves over a particular field—depending on applications that you may have used before, this may have been called Tool Tips or Bubble Help, but the concept is similar. You can use the Screen Tip text box to enter some text that will appear when the user moves her mouse near the field and holds it there for a few seconds.

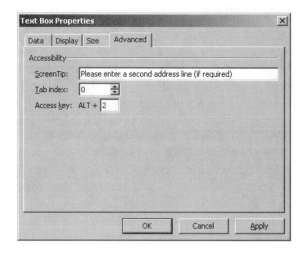

FIGURE 6-4   Advanced properties

The Tab Index setting, which is often overlooked, will be used often as you develop different forms. When creating a form, InfoPath sets the tab order based on the way the fields are arranged on your form—this means that when you open the form, the focus generally is given to the field that appears in the upper-left corner of your form, from which pressing the TAB key will take you through the different fields, moving from the left side of the page to the right.

You can change the tab order that is associated with a form by using the Tab Index setting provided in this dialog box—enter a value from 1 to the total number of fields, where 1 is the first field that will be selected when the form is opened. When the user presses the TAB key, this index is used to determine where the cursor goes next—if you don't set the Tab Index for every field on your form, leaving the default of 0, InfoPath follows the index values it does have and then defaults back to the left-to-right method for moving through the form fields.

You can also use the Text Box Properties dialog box to set an access key for a particular Text Box object. For example, you could establish ALT-2 as the shortcut key for the Address2 field on a form by typing 2 in the Access Key field. Then, when the user presses ALT-2, they jump directly to this field on the form.

In either case, you will spend the majority of your time working with InfoPath when dealing with objects that capture data, and in the following sections, you will be looking at all the different types of objects that you can use for data entry, starting off with Text Boxes.

Working with Text Boxes

The majority of data entered into an InfoPath form is entered using simple Text Boxes, like the one shown here.

To insert a Text Box onto your form, you can simply drag it from the Controls view of the task pane or from your Data Source and drop it on your form. You can set the formatting attributes for a Text Box to change its appearance or how text is displayed inside the box itself, but the information that is entered into a Text Box is entered into the underlying database or XML file as plain text.

TIP   *If you want to let the user enter some text formatting and retain that formatting in the field in the underlying data source, you need to use a Rich Text Box, which we will look at later in the chapter.*

To change the properties of a Text Box, right-click the object and select Properties from the right-click menu to open the dialog box shown in Figure 6-5.

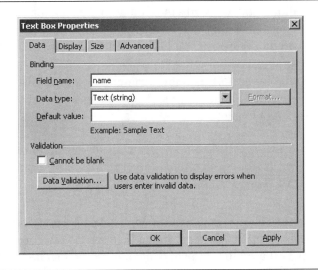

FIGURE 6-5   Text Box Properties dialog box

Working with Basic Properties

If you have added a field from an existing data source, you will not be able to change the Field Name or Data Type on the Data property page, because this information is defined by the underlying data source. If you are using the on-the-fly method to build your form, you can specify the name and select one of the data types shown here from the drop-down list provided.

- Text
- Whole Number
- Decimal
- True/False
- Hyperlink
- Date
- Time
- Date and Time

As you work with these different data types, a Format button may appear beside the Data Type drop-down list. This button is enabled only for certain data type formats and allows you to specify the format of the data that is entered. For example, if you were to select a Data Type of Date and click the Format button, the dialog box shown in Figure 6-6 would open and allow you to set the formatting options available for this data type.

You can select the format "by example" using the list of formats provided; the Locale drop-down list at the bottom of the dialog box provides access to different formats used in different countries.

NOTE *"Format by example" is available for a number of different data entry objects (text boxes, and so on) to allow you to control the format of data entered using those objects.*

Also, by using the Default Value option on the Data property page, you can specify any default text that will appear in the field when your form is to be filled out. This option is best used to set the default values for a text box (for example, entering USA in a text box for Country).

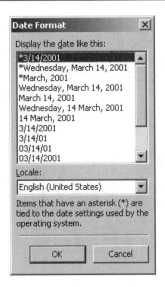

FIGURE 6-6	Formatting options for dates

TIP *You also have the option of placing some "placeholder" text in your text box to provide instructions (for example, "Click here and type your name"), which is discussed later in this section.*

At the bottom of the Data property page are some options for validation of the data that has been entered. Validation works on the basis of rules that you can establish by using this dialog box. When the criteria for one of the rules is met, you can show an error message or pop up an error message box to allow the user to correct their entry. If this seems a little confusing now, don't worry—data validation is covered in Chapter 9.

One validation option that is easy to set is the Cannot Be Blank option at the bottom of the dialog box, which forces users to enter data into this field before they can proceed with submitting the form.

Controlling Display Settings

In addition to controlling the default value and basic validation settings, you can also control how a text field will appear, by using the Display property page of the Text Box Properties dialog box, shown in Figure 6-7.

You can use the Display property page to enter a placeholder for the field—a placeholder is similar to a default value, with the exception that when a user clicks

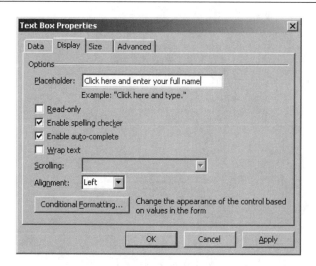

FIGURE 6-7   Text box display options

or tabs into a field to enter some data, the entire placeholder is highlighted. This allows the user to immediately overtype the placeholder without having to highlight and delete the text. Another distinction is that placeholder text never gets written back to the underlying data source, while default values could be saved or submitted to the underlying data source.

Selecting the Read-Only option will lock your text field so that the user cannot enter or edit any field information. Referring to the earlier example in which a default value of USA was set for a Country field, you could also make the field read-only so that the user wouldn't have to worry about changing the Country field each time. Also, for forms that are prepared for specific use (with fixed department or expenditure codes, for example), you can easily set the default values and then make these fields read-only.

InfoPath also has an integrated spell-checking facility that you can use to check the data that has been entered onto a form through a standard interface. By default, all the fields that you create on your form are enabled for spell-checking—when a user enters a word into the form that is not in the dictionary, the word is underlined, as shown here.

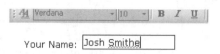

If you don't want this field to be checked for spelling or if the field is used to enter a proper name that may not be in the dictionary, you can turn this option off. InfoPath also enables an Auto Complete function by default, which completes for you commonly used text, URIs, and URLs after you type the first few characters. You can turn either of these options off by using the check boxes provided on the Display property page.

You can determine whether or not the text in your text box will wrap by using the Wrap Text check box. If you select this option, users will be able to enter text into a text box and have that text wrap to the next line, increasing the size of the text box, as shown here.

```
                                  ┌─────────────────────┐
                                  │Apt. 505, 37         │
                                  │Crown Street,        │
                                  │Crown Towers         │
                                  │Complex, Atlanta     │
                  Home Address:   │GA 40404             │
                                  └─────────────────────┘
```

This behavior is set by default, because the size of a text box object is automatically set to Auto, which causes the field to expand as more data is entered. You can stop this from happening by using the technique described earlier (refer to the section "Working with Control Size") to change the size of the object to specify a precise height instead of the default Auto setting.

After you set a definite size for your Text Box object, you will find that the options provided in the Scrolling drop-down list (immediately below the Wrap Text option) come in handy for controlling how this text appears when scrolling in a fixed-size text box. These options include

- Show scrollbar when necessary

- Scroll automatically while typing

- Show scrollbars

- Expand to show all text

Of these options, you will probably use the Show Scrollbar When Necessary option the most—this eliminates showing the scroll bar unless the text in the text box wraps to the next line.

The last settings on the Display property page are used to control the alignment of your field contents (Left, Right, Centered, and so on) and to apply any conditional formatting that you want to specify for this Text Box object. Conditional formatting works on the basis of creating a condition and where that condition is true, some formatting attribute will be applied (for example, If Country is equal to "USA" then you can make the text box background Blue.)

Since conditional formatting can be applied to many different types of objects, it's actually covered in its own section in the next chapter, so you can flip ahead to Chapter 7 if you just can't wait.

One more important note about formatting Text Box objects: You can use the Formatting toolbar to apply formatting attributes to your Text Box object, including fonts and alignment, but this formatting only applies to how the Text Box object appears on your form. When users enter data using this control, it is still passed to the back-end database or XML file as plain, unformatted text.

You can apply the same font formatting to other Text Box objects that appear on your form by right-clicking the object you have formatted and selecting Apply Font to All Text Box Controls. This trick also works with other types of objects.

Working with Rich Text Boxes

If you do need to allow the user to format text in a data entry control, the Rich Text Box object would be a much better choice than the Text Box object. Using the Rich Text Box object, you can give users a way to enter and format their own text, and the formatting will be retained and stored in the back-end data source or XML file, including fonts, tables, graphics, and so on.

When you add a Rich Text Box object to a form from the Controls view of the Task Pane or your own Data Source, it will default to approximately 540 pixels wide by 50 pixels high, similar to the box shown here.

You can change the size and appearance of a Rich Text Box object by using some of the common formatting techniques reviewed earlier in this chapter. By default, a Rich Text Box object can be used to enter formatting text, tables, horizontal lines, pictures, and so on, and is ready to use without any additional formatting required.

> **TIP** *For a review of how to use Rich Text Box objects to enter data, flip back to Chapter 3, which looked at InfoPath from the end-user's perspective.*

Controlling Display Settings

If you want to limit what users can enter into a Rich Text Box, you have some control over what can be entered through the object's property pages. To access these pages, right-click your object and select Properties from the right-click menu to open the Rich Text Box Properties dialog box. Click the Display property page, shown in Figure 6-8.

Under the Available Formatting section, you can select what elements a user is able to use when entering text into a Rich Text Box, including

- Paragraph Breaks

- Character Formatting

- Full Rich Text (images, tables, and so on)

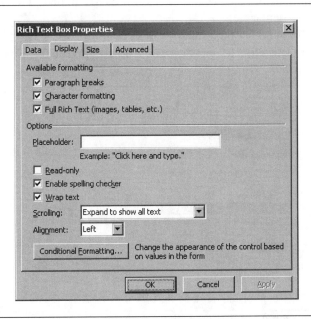

FIGURE 6-8 Rich Text Box object display settings

You can select these options independently without affecting the other formatting options—if you don't want users to be able to add larger images, tables, and so on, you can turn off the option for Full Rich Text, which will then limit users to entering only formatted text.

In the Options section, you have some of the same formatting options that are available for plain text boxes, including the options to make the field read-only, enable spell-checking, enable text wrapping, and so forth, but there are not a lot of other options available for rich text boxes, because the user will be doing the majority of the formatting.

Working with Drop-Down Lists and List Boxes

While text boxes provide an easy method of entering data on a form, the consistency of data entered can sometimes be a problem. InfoPath provides a robust set of tools for validating user input, but for commonly entered data (for example, States, Countries, Product Codes, and so on) it may be easier to use a drop-down list to enter data instead of a simple text box.

A drop-down list or list box, like the ones shown in Figure 6-9, can be used to present the user with a number of choices that appear in a list. When using a drop-down list, these choices appear when the down arrow to the right of the field is clicked, and when using a list box, these items appear by default.

Users can then select an item from the list without having to retype the data. This helps to eliminate inconsistent data and limits the choices a user has for data entry for a particular field.

Drop-down lists and list boxes can work in either of two ways. If you know which items you would like to appear in the list and those items are not stored in

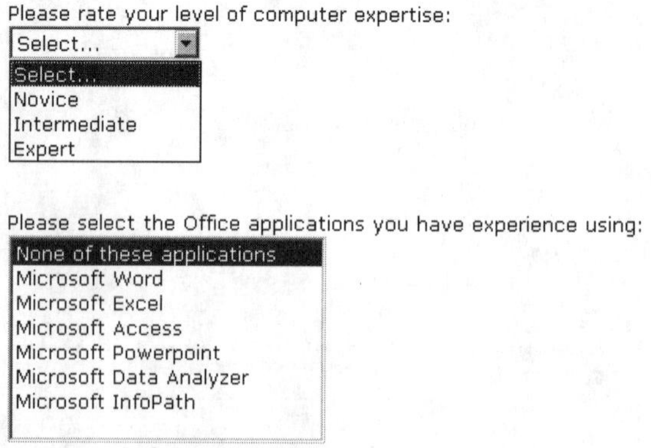

Please rate your level of computer expertise:

Select...

Select...
Novice
Intermediate
Expert

Please select the Office applications you have experience using:

None of these applications
Microsoft Word
Microsoft Excel
Microsoft Access
Microsoft Powerpoint
Microsoft Data Analyzer
Microsoft InfoPath

FIGURE 6-9   A drop-down list and list box on a form

an existing database or other data source, you can enter those items manually. If you do have those items stored in an existing database, you can hook directly into that data source to populate your drop-down list. The following sections look at both of these methods.

Creating List Box Entries Manually

To create the list box entries manually, first add a drop-down list or list box to your form. Then, right-click the drop-down list or list box and select Properties to open the dialog box shown in Figure 6-10.

The option Enter List Box Entries Manually is selected by default—to add a new entry, click the Add button to open the dialog box shown here.

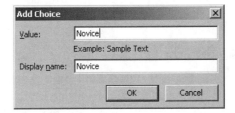

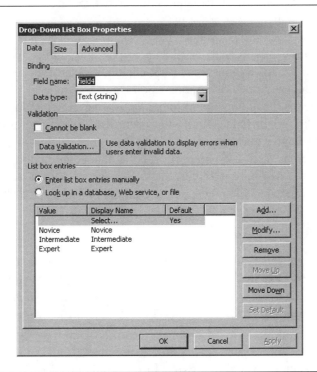

FIGURE 6-10   Drop-down and list box options

Enter a value and a display name for this item—the user will see the display name in the list, but the actual value is what will be passed back to the database or XML file when the form is submitted or saved. Click OK to return to the Data property page.

You can use the Modify and Remove buttons to modify or delete any entries you may have created, and you can use the Move Up and Move Down buttons to change the order in which your items appear in the list. Finally, to choose the value that is initially selected, highlight an item and use the Set Default button to make it the default value to be used.

When you are finished, click OK to accept your changes to the item list and property pages and return to your form. You should now be able to preview the form and view the items you have created in your drop-down list or list box and the display names you have created.

Looking Up List Box Entries

While manually creating the list box entries can be the easiest way to quickly get a new form up and running, it is a better practice to store list information in a database or other data source. This enables you to reuse these items in multiple forms without having to re-create them each time, and as new items are added to the database, they will automatically appear in the list.

To look up list box entries, you need to create a secondary data source that will be used to look up values in an external database or data source. To do this, add a drop-down list or list box to your form, right-click it, and select Properties. Click the Data property page and select the option Look Up in a Database, Web Service, or File, which changes the dialog box to look like the one shown in Figure 6-11.

To create a link to the data source where your list box entries reside, click the Secondary Data Source button to show a list of secondary data sources already associated with your form—if you don't see the data source you wish to use in the list, click the Add button to open the Data Source Setup Wizard. Following the same steps covered in Chapter 5, select the type of data source (XML Data File, Database, Web Service) and walk through the wizard to select where the data item resides.

NOTE *If you are using a data source that is not in the list, you may need to consider writing an XML Web Service as a "wrapper" to connect to your data source or consider using SQL Server or Access as an intermediate database format.*

After you have set up your data source, you will be returned to the list of secondary data sources available for your form—click the Close button to return

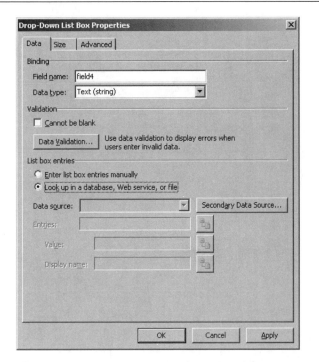

FIGURE 6-11   List box options

to the Data property page of your drop-down list or list box. You should now be able to see your secondary data source in the Data Source drop-down list, as shown in Figure 6-12.

In order to look up the list box items from your data source, you need to specify the field or group that you want to use for the Entries field in your drop-down list or list box. Click the icon beside the Entries field to open the standard InfoPath field picker dialog box, shown in Figure 6-13, and select the field where the data for your list resides.

When you are finished selecting your field, click OK to return to the Data property page—your selection will be translated into an XPath reference and should now be displayed in the Entries text box. If your secondary data source had two fields that were used and grouped together (for example, a state abbreviation field and the full description, like CA and California), you could have selected this grouping and then used the icons beside the Value and Display Name settings to match the name that would be displayed in your list to the actual value that would get passed back to the underlying data source or XML file when your form was submitted or saved.

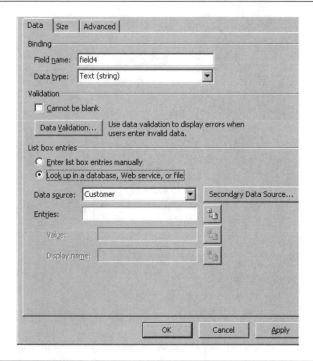

FIGURE 6-12   List box options with the secondary data sources showing

FIGURE 6-13   Selecting a group or field

6

TIP

As it is, by selecting one entry, both the value and the display name are the same. Regardless of which one the user selects from the list the same value will be returned to the data source or XML file.

Keep in mind that when looking up a value to display in a drop-down list or list box that InfoPath submits a simple SELECT query against the data source. From the earlier example in which you were selecting from a State field, you would

How to ... **Work with the Date Picker**

Another handy object for data entry is the Date Picker, shown in the following illustration, which can be used to select dates using a calendar instead of actually entering the entire date by hand.

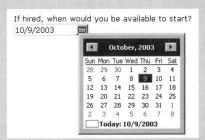

A Date Picker object looks similar to a Text Box object, but features a small calendar icon on the right side of the field. Clicking this icon causes a small calendar to pop up that allows you to navigate through the calendar and select a date.

The Date Picker control can be added to your control in the same way you add the other data entry objects you have looked at so far, by dragging and dropping it from your data source or from the Controls view of the Task Pane.

There aren't a lot of properties associated with this object, because its use is pretty straightforward—the calendar that appears when the icon is clicked defaults to the current month, and the current date is highlighted with a red outline. You can use the right and left arrows at the top of the calendar to navigate through the months of the year, and then click to select the date you want. This date in turn is displayed in the associated text box, and its value is passed back to the underlying data source or XML file.

get multiple values for each state in the list (for example, CA, CA, CA). To eliminate these duplicate values, either use a lookup table specifically created for the purpose that only contains one of each item or change the SQL query in your secondary data source to SELECT DISTINCT to eliminate duplicate records.

Check Box Objects

Check Box objects are a great way to enter data from a two-state control. Most people think of check boxes as a method of entering only Boolean data (that is, True and False). When the check box is checked, it is set to True; when it is unchecked, it is set to False. Check boxes in InfoPath can go beyond this simple implementation by allowing you to select both a different data type and values that should be passed when the check box is checked or unchecked.

To see this in action, drag a Check Box object onto a form, right-click the object, and select Properties from the right-click menu to open the dialog box shown in Figure 6-14.

By default, when you add a Check Box object to your form using the on-the-fly method of form creation, the Data Type field will be set to True/False. You can set the Default State (in other words, whether the box is checked or cleared) and then specify what value should be passed along when either of these states occurs. This is the simplest way to use the check box, but you will find that if you change the Data Type field, you can actually set the values that will be passed when the check box is checked.

Check Box options

FIGURE 6-15   A check box used to enter

For example, in the dialog that is shown in Figure 6-15, a Check Box has been used to prompt the user for whether they want Priority Shipping for an extra $20. In this instance, regular shipping is only $10. The object has been set up so that the Unchecked state will pass a value of $10—if the user checks this option, the value of $30 is passed to the underlying data source or XML file. An example of how the properties for this object might look is shown in Figure 6-15.

You can use check boxes with all different sorts of data types in the same manner—simply specify the values that will be passed when the option is checked or cleared.

Option Button

The last object you will use for data entry is the Option Button, which sometimes is also called a Radio Button. Option buttons are used on a form to give the user a list of options that are bound to a single field, from which they can select only one, as shown in the shipping options shown here.

For outside the Sydney Metro Area, please select a shipping option:

○ Will Pick-Up
○ Standard Mail Service
○ Courier Service
○ Priority Shipping

When you first go to add an option button to your form, you will be presented with a dialog box like the one shown in the following illustration, which allows you to enter the number of option buttons that you want to create. This process is important as you can have multiple option buttons associated with a group and you can only select one of them.

After you have added option buttons to your form, you can edit the label that is associated with each as you would normally edit text on your form, and you can also specify the value that will be passed when the option is selected through each individual option's property pages. To set the value and default selection, right-click one of the options on your form and select Properties to open the dialog box shown in Figure 6-16.

Enter a value in the Value When Selected field to be passed back to the underlying data source or XML file when the form is submitted or saved. If you want to save the user some time and already have one of the options selected when they fill out the form, select the This Button Selected by Default check box.

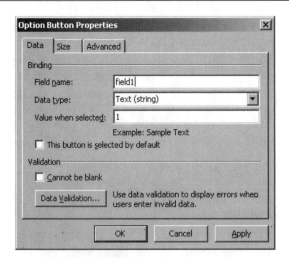

FIGURE 6-16   Option button properties

Summary

By now, you should be fairly confident using the data entry controls within InfoPath, but that is just the tip of the iceberg. There are a number of other controls that can be used on your InfoPath form for everything from repeating sections to command buttons, lists, and more. It's these objects that we will discuss in Chapter 7.

6

Chapter 7

Work with Form Controls

How to...

- ■ Insert different types of sections
- ■ Create repeating tables
- ■ Utilize plain, numbered, and bulleted lists
- ■ Use Picture controls to capture graphics on a form
- ■ Insert hyperlinks into a form
- ■ Create expressions using XPath

Chapter 6 presented some of the standard controls that you can place on a form to enter data. In this chapter, you are going to look at some of the other controls that you can use to add more features and functionality to your forms.

To start, you will look at the different types of sections that you can add to a form, including repeating and nonrepeating sections as well as optional sections (for optional user input). Then, the discussion switches to working with tables and lists. The chapter wraps up by describing how to use pictures, hyperlinks, and expressions in your forms.

Working with Sections

In the previous chapters, you have been presented with a simplistic view of form design—placing individual data entry objects on a form from some fairly simple data sources. These data sources have typically just been a list of fields relating to an underlying data source. While InfoPath makes it easy to create simple forms from these data sources, it can be used to do so much more. This chapter introduces not only some new objects, but also a new data source concept: groups. Groups are collections of fields within a data source. A typical group might look something like the one shown in Figure 7-1.

This is an actual data source from the sample Expense Report form presented in Chapter 3 and includes groups of fields for the name and address information, as well as the expense items in the form and other repeating information. So, why would you have groups of fields in a data source? To start, the underlying data source may require more than a 1:1 relationship in the data. In addition, you may want to organize the fields in your data source according to the hierarchy of the form or an

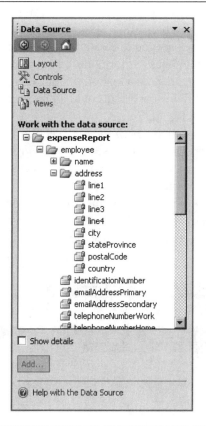

FIGURE 7-1   A typical group

existing data source. You could also use groups to hold information that would appear more than once—such as multiple addresses for a single customer or employee.

For example, in the data source for the sample Expense Form, there are multiple expense items that are included on the form—those fields will eventually be used to populate another data source where the Expense Details table may require those detailed expense items. Grouping within a data source allows you to create more complex data structures that break the 1:1 relationship with the data in favor of a 1:many relationship.

With this technique, you can create complex forms from a single data source without resorting to multiple data structures (databases, tables, and so on) for the different types of information gathered on your form. When the resulting form data is submitted or processed, back-end processes can denormalize this data and place it into the correct tables.

One of the tools that enables you to create this type of complex form are sections. Sections are special areas within your form that can be used for a number of different purposes. Sections in a form are bound to groups. For example, in the sample Expense Report form, the group of fields for Name could all be organized into a single section on your form, as shown in Figure 7-2.

This type of section is called a *nonrepeating* section, because the fields within the Name group don't repeat in the data source—this group of fields is used to enter the name of the person who is filling out the expense report, and the name appears only once on the form.

If you were to look at the Item group instead, you would see that you could insert a section bound to this group, but it would have to be a *repeating* section, because the fields in the Item group are used to collect the detailed expense item

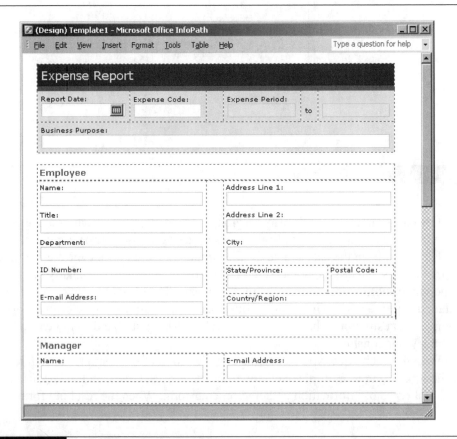

FIGURE 7-2   A nonrepeating section

information, as shown in Figure 7-3. Users can utilize this section to add one item or many, depending on how many expenses they have incurred for the month.

The last type of section is an *optional* section, which is not required to be completed when the form is filled out. Like the other types of sections that have been described, optional sections are bound to a particular group of fields, but the difference is that the user can add or remove the optional section of the form.

For example, in the Expense Report form, you could add an optional section at the bottom of the form that enables the user to enter the names of the clients they have entertained. If they don't have any client-related expenses, they can leave this section off, but if they need to fill out this section, they can click either the icon or text link to insert the section.

Now that you have had a brief overview of sections, you are actually going to create some sections on your own forms. Throughout the following sections, you

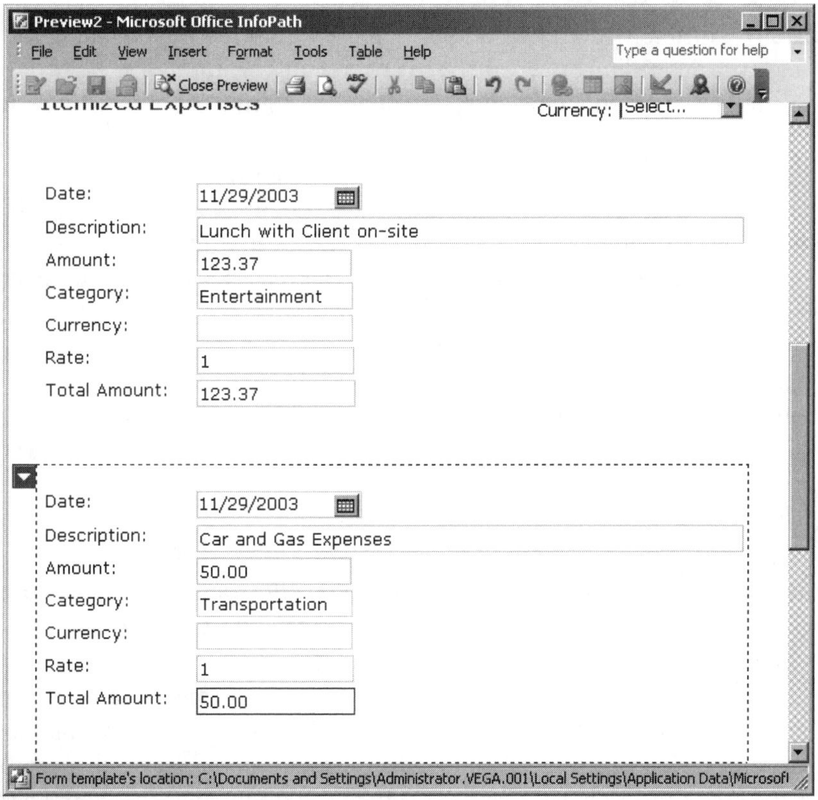

FIGURE 7-3   A repeating section

are going to be working with a data source that is available with the downloadable files available at www.osborne.com.

Working with Nonrepeating Sections

Nonrepeating sections are sections that are shown once within a particular form. There are a number of reasons that you would want to use a nonrepeating section (as opposed to just showing the fields in a particular area) but they are mainly used to organize your form and to enable you to format an entire section of your report without having to format each individual element.

For example, when you want to validate a particular field, you can change the color of the background of the entire section to draw attention to the validation error. The following section explains how to use nonrepeating sections in your own forms and how to format them.

Inserting Nonrepeating Sections

There are two different methods that you can use to insert a nonrepeating section into your form, depending on whether you are creating the form on-the-fly (creating the data source as you go along) or are creating the form from an existing data source.

If you are working with a blank form and creating the data source as you go, you can create a new section by simply dragging the Section control from the list of Controls and dropping it onto your form, as shown in Figure 7-4.

A new group called Group1 will be created in your data source and bound to the section you have just created. To rename this group, select View | Data Source to open the Data Source task pane, locate the group, and then right-click the group name and select Properties from the right-click menu to open the Properties dialog box. You can then change the name to something more meaningful.

TIP   *You can also change the name through the property pages for the individual section.*

You could then add data entry objects to this section, and with each data entry object, a new field will be added to your data source, until your form and data source look something like the ones shown in Figure 7-5.

The second method of creating a section is used for forms that are created from an existing data source. When you add a section to this type of form from the Controls task pane, the Section Binding dialog box opens, as shown in Figure 7-6, and prompts you for the group to associate with this section. After you have inserted the section into your form, you can add data entry objects from this group and format them as you normally would.

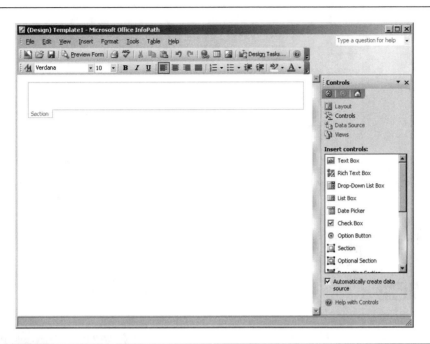

FIGURE 7-4   A new section

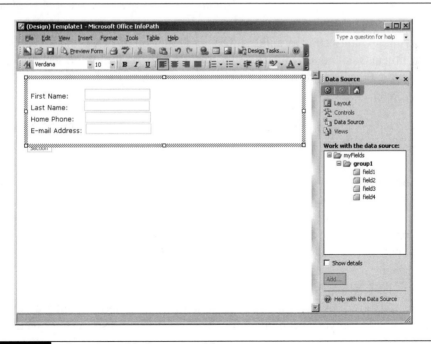

FIGURE 7-5   A section with data entry objects

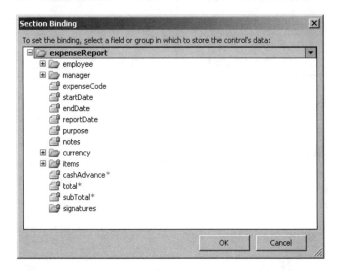

FIGURE 7-6 A section created from a group in an existing data source

 *To see the data source that a particular section is bound to, right-click the section and select Show Data Source from the right-click menu. This opens the Data Source task pane and highlights the group your section is bound to.*

If at a later date you would like to change the group of fields that this section (or any other) is bound to, you can right-click directly on top of the section and select Change Binding from the right-click menu to open the Section Binding dialog box again and select a new group to bind to.

 *Changing the binding may cause errors if the controls within a section do not correspond to the fields in the group.*

If you already have an existing data source, there is an even easier method you can use to insert a section directly from the Data Source task pane. Locate the group you want to bind to the section and drag the group onto your form. A drop-down menu appears that enables you to insert a section or a section with controls, so you don't actually have to add the data entry objects by hand.

Formatting Sections

Nonrepeating sections have some of the same formatting options that are available for other objects on your form, including size, position, and so forth, as well as

some attributes that are unique to sections. To format the section you have just
inserted, right-click the section and select Properties from the right-click menu
to open the dialog box shown in Figure 7-7.

You can use the Field or Group Name text box to rename the group that this
section is bound to, but remember to check the spelling of the group you are
binding to, because a misspelling could cause a binding error. In the Default
Settings area, the default setting for a nonrepeating section is Include the Section
in the Form by Default. Don't worry about the other settings on this page for the
moment; they are described later in the chapter, in the context of optional and
repeating sections. However, you now are going to look at some of the generic
section-formatting options, which apply to all three different types of sections
and thus won't be repeated later in the chapter (so pay attention to them now!).

After you add a section to a form, you can resize the section by using the
"handles" that appear on each side of the section when you click to select it. Like
the other objects you have looked at in previous chapters, you can gain more precise
control over the size and appearance of a section through the Size tab of the Properties
dialog box. The Height setting of a new section is set to Auto by default, which
means that the height of the object is set in proportion to the objects that are placed
inside of it. You can change this setting and the Width setting of the field by entering
values in the fields provided and then selecting a unit of measure (cm, px, and so on).

7

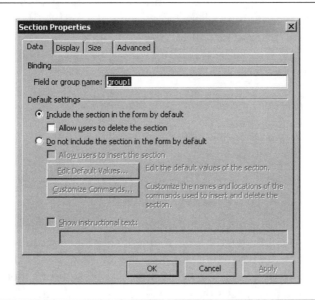

Section Properties dialog box

If your section has objects inside of it, you will never be able to set the height below the size taken up by these objects.

The two other dimensions that you can set on the Size tab are the padding and the margins. *Padding* refers to the buffer of space on the inside of the section, in between the perimeter of the section and the other objects inside the section. Increasing the Padding setting results in a white border that appears around the inside of your section. Padding can be useful to add some white space to your form and evenly space the text boxes and text that appears on your form.

Margins, just like with other objects, refers to the buffer of space on the outside of the box, between the perimeter of the section and any other objects that may appear on your form.

The final property page associated with sections is the Advanced tab, which is used as a catch-all for properties that are associated with a section but really don't belong anywhere else.

Screen tips are used to display text when your mouse moves over a particular section. You can use the ScreenTip text box to enter text that will appear when the user moves their mouse near the section and holds it there for a few seconds.

As when working with data entry objects, you can change the tab order that is associated with a form by using the Advanced tab's Tab Index setting. Enter a value from 1 to the total number of fields, where 1 is the first field that will be selected when the form is opened. When the user presses the TAB key on their keyboard, this index is used to determine where the cursor will go next—if you don't set the Tab Index for every field and section on your form, InfoPath follow the index values that it does have and then defaults back to the left-to-right method to move through the form field and sections.

This section does not cover the properties on the Display tab, which include Conditional Formatting for sections. Because Conditional Formatting can be used on a wide variety of objects, it has been given its own section in Chapter 8.

Working with Optional Sections

Optional sections are a special type of section that can be used on a form to collect information that is not required by all form users. The advantage of using optional sections is that they can be used to eliminate clutter on a form by displaying only the required sections of a form—objects that are used to collect optional information are hidden until the user inserts the optional section into the form. An example of a form with an optional section is shown in Figure 7-8. When the user clicks the

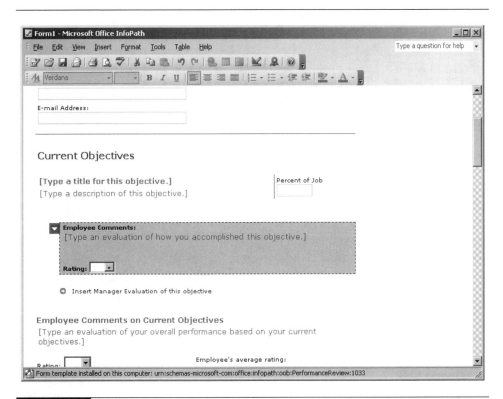

A form with an optional section

link provided (Insert Manager Evaluation of this Objective), the optional section is inserted into the form.

In addition to links that appear on the form, you can also insert optional sections by using commands added to the different InfoPath menus or from toolbar buttons, like the buttons shown in Figure 7-9.

This provides a quick and easy method to build flexible forms that have a wide variety of uses—you don't need to create one massive form with all the different sections, but instead can just let the users insert the sections they need.

Inserting Optional Sections

Again, to insert an optional section into a form, you can user either of two methods. If you are building the data source on-the-fly, dragging the Optional Section control onto your form creates a new group in your data source. You can then add data entry objects and build up your form and data source at the same time.

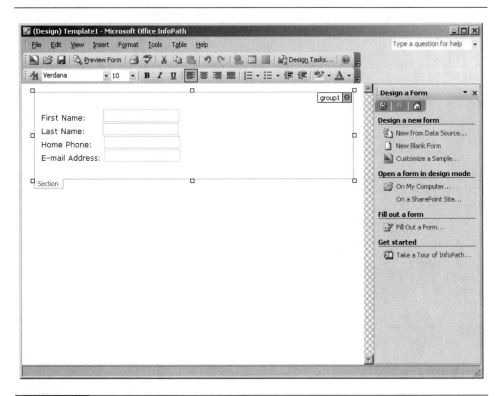

FIGURE 7-9 Optional methods of inserting sections

If you are creating a form from an existing data source, the Section Binding dialog box opens (refer to Figure 7-6), prompting you to bind your Optional Section control to a group within your data source.

In either case, once your optional section has been added to your form, it will appear as an outline of the section. When your form is previewed, this section is collapsed to a single line that the user can click to insert the section you have created. By default, the user is prompted with the text shown at the bottom of Figure 7-10. In InfoPath, this is called "instructional text," but you don't have to use the default text or even show it all.

Formatting Optional Sections

To change the instructional text and other options, right-click the section you have inserted and select Properties to open the Section Properties dialog box, shown in Figure 7-10. The properties for an optional section are the same for the other types

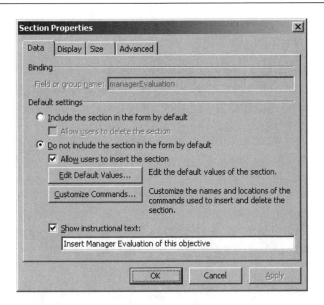

FIGURE 7-10   The default text for inserting an optional section

of sections we have looked at, except that the option Do Not Include the Section in the Form by Default is selected. This means that the section itself will not appear on the form—when the user is filling out the form, they see only the instructional text that you have entered (for example, "Click here to insert") and they have to click the link to insert the optional section into their form.

To set the default values for this section, click the Edit Default Values button to open the dialog box shown in Figure 7-11.

By using the radio buttons at the top of the dialog box, you can select whether you want to use these default values in all occurrences of the section or only when the user inserts the section; all the fields in the associated group are listed in the middle of the dialog box. To add a default value, click to select a field from the list and enter some text in the Default Area text box. These values will then be used to indicate what type of data should be entered into the data entry object when the form is filled out. When you are finished entering the default values, click OK to return to the Section Properties dialog box.

Earlier, we looked at the different ways you could insert an optional section and saw that you could show both an icon and some instructional text on your form to alert the user that there was an optional section available. But that is not the only way you can advertise an optional section—the Customize Commands button

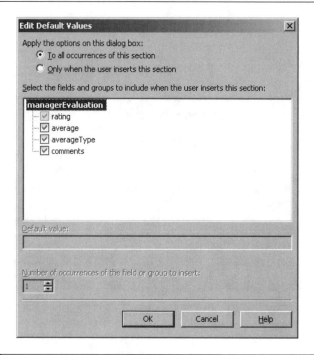

FIGURE 7-11   Edit Default Values dialog box

is used to specify the commands that are used to insert and delete these sections. When you click the Customize Commands button, the Section Commands dialog box (shown in Figure 7-12) appears, enabling you to specify where these commands should appear.

The two actions that are available for optional sections are Insert and Delete. Use the Action drop-down list to select the action you want to work with and then use the check boxes to specify where the commands should appear. The majority of the locations shown are in existing InfoPath menus (File, Edit, and so on); check the location to select it and use the Command Name text box at the bottom of the dialog box to specify what label should appear on the menu.

If you want to add a command to a toolbar, check the Form Toolbar box. Note that, below the Command Name text box, the ScreenTip text box enables you to customize what text will appear to the user when they move their mouse over the toolbar button.

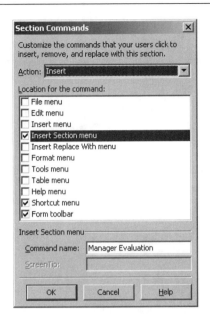

FIGURE 7-12   Customizing the commands that users click

> **TIP**
>
> *If your group names are well thought out, working with group names will be much easier. For instance, the menu for a group named Item will be labeled Insert New Item, whereas the menu for a group named inv_item_ with_product will be labeled Insert New inv_item_with_product.*

When you are finished setting the command options, click OK to return to the Section Properties dialog box. The last formatting option that you need to look at is the Show Instructional Text check box and its accompanying text box at the bottom of the dialog box. You can enter some text that will appear on the form beside the Optional Section icon, as shown in Figure 7-13.

You also have the option of not showing any instructional text at all, but you need to provide an alternate method to insert the section (for example, with a menu or toolbar command, as just described).

> **TIP**
>
> *If you decide not to display the instructional text for an optional section on your form, you may want to put a note on the form reminding users that other sections are available to be inserted.*

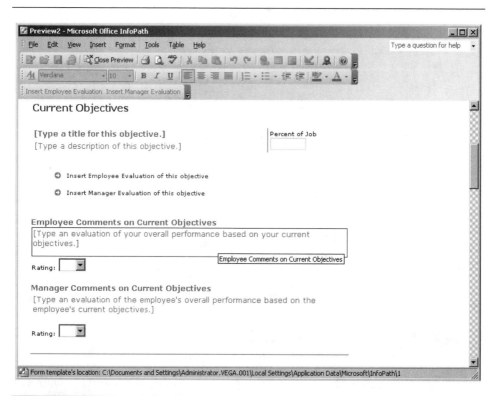

FIGURE 7-13   An optional section icon with some instructional text

Working with Repeating Sections

Repeating sections are used in forms to add information that has a 1:many relationship with your data. By using repeating sections, you can create a form that can be used to enter a number of different records. For example, the Employee Roster form shown in Figure 7-14 uses a repeating section that allows the user to enter information for one or more employees on the roster—the user can insert as many sections as required to enter all the information required.

Inserting Repeating Sections

To insert a repeating section into your form, drag the Repeating Section control from the Controls task pane onto your form. If you are creating your data source

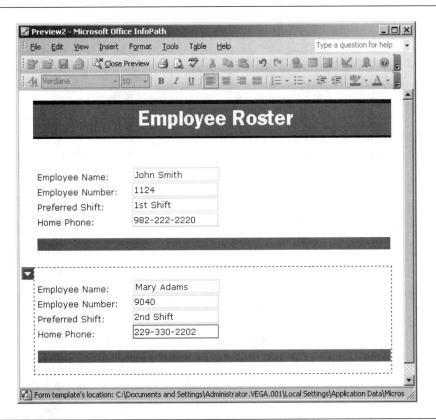

FIGURE 7-14   A form with repeating sections

on-the-fly, this creates two new nested groups (a standard group containing a repeating group); if you are working with an existing data source, this opens the Section Binding dialog box and allows you to select the group of fields to be associated with this section. You need to select a repeating group—otherwise, you will receive an error message like the one shown in the following illustration and you will not be able to insert the section into your form.

After you insert the section into your form, you can then start adding all the data entry objects that you want to use in the section. Remember, if you don't want to go to the trouble of creating all the data entry objects by hand, you can also create a section from the Data Source task pane. Simply drag a repeating group onto your form to open the dialog box shown in Figure 7-15, and then select Repeating Section with Controls.

A section will be inserted with data entry objects added for all the different fields that are in your group.

You'll notice that when you preview the form (File | Preview Form | Default), the section is displayed with a small arrow icon shown to the left of the section—click the icon to open a drop-down menu similar to the one shown in Figure 7-16.

When filing out the form, users can use this menu to insert or remove sections as required—the standard Windows Clipboard shortcuts (Cut, Paste, Copy, and so on) can also be used with repeating sections and are available from the same menu.

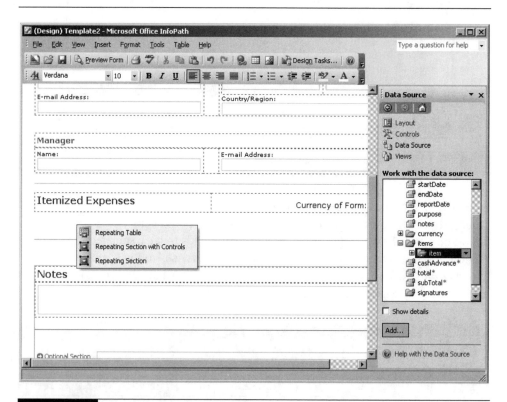

FIGURE 7-15   Repeating section options

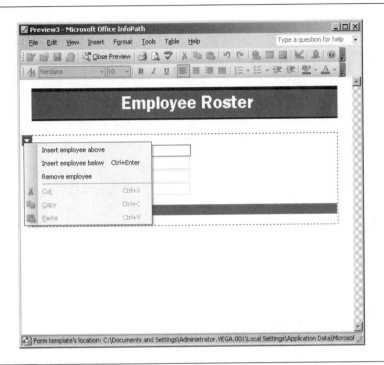

FIGURE 7-16   Repeating section menu

Formatting Repeating Sections

To format a repeating section, right-click the section and select Properties to open the dialog box shown here.

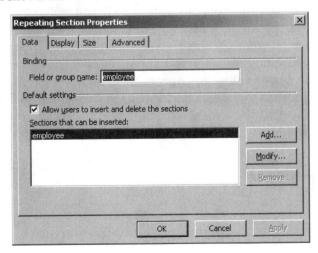

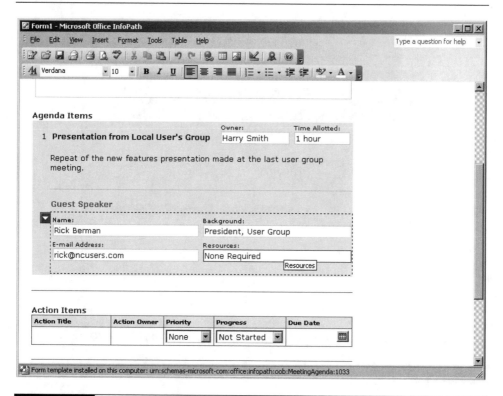

FIGURE 7-17 A repeating or nested section

When working with a repeating section, you can specify which sections you will allow users to insert—this option can be used to add multiple sections on the same form. For example, in the Meeting Agenda sample form that is included with InfoPath (shown in Figure 7-17), there is a repeating section for the Agenda Items and then another repeating section within the Agenda Items for entering any guest speakers who may be presenting that Agenda Item.

To add a new section to the option list, click the Add button on the Data tab and enter a name for the group. To modify settings for an existing section, highlight the section and click Modify to open the Section Properties dialog box, shown next.

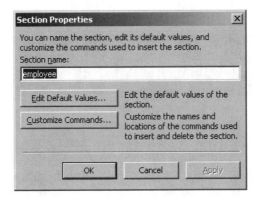

You have similar options to the ones that you have when formatting a normal section, including the ability to edit the default values that will be used in this section and the ability to customize the commands that can be used to add additional sections to your form. When you are finished formatting your section, click OK to return to your form's design.

Working with Repeating Tables

Tables are another easy way to organize data entry objects on a form and provide an easy way to enter multiple rows of data, as shown in Figure 7-18, which is the sample Expense Report form used earlier in this chapter.

Inserting a Repeating Table

To insert a table into your form, you have two choices. If you are building your data source as you go, you can drag the Repeating Table control from the Controls task pane directly onto your form. This opens the dialog box shown in the following illustration, in which you can enter the number of columns that you want to use in your repeating table.

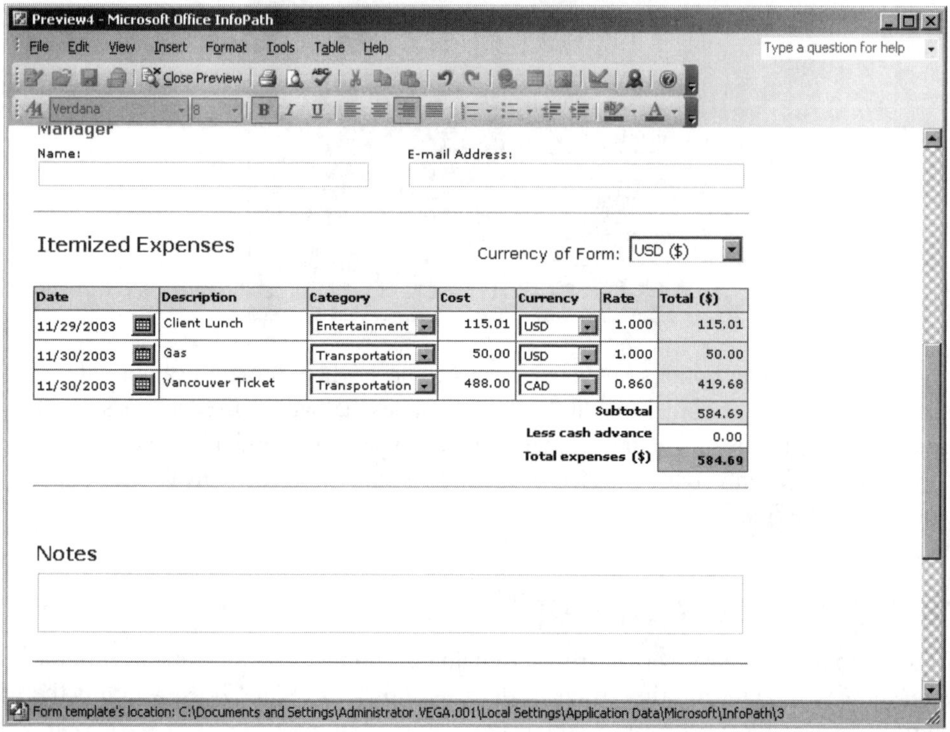

FIGURE 7-18   Expense Report form with a repeating table

If you are working with an existing data source, you can use the same process instead of specifying the number of columns, the Repeating Table Binding dialog box shown in the following illustration will appear and prompt you for a group within your data source to bind to.

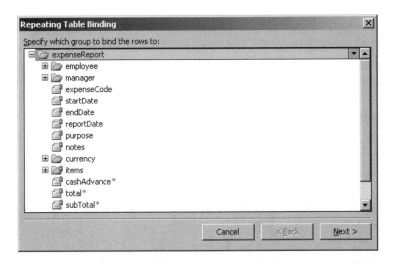

Notice that this dialog box is slightly different from the Binding dialog boxes that you looked at when creating sections—this dialog box has a Next button, because now you need to select which fields are going to be shown in your repeating table. Click Next to go to the second step, where you use the dialog box shown in the following illustration to select the fields to appear.

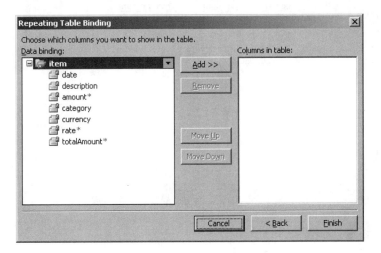

To select a field, highlight it in the list on the left and click the Add button to move it to the list of selected fields on the right. When you are finished selecting fields, click the Finish button to accept your changes and return to your form design. Your repeating table will be inserted into your form (shown in Figure 7-19) using the fields you selected.

Keep in mind that all the fields were inserted using the default data entry object for that field type. For example, you may have a text box inserted for a particular field, but you really may want to use that field as a drop-down list. To change the

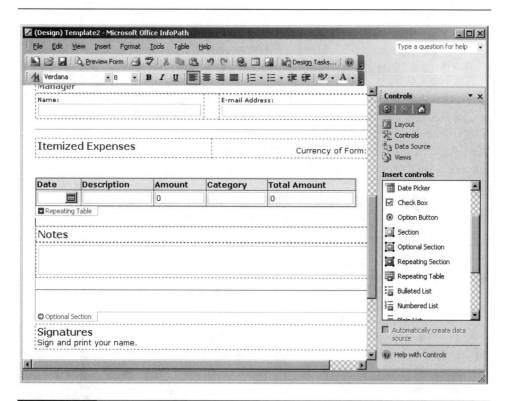

FIGURE 7-19 A typical repeating table

object type, right-click an object and use the Change To menu, shown in the following illustration, to change the object to the desired type.

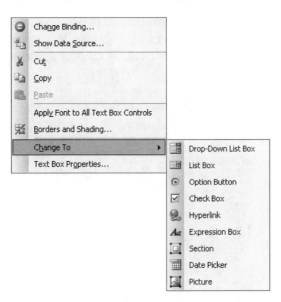

7

NOTE   *The Change To menu is not specific to sections and can be used to change fields and sections to different types. For example, you could have a text box in which you want to display a date. You could right-click the text box and use the Change To menu to change to another type of data entry control.*

Like sections, when you preview your form, an arrow icon appears to the left of the table that enables you to insert and remove rows.

TIP   *You can also use* CTRL-ENTER *at the end of each line to insert a new line, a shortcut that you may want to point out to form users to enable them to enter data quicker.*

Formatting Tables

Two sets of properties are associated with a repeating table: the generic properties that are normally associated with a table (for example, rows, columns, alignment, and so on) and the formatting options that are specific to a repeating table.

To format just the table itself, right-click the table and select Table Properties to open the dialog box shown here.

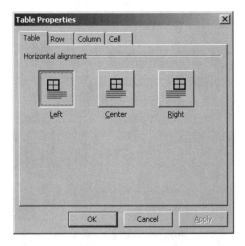

A number of different property pages are associated with the table itself, enabling you to select the alignment for the table, as well as the height and width of the rows, and the alignment and padding for the cells in the table.

In addition to these formatting options, you can also control the look and feel of your table through the right-click menu associated with the table, as shown here.

From this menu, you can insert or delete rows, as well as set the borders and shading for the table (discussed in Chapter 8, which is all about formatting).

To access the formatting options that are specific to repeating tables, right-click the table and select Properties. The formatting options for repeating tables are similar to those for sections, so the only thing to note here is that if you want to change the binding for your table, click the Change Binding button to invoke the Binding dialog box previewed in Figure 7-6 and select the group and fields to be used for your table.

Working with Lists

Another handy method for entering multiple items onto a form is through the use of lists. There are a number of different types of lists available within InfoPath, including plain lists, numbered lists, and bulleted lists like the one shown in Figure 7-20.

The concept behind lists is that users can choose the number of items they would like to enter—as a user finishes entering an item, they can simply press

7

FIGURE 7-20   A typical bulleted list

ENTER to move on to the next line. This simple data entry method is effective for creating forms for everything from capturing agenda items to entering detailed instructions, and it doesn't require any additional training for users to be able to use this feature. (If they are familiar with other Office products, they have probably used some sort of lists before.)

Inserting a List Control

To insert a list into your form, drag one of the List controls from the Controls task pane to your form. There are three different List controls available:

- Plain List
- Numbered List
- Bulleted List

If you are creating your data source on-the-fly, a group and a field are inserted for your list; otherwise, the standard Binding dialog box appears, enabling you to bind your list to an existing group within your data source.

Formatting a List Control

To access the formatting options for a list, right-click the list and choose Properties from the shortcut menu shown in the following illustration. The Properties dialog box for a list is similar to the Properties dialog boxes for the other objects that you have previously looked at. You can set a default value for your list (that is, the values that will appear by default when filling out the form) by using the text box provided, and use the other property pages to set other general options.

Working with Pictures

The last type of control you are going to look at in this chapter allows users to add pictures to their forms. For example, in the Employee Information form shown in Figure 7-21, the user can add an employee photo to the form by clicking the icon.

   This feature is where InfoPath really expands on functionality you might have found lacking in traditional electronic forms. It can be used to capture photographs, images, and other graphics to be stored in an XML file or database. Typical uses for this feature include storing photographs of employees, assets, and so on, as well as graphic elements normally submitted in other forms or reports, including charts, graphs, plots, and more.

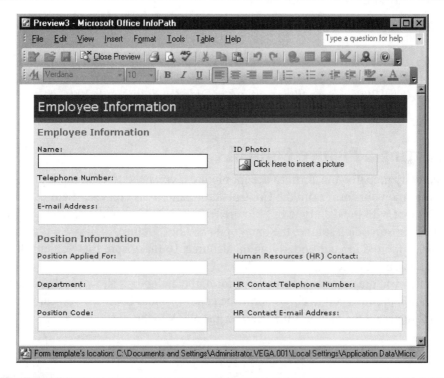

FIGURE 7-21   Adding a picture through a form

For adding pictures to a form, InfoPath supports the following graphics file formats:

- Enhanced Metafile (.emf)

- Graphics Interchange Format (.gif)

- Joint Photographic Experts Group (.jpg)

- Portable Network Graphics (.png)

- Microsoft Windows Bitmap (.bmp, .rle, .dib)

- Windows Metafile Graphics (.wmf)

- Tagged Image File Format (.tiff)

- Encapsulated PostScript (.eps)

NOTE *You can also insert other pictures in other graphic formats by using the filters that ship with Microsoft Office 2003 or stand-alone versions of Word 2003. These filters are not included with InfoPath 2003, so you need to either install Office or Word to use these filters.*

Inserting a Picture Control

To actually prepare your form to accept pictures, you need to drag the Picture control onto your form from the Controls task pane. This creates a field in your data source with the data type of "Picture." If you want to create a Picture object from an existing data source, the data type *must* be "Picture." This data type may not be supported in your underlying data source, so make sure that you check before you use this feature.

When you drag the object onto your form, the dialog box shown in the following illustration prompts you to choose how the control should behave—you can set the control to accept the graphics file itself or just a link to the file.

If you select the Included in the Form option, keep in mind that the size of the resulting data could be quite large, depending on the size and resolution of the graphic. If you instead select the As a Link option, remember that only the following graphics formats are supported:

- Joint Photographic Experts Group (.jpg)
- Graphics Interchange Format (.gif)
- Portable Network Graphics (.png)

Formatting a Picture Control

When displaying a Picture control on a form, you have the choice of showing the default picture or specifying your own image. To set this and other formatting options, right-click the Picture Control and select Properties to open the dialog box shown here.

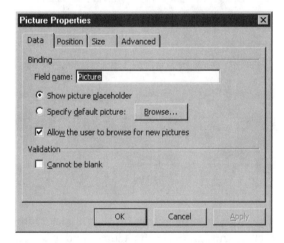

To specify the default picture that is used, select the Specify Default Picture radio button and then click the Browse button to open a standard Open dialog box and browse for the picture that you want to use as your default. Like other objects we have looked at, you can also control the size and position of your Picture control by using the other property pages in the Properties dialog box.

TIP   *InfoPath also includes an Ink Picture control that allows you to enter ink directly onto your form, which then can be stored as a picture within your data source. For more information on using InfoPath with a Tablet PC, select Help | Microsoft InfoPath Help and search on the term Ink.*

Working with Hyperlinks

In addition to inserting pictures into an InfoPath form, you can also insert hyperlinks. A hyperlink within InfoPath is a text object that is linked to a web page or e-mail address. When the user clicks a hyperlink to a web page, a separate browser window opens with the hyperlink's URL (for example, www.microsoft.com). If an e-mail address has been specified with a "mailto" command (for instance, mailto:user@ domain.com), the user's default e-mail client opens a blank message to the e-mail address specified.

Inserting Hyperlinks

To insert a hyperlink into your form, select Insert | Hyperlink to open the dialog box shown here.

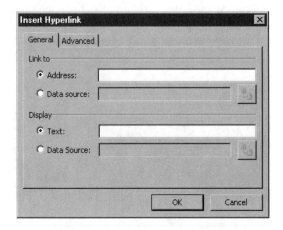

You can either hard-code your hyperlink by entering an address and some text to display or you can pick up the values for the address and text from your underlying data source. For example, if you want to put a link to a web page on your intranet that contains more information on filling out this particular form, you could enter the address and display text by entering the information in the two text boxes provided. This is the default method when creating hyperlinks in InfoPath.

On the other hand, if you are designing the query view of a form and have a list of companies and their web sites being returned from your data source, you could specify both the text to be displayed and the link address by picking the field that contains this information. To set the address and text from fields within your data source, click the Data Source radio button and use the icon to the right of the text field to select the field to use.

TIP *The field will be displayed using its XPath reference, which will be defined in the following section.*

Working with Expression Boxes

The final type of control to look at is the expression box, which is used to perform calculations using formulas written as XPath expressions. XPath is a query language for XML documents that can be used to address different parts of XML schemas, so you can select the specific part you want.

This is similar to how spreadsheet formulas are created. If you have two columns of data and want to add them together, you reference them using their cell addresses (for instance, +E4 +F4). In InfoPath, you use the same method to reference parts of your form, but instead of using cell references, you use XPath to describe where these elements can be found on your form. In addition, XPath also provides functions and operators for working with the data held in these elements.

For example, in this section, you are going to be working with an InfoPath form that is a simple commercial invoice. This invoice has a repeating table with data entry objects that can be used to enter the Item Number, Description, Price, Ship Cost, and so on. These objects tie directly back into the underlying data source, which is shown in Figure 7-22.

If you want to create a simple expression to add the Price and Ship Cost together, you could simply use the expression shown here:

```
my:shipping+my:amount
```

When referencing fields in your data source, you will always use the "my" prefix, which refers to the XML namespace, along with the field name:

```
my:shipping
```

or

```
my:price
```

You can also refer to groups using the full path:

```
my:items/my:item/my:price
```

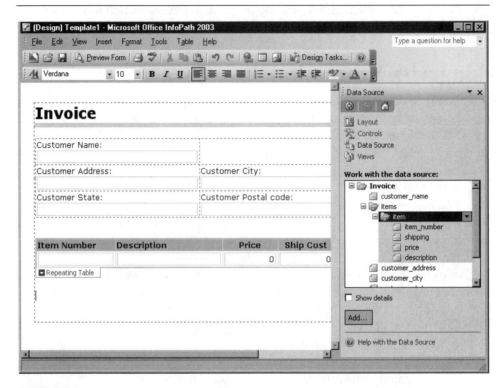

FIGURE 7-22   The invoice form and underlying data source

If this all seems a bit confusing at first, don't worry! When working with expression fields, you can use the GUI tools provided within InfoPath to select the field or group without having to write the entire expression yourself. The easiest way to learn how to create and modify expressions is to create some of your own, which you will do next.

Inserting Expression Boxes

To insert a new expression into your form, select View | Design Tasks and then click Controls and drag an Expression Box control onto your form. This opens the dialog box shown in the following illustration and allows you to enter an XPath expression to be displayed on your form.

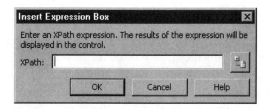

7

If you need some help creating your XPath expression, you can use the icon to the right of the XPath text box to select a field or group to use as the basis for your expression. The following sections look at some of the most common types of XPath expressions and how they are created and used.

Simple Arithmetic Calculations

Most of the expressions you will write within InfoPath will be simple arithmetic calculations: adding, subtracting, multiplying, and dividing one or more fields or constants. There are five simple arithmetic operators, listed in Table 7-1.

The reason the Description column states "two or more fields or constants" is that you can use expressions to perform calculations by using the fields that appear in your data source, by using constants that you enter (for example, 3.14), or by using both. From the form we have been working with in this section, you could use an expression box to calculate the sales tax for each item on your invoice. If we knew the sales tax to be 10 percent, you could insert an expression such as this into a repeating table:

```
my:amount*.10
```

Since you placed this expression in a repeating table, it would be evaluated and displayed for each row in the table. Likewise, if you wanted to add the price of each item together with the shipping costs, you could add the two fields together:

```
my:amount + my:shipping
```

Operator	Use
+	Add two or more fields or constants
-	Subtract between two or more fields or constants
*	Multiply two or more fields or constants
Div	Divide two or more fields or constants
Mod	Return the remainder when dividing between two or more fields or constants

TABLE 7-1   Simple Arithmetic Operators

You may notice that, when working with expressions, InfoPath sometimes displays "NaN" or "1. #QNAN" as the result of an expression. This is shorthand for "Not A Number" and this message will be displayed when the results of an expression cannot be identified as numeric. To fix this problem, make sure the fields that are used on your expression have default numeric values (for example, 0). To set the default values for a particular field, right-click the field and select Properties. Enter a value in the Default Value text box. This should eliminate the error message and allow you to continue working with your expression.

Using Numeric Functions

In addition to the simple arithmetic operators listed in Table 7-1, InfoPath also has a number of functions that you can use to create formulas, as listed in Table 7-2.

To sum a column of numbers that appears in a repeating table or section, you need to insert an expression box outside of the table or section boundaries. In this example, you are going to look at summing the Amount column of your invoice. After you insert an expression box below the repeating table, you can click the icon in the Insert Expression Box dialog box to select the path to use in your expression. In this case, you are summing up the Amount field, so the path would look like this:

```
my:items/my:item/my:amount
```

To use any of the functions mentioned earlier, you would need to enter the function name and surround the field reference in parentheses, as shown here:

```
Sum(my:items/my:item/my:amount)
```

This would return the sum of the Amount column that appears in the repeating table, so your form might look something like the one shown in Figure 7-23.

Function	Use
Sum	Sum a column of numeric fields
Count	Count the items in a column
Round	Round numerical values up to the nearest integer

TABLE 7-2   Numeric Functions

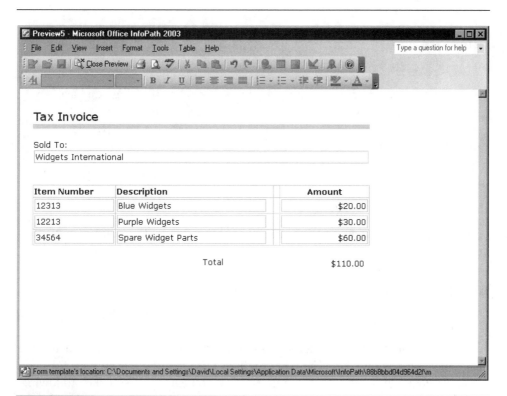

FIGURE 7-23   A sum of column values

The other numeric functions work in the same manner—the Count function can be used to calculate the occurrences of a certain field. You could use this function to count the total number of items shown in the invoice by using the expression shown here:

```
count(my:items/my:item/my:itemnumber)
```

The Round function is used to round off numbers to the nearest integer. For example, if you wanted to sum the total shipping costs and then round off to the nearest dollar, you could write an expression like this:

```
round(sum(my:items/my:item/my:itemnumber)))
```

Formatting Results May Differ

Your actual results may be different depending on the formatting you have applied to your expression box. The preceding example assumes that you have formatted your expression box to display a currency format with two decimal places. More information about formatting options is provided in the upcoming "Formatting Expression Boxes" section.

If the sum of the shipping costs is $320.56, for example, the expression would round this number up to the nearest whole integer and display $321.00.

Working with String Functions

The last category of XPath functions you'll look it is for manipulating strings, using the functions listed in Table 7-3.

The most commonly used function is Concat, which can be used to concatenate two or more strings together. These strings aren't limited to fields on your form— you could combine fields with string literals that you enter yourself. The following example uses the Concat function to concatenate a First Name field and a Last Name field that appear on a form, with a space in between:

```
concat(my:firstname, " ", my:lastname)
```

Function	Use
Concat	Concatenate two or more strings together
String-length	Return the length of the string
Substring	Return part of a string based on a starting position and length

TABLE 7-3   String Functions

> **NOTE** *Any string literals that you want to concatenate have to be enclosed in double quotes.*

You can also use this technique to concatenate multiple fields and string literals, as in the following example, where the e-mail address is built and displayed based on the pattern of *firstname.lastname@company.com*:

```
concat(my:firstname, ".", my:lastname, "@company.com")
```

In addition to putting strings back together, you can also pull them apart and return parts of a string using the Substring function. To be able to use Substring, you need to imagine that the string itself is an array and that each letter within the string is assigned an index number. For example:

```
John Smith
12345678910
```

Substring can work in two ways. First, you can specify a string and a starting point, and the Substring function will return the part of the string from the starting point to the

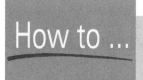 **... Format an Expression Box**

You also may notice that when you are working with expression boxes, the manner in which the results are displayed isn't quite as you expect. The reason is that when you create an expression box, InfoPath has no way of knowing what the output from the expression box will look like—whether it will be a string, currency, number, or something else—so there are no formatting attributes applied to the object when you create it.

You can format expression boxes and the results they contain by right-clicking the box and selecting Properties. On the General tab, you can use the Format As drop-down box to select a generic format type (for instance, Text, Decimal, Whole Number, and so on) or you can click the Format button to open a standard formatting dialog box in which you can select the format for your field by example.

end. For example, using the preceding string, the following expression would return the substring "Smith":

```
substring("John Smith", 6)
```

The other way that Substring works is to specify both the start and end point. The following example specifies to start at the sixth character and continue to the ninth character:

```
substring("John Smith", 6,9)
```

This would return a substring of "Smit". You can use this function on fields and string literals, and it is handy to use if you have product codes or other fields that are made up of components (for example, where the first two digits are the department).

 *The formatting options for the different fields are identical to the formatting options for data entry objects, as covered in Chapter 6.*

Summary

This chapter looked at a number of different types of sections and objects that you can use to create more complex forms. The next chapter takes that theme a little further with some advanced formatting techniques to make your forms really shine.

Chapter 8

Form Formatting

How to…

- ■ Use layout tables
- ■ Create and manage form views
- ■ Work with borders and shading
- ■ Use color schemes
- ■ Conditionally format objects

Now that you have had a chance to look at the different types of controls and sections that you can use in your forms, it's time to look at where you will spend the majority of your development time—formatting forms.

This chapter covers the whole gamut of formatting options for your forms, starting with organizing your form using layout tables, views, and more. You'll then move on to working with borders and shading, as well as how to use InfoPath's built-in color schemes to apply a coordinated look to your forms.

The chapter ends with a look at conditional formatting. Conditional formatting works on the basis that if some condition is true, then a formatting attribute will be applied. You can use this formatting technique to draw attention to invalid data entries, incorrect values, and more—most of the objects that you have looked at so far in InfoPath can use conditional formatting, so the possibilities are endless!

Before you get to that point, you need to look at how to better organize your form design, which is where you will start using layout tables.

Controlling Form Layout

You have probably noticed that the InfoPath Designer behaves a lot like a web development tool. Objects are placed on the page and flow down the page as if your form were a web page that the user could scroll through. While InfoPath makes it easy to quickly create new forms, you are going to need to use a couple of tricks from some old web developers to make your form look like you want it to.

When the Internet first became popular, users weren't too worried about how the individual pages looked—most pages were just simple text and didn't have any formatting applied, other than a few changes to the font and size for emphasis. As the Internet has grown, web developers have pushed the boundary of web page design and can now create complex, highly formatted pages in just about any configuration you want.

One of the tricks they use to create these pages is a layout table. A layout table is an invisible table of rows and columns that provides the structure for the page. Using layout tables, web developers can create any number of different layouts and designs, ensuring that each component will be placed correctly on the page.

InfoPath also features its own layout tables, which you can use to help add some structure and spacing to your form. Most of the sample forms you have looked at so far have used layout tables to control the spacing and placement of objects within the form. In the Time Card form shown in Figure 8-1, a layout table has been used to hold the Employee information and separates the fields into two columns with a "spacer" column in between.

The following sections look at how to insert and format this type of table.

> NOTE   *Don't confuse layout tables with repeating tables—repeating tables are used to hold fields that are part of a group and can be a variable number of rows depending on how many items the user enters. Layout tables are of a fixed size and are used to hold individual fields that do not repeat.*

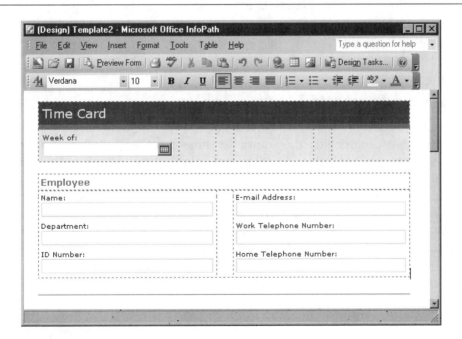

FIGURE 8-1   A typical form with a layout table

How to ... Insert Layout Tables

To insert a layout table into your form, select Insert | Layout Table to open the small dialog box shown here.

You need to enter the number of rows and columns for your table. After you enter the required information, click OK and your new table will be displayed on your form. By default, a layout table is displayed with a single dotted-line border. This border only appears when you are designing your form. When you are previewing or filling out your form, the table or its boundaries do not appear (unless you specifically added a border or shading to the table or cells).

To add objects to a layout table, you can either drag and drop them directly into the cells within the table or click within the cell and then use any of the insert methods described in the preceding chapter. For example, if you want to insert a hyperlink into your table, click within the cell where you want to place it and then select Insert | Hyperlink.

Inserting Formatted Layout Tables

You can also insert preformatted layout tables into your form by selecting View | Task Pane and then using the drop-down list at the top of the Task Pane to select Layout. This opens the dialog box shown in Figure 8-2, with all the preformatted layout tables that are available.

Selecting the Table with Title option inserts a one-column, two-row layout table with a border between the two rows, as shown in Figure 8-3.

There are placeholders within the table for the form title and content, and you can change the color, width, and style of the border that appears between the two rows by using the Borders and Shading options, which are described later in this chapter in the section "Working with Borders and Shading."

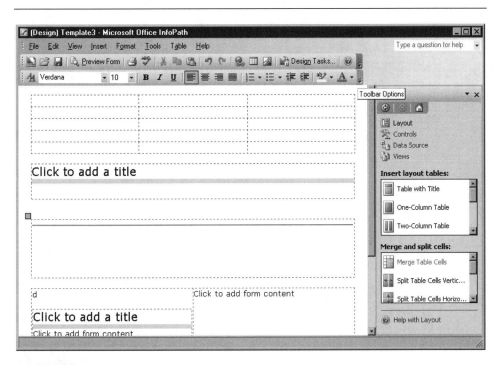

FIGURE 8-2   Layout options

The rest of the preformatted layout tables are pretty simple, with options for inserting a one-, two-, or three-column table. Most times you will want to create your own tables either by using Insert | Layout Table or by selecting the Custom Table option from the Layout view of the task pane.

Again, regardless of how the layout table has been created, the process for adding objects to the table is the same. In the case of some of the preformatted tables, there may be some placeholder text that appears in the table or cell (for example, "Click to add form content"), but once you click in the cell where this text appears, it quickly disappears.

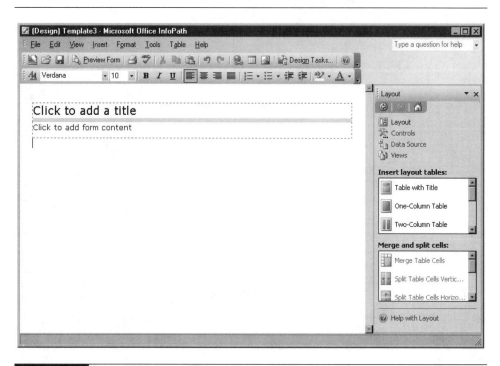

FIGURE 8-3 Layout table created by selecting Table with Title

Formatting Layout Tables

If you are an experienced Office user (current or previous versions), most of the formatting techniques that you are going to look at in this section will seem familiar to you. One of the design goals of the developers of InfoPath was to share a common user interface with other Office applications, and you can see the results of that focus at work when you are formatting tables.

Once you have inserted tables in your form, you can control the majority of formatting options through the right-click menu, shown here.

To insert a new row or column into your table, right-click within a cell at the point where you want to insert the row or column. Then, select Insert from the right-click menu, and choose one of the following options from the Insert menu:

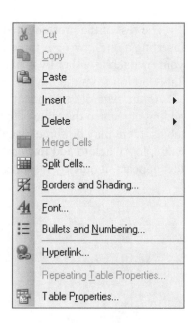

- Columns to the left

- Columns to the right

- Rows above

- Rows below

TIP *Alternately, you could also select an entire row or column by using your mouse pointer and then right-clicking to select an option from the Insert menu.*

Similarly, if you want to delete rows or columns (or even the entire table itself!), right-click anywhere within the table (or highlight a row or column and then select the Delete menu) and select one of the options from this list:

- **Table**   Deletes the entire table

- **Rows**   Deletes the currently selected row(s)

- **Columns**   Deletes the currently selected column(s)

In addition to inserting and deleting rows and columns, you can also perform other table operations, like merging and splitting cells. To merge two cells together, highlight two or more contiguous cells within your layout table and then right-click the highlighted selection and select Merge Cells.

TIP *You could also select a number of merge and split operations from the options found at the bottom of the Layout task pane.*

To split a cell, right-click within the cell that you want to divide, and select Split Cells to open the dialog box shown here.

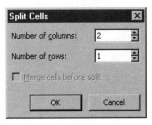

You can specify the number of resulting rows and columns you want to create and click OK to return to your form design. Another option for splitting cells is to merge them first before you actually split them. In this scenario, you may have two columns that you actually want to split into three columns and two rows. Instead of merging the cells first and then splitting them, you could simply highlight both columns and then select Merge Cells from the right-click menu. The Merge Cells Before Split option will be enabled, which allows you to merge the cells before they are split apart into the new configuration.

Working with Table Properties

In addition to all the options found on the
right-click menu, there is also a set of property
pages associated with each layout table. You can
access these property pages by right-clicking
anywhere within the table and selecting Table
Properties to open the dialog box shown here.

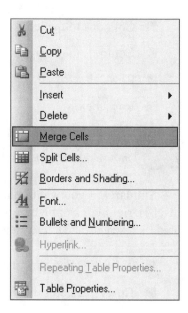

You can select how your table will be aligned
on the page from the default property page—there
are also property pages for the rows and columns
that appear in your table, and you can use the
options on these pages to control the height and
width of the same. The Cell tab, for instance, is
used to set the vertical alignment for the text and
other objects within a cell. You can specify the
padding you would like to use for the inside of
the cell as well.

Working with Views

When you are trying to design an efficient, well-structured form, layout tables can
go a long way toward helping you organize your form content on a page. But what
about when you have more than one page worth of content? You could leave all of
this content on a single (but very long) page and allow users to scroll down to see
the rest of the form content, but there is a much easier way to organize your forms.

Views within an InfoPath form allow you to separate form content onto
separate pages within a single form. When users open a form, they will be
presented with a default view and can then change to other views as required to see
the other "pages" of form content. In addition to helping organize form contents,
you can also use views to apply the same formatting to multiple objects that may
appear on a view. Another handy use for views is that they can be used to create
a "print version" of the form that is optimized for printing on a printer (that is, it
may have a header, footer, page numbers, and so on).

The following sections describe how to create new views and format the same.

Creating New Views

When you are designing a form, you can see all the views that are available by
selecting View | Manage Views to open the Views task pane, as shown in Figure 8-4.

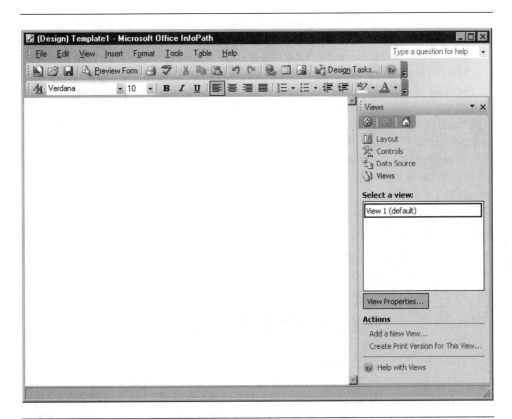

8

FIGURE 8-4   Views task pane

When you first create a new form, a view labeled View 1 is automatically created and is set as the default view. To create a new view, click the link at the bottom of the Task Pane marked Add a New View, which opens the dialog box shown here.

Enter a name for your new view and click OK to add a new blank view to your form. InfoPath immediately displays your new view, and you then can add controls and other elements to the view as you normally would. When working with a form,

you can switch between views by selecting View | Manage Views to open the Views
task pane and then clicking to select the view you want to work with.

When previewing or filling out a form, you can switch between views by using
the View menu. In the example shown in the following illustration, the View menu
includes three different views (Customer Information,
Contact Information, Sales Opportunities) for a form
that has been created for entering information about a
prospective customer.

By default, all views appear in the View menu, but
you can change this behavior by editing the view's
properties.

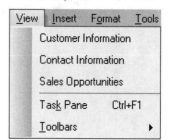

Formatting Views

To view the properties for a particular view, select View | Manage Views, choose
the view from the list, and then click the View Properties button to open the dialog
box shown here.

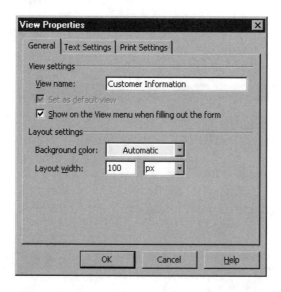

You can use the General tab to change the name of a view. The options
immediately below the View Name text box control whether this view is the default
(that is, it is shown when the form is opened) and whether or not the view is shown
in the Views menu when the form is previewed or filled out.

Using the drop-down list at the bottom of the General tab, you can control the background color for your view, as well as the layout width. This doesn't actually physically change the size of the page but it does set the default width of any layout tables that you may have added to your view.

To set the default font, font size, and color for objects within your view, click the Text Settings tab, shown here.

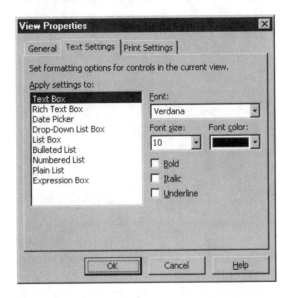

This tab enables you to set the font for a particular type of object that appears on your view. For example, if you decide that you want all the text boxes on your form to be 12-point Arial, you could go through and format each text box the old way (which would be tedious). Instead, you could use this tab to select a particular type of object (for example, Text Box) and a font, size, and so on and that formatting would be applied to every text box that appears on the view you are working with. This is especially handy if you are working with a number of fields and quickly need to format them all at once.

Creating Print Views

Another important use of views is to provide an alternate version of a form for printing purposes. You can set the printing options for a particular view through the Print Settings tab, shown here.

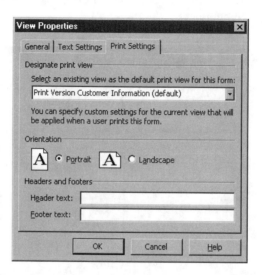

You can use these options to specify which view will be used when printing out a particular view. Seem confusing? Think of it this way—say you had a form that had three different views in place. You could create a separate print view for each of these views so that you could print each individually, or you could create a single print view that would display the contents of all three views.

The choice is up to you whether you have a 1:1 relationship between views and their print views—in fact, you don't even have to display the same objects on each. You could have a view in an Expense Report that shows the employee's name, detailed expenses, and so on, and a print view that shows only the total for the expenses, with a place for a manager to sign. How you choose to use print views is up to you (and your imagination).

You can also create a print view for an existing view by highlighting the view in the Task Pane and clicking the Create Print Version for This View link at the bottom.

In the Orientation area of the Print Settings tab, you can select whether your view will be printed Portrait or Landscape. At the bottom of the tab, you can enter text for a header and footer for your view, which will appear at the top and bottom of the printed page.

 *To see what your view will look like printed, preview the form and then select File | Print Preview to get a WYSIWYG view of your printed form.*

Advanced Form Formatting

So now that you have had a look at some of the formatting options associated with views, you are ready to look at some of the formatting techniques that haven't been covered up to this point. Since the majority of the time that you will spend developing an InfoPath form will be spent working on the layout and formatting of both the form and the objects on the form itself, you should be able to pick up some tricks in the following sections to make your forms look like they were designed by a pro.

Working with Borders and Shading

The task of adding borders and shading to a particular object has been saved for this chapter because the process of adding these formatting attributes is similar regardless of what type of object you are attempting to apply them to.

To add a border to an object (Text Box, Table, and so on), right-click the object and select Borders and Shading from the right-click menu. This opens the dialog box shown in Figure 8-5.

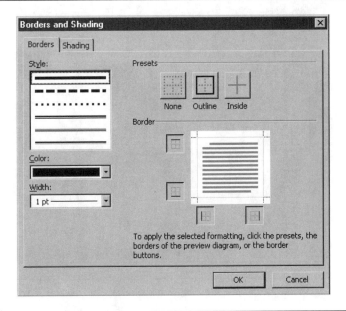

FIGURE 8-5 Borders and Shading dialog box options

With an interface similar to the Borders dialog box in Microsoft Word, you can select the style, color, and width of the border to be applied by using the drop-down lists on the left side of the dialog box. On the right side of the dialog box are a number of preset border styles and a graphic that shows you the effect of your border selection on the object that you have selected. You can click the icons around this graphic to apply a border to the top, bottom, left, and right of your object and the display will show you how the object will look when finished.

To add shading to an object, click the Shading tab, shown in Figure 8-6.

By default, each object is set to No Color, but you can select a color from the Color drop-down list. If the color that you want to apply is not in the list, you can use the More Colors option to open the standard Windows color picker, where you can select from a spectrum of colors or enter your own RGB values to create a custom color.

Using Color Schemes

If you are a bit leery of selecting colors that clash, there is no need to be. In addition to the format tools that you have looked at so far, InfoPath has some predefined color

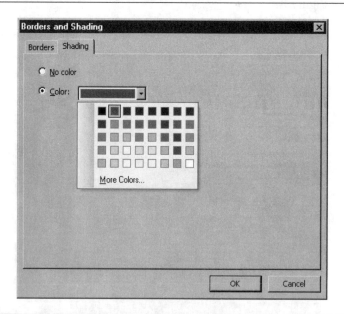

FIGURE 8-6   Shading options

schemes that can add a bit of pizzazz to your forms. To apply a color scheme to your form, select View | Design Tasks (just to open the Task Pane) and then use the drop-down list at the top of the Task Pane to select the option for Color Schemes. This opens the dialog box shown in the following illustration and allows you to select a color scheme for your form.

As you add different objects to your form, these colors will be applied. For example, if you select the Blueberry color scheme and then add a Table with Title layout table, your form might look something like the one shown in Figure 8-7.

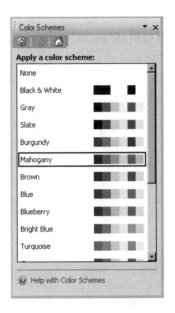

 *To answer that frequently asked question: No, you can't change any of the colors in a scheme or create your own.*

8

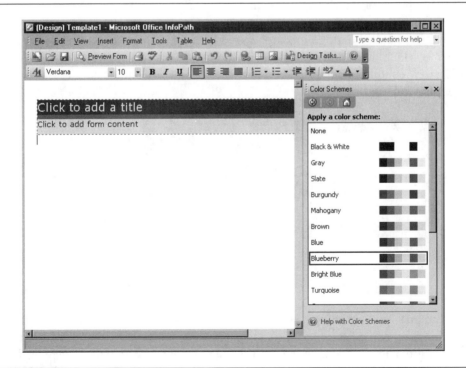

FIGURE 8-7   A color scheme applied

Conditional Formatting

The basic concept behind conditional formatting is simple—if a condition is true, then some formatting attribute (or attributes) will be switched "on." Conditional formatting can be applied to a number of different types of objects, including data-entry controls and sections. The reason that this chapter looks at conditional formatting is that the process of setting up conditional formatting is the same regardless of what type of object you are working with.

To set up conditional formatting on a text box, for example, click to select the text box object and then select Format | Conditional Formatting. This opens the dialog box shown in the following illustration and allows you to create the conditions that will trigger your formatting choices. You can also add conditional formatting by right-clicking the control, choosing properties, the Display tab and Conditional Formatting.

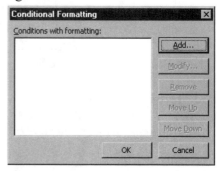

Notice that this dialog box can be used to enter multiple conditions—the order in which the conditions appear in the list determines the precedence. To add a new condition, click the Add button to open the Conditional Format dialog box, shown here.

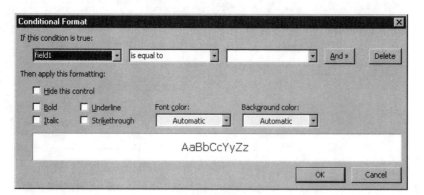

The first step in creating a new condition is to select a field or group to use from the first drop-down list (you'll look at expressions in Chapter 10). By default, the field or group that is bound to the control you are working with will be displayed, but you can use the drop-down list to select another field or group from your form's data source.

Once you have selected a field, you need to choose an operator from the next drop-down list. You can select from the following operators:

- Is equal to
- Is not equal to
- Is less than
- Is less than or equal to
- Is greater than
- Is greater than or equal to
- Is present
- Is not present
- Is blank
- Is not blank
- Contains (to check whether a field contains a string you enter)
- Does not contain
- Begins with (to check whether a field starts with a string you enter)
- Does not begin with

After you have selected an operator, you can use the third drop-down list to enter the value, field, or group you want to compare against. The available options are shown here.

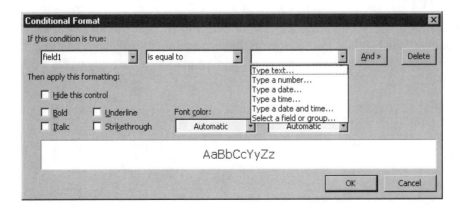

If you want to add compound criteria, you can click the Add button to add another line to your list of conditions and keep on going. Conditions can be put together using either an And or an Or. For example, if you want to conditionally format a field to be displayed in red when the Expense Total field is over $1000 and the Cash Advance field is over $250, you could put these two conditions on separate lines and use the options in this dialog box to select the And operator.

With any of the conditions you may create, where the condition is true then a formatting attribute will be applied. Your options for these attributes include

- Hide this control
- Bold
- Italic
- Underline
- Strikethrough
- Font color
- Background color

The box at the bottom of the dialog box will display what your field or object would look like if the condition were true. After you finish selecting your formatting attributes, click OK to return to the list of Conditional Formatting criteria to be applied to this object. You can use the Add button to add as many sets of criteria as you like and use the Move Up/Move Down buttons to set the precedence of the criteria.

Summary

With a bit of form formatting under your belt, you are ready to turn your attention to some of the behind-the-scenes work that is required to make sure that the data entered into an InfoPath form is valid. Thus, validation is the topic of the next chapter.

Part III

Advanced Form Design

Chapter 9

Validate Form Data

How to…

■ Eliminate blank fields

■ Create validation rules

■ Use validation operators

■ Create alerts inline and with dialog boxes

If you have ever worked on a database-reporting or data-warehousing project, you know how important data quality is to turning raw data into decision-making information. While there are a number of good data-cleansing applications available on the market, it is much easier to catch any data entry errors at the beginning. InfoPath has a robust toolset for ensuring the quality of the data that has been entered via an InfoPath form.

Validation within InfoPath can be used to ensure that users enter the correct values on a form and that these values adhere to the business rules in place within your organization. This chapter surveys the validation features within InfoPath and shows how they can be used to ensure that the data entered into your forms is correct. The chapter starts with an overview of how validation works and then moves on to describe how to create your own validation rules by using the tools provided within InfoPath.

How Validation Works

Validation in InfoPath is used to check values entered against some criteria that the form designer has established. This criteria could be used to enforce something very simple, like making the user fill out all the blank fields in a form, or it could be used to check values against certain company policies using a complex, compound set of criteria. When the criteria is true, an error message is generated, allowing the user to correct the problem before submitting or saving the form.

This criteria is called a *validation rule,* which is created within InfoPath using a standard set of validation operators (explained later in the chapter, in the section "Using Validation Operators"). You can use these operators to create complex sets of validation criteria—when the criteria is true, a validation error will occur.

Validation errors within an InfoPath form can manifest themselves in two ways. The first is with an inline error message, like the one shown in the illustration. If a control is marked as "Can't be blank," an inline error message appears as a red underline "in line" with the field where the error has occurred.

Otherwise, the inline error appears as a red-dashed border around the control. As a user moves their mouse over the field, ScreenTips text appears with an error message that the form designer has specified. The user can also right-click the field in question and obtain the full error description (which has also been specified by the form designer).

The other method used to display validation errors is a standard Windows dialog box that displays some text that the form designer has specified, as shown in Figure 9-1.

For larger or complex forms with a number of different data entry controls, the dialog box method can quickly draw attention to validation errors, but the inline method also has the advantage of being unobtrusive. Regardless of which method you decide to use, validation rules are created in the same way, which is what you will be looking at in the following sections.

> **NOTE** *You may also notice that you can perform validation by using scripting within InfoPath. If you are interested in using this method of validation, check out Chapter 10, which covers this and other scripting applications.*

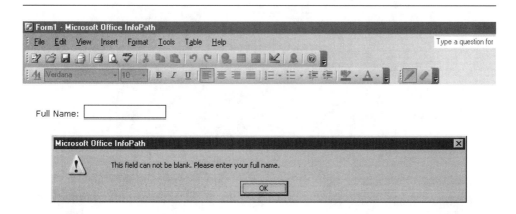

FIGURE 9-1   An example of a dialog box alert

Eliminating Blank Fields

On the most basic level, you can check the objects on your form to ensure that something has been entered into each. To force the user to enter a value into a data entry control, right-click the object and select Properties to open the dialog box shown in Figure 9-2.

To force the user to enter some value, select the Cannot Be Blank check box in the Validation area. When the form is viewed, the object will be shown with a red underline, like the object shown here.

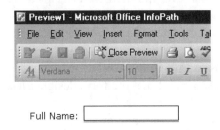

In addition, if the user attempts to save or submit the form, they will receive the error message shown in the following illustration, which indicates that the form

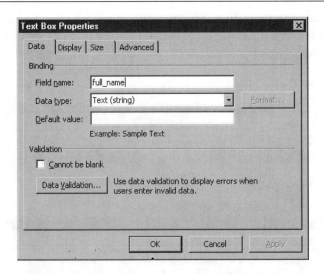

FIGURE 9-2　Object properties

has errors and asks the user if they still want to save it (keep in mind the user won't be able to submit it, however).

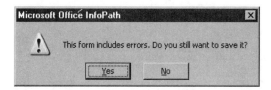

If the user selects No, they can go back and correct any errors in the form before saving or submitting it.

Creating Validation Rules

If you have more complex validation requirements, you probably want to consider using validation rules, which are sets of criteria that you can establish. If the value entered into the field does not meet that criteria, you can trigger either an error message inline with the field or an error message that is visible through an alert box, as described earlier.

Validation rules are created at the object level; in other words, rules are associated with the individual data entry controls that are present on your form. To create a new validation rule, right-click an object and select Properties.

On the Data tab of the Properties dialog box, click the Data Validation button to open the dialog box shown in Figure 9-3.

Click the Add button to open the Data Validation dialog box, shown in Figure 9-4.

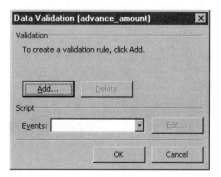

FIGURE 9-3   Data validation options

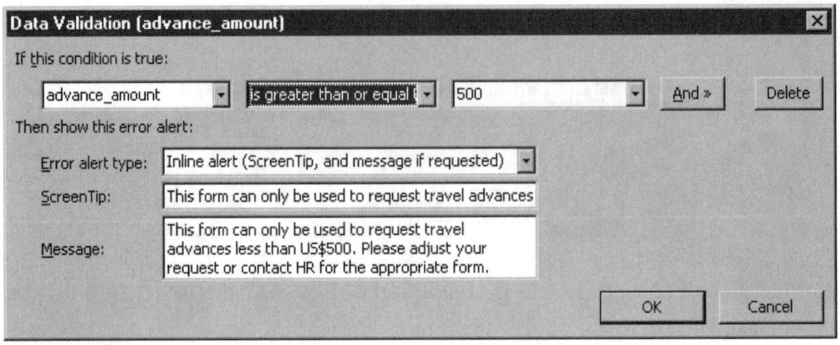

Data Validation (advance_amount)

If this condition is true:

| advance_amount ▼ | is greater than or equal t ▼ | 500 ▼ | And » | Delete |

Then show this error alert:

Error alert type: Inline alert (ScreenTip, and message if requested) ▼

ScreenTip: This form can only be used to request travel advances

Message: This form can only be used to request travel advances less than US$500. Please adjust your request or contact HR for the appropriate form.

OK   Cancel

FIGURE 9-4   Validation rule options

The way that validation rules work is that you can select a data entry control, or a field or a group of fields that appear within your data source and use a number of operators (Is Equal To, Starts With, and so on) to make a comparison against a value you enter or the contents of another field.

For example, you may have a Travel Request form with a numeric data entry control for the user to enter the travel advance they would like to receive. This object could have a criteria set so that if the user enters an amount over $500, an inline error or dialog box would be shown, indicating that the form couldn't be used to authorize these amounts.

The criteria in this case would be similar to the one shown in Figure 9-4, which specifies that if the condition is true that the advance_amount field is greater than or equal to 500, then the user receives an error alert stating that the form can only be used to request travel advances less than $500.

At a basic level, you can establish one set of criteria to check using the dialog box provided, or you can use the Add button to add extra criteria. Continuing the preceding example, you may want to allow people who have the title of "Manager" to request a larger travel advance. In this case, your criteria might look similar to the dialog box shown in Figure 9-5.

By default, the relationship between multiple validation rule criteria is And, but you can use the drop-down list provided to change this to Or. If you no longer need one of the sets of validation criteria you have added, you can use the Delete button to remove it from your rule.

So that you can learn how to create the different types of validation rules, the following section presents the different types of validation operators that you can use and leads you through some examples of where you would use each.

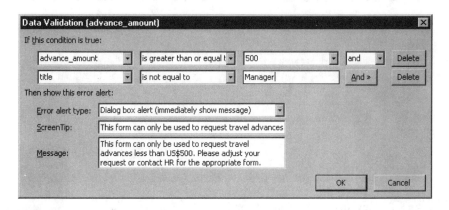

Data Validation (advance_amount)

If this condition is true:

| advance_amount ▼ | is greater than or equal t ▼ | 500 ▼ | and ▼ | Delete |
| title ▼ | is not equal to ▼ | Manager | And » | Delete |

Then show this error alert:

Error alert type: | Dialog box alert (immediately show message) ▼

ScreenTip: | This form can only be used to request travel advances

Message: | This form can only be used to request travel advances less than US$500. Please adjust your request or contact HR for the appropriate form.

[OK]   [Cancel]

FIGURE 9-5   Compound validation rule criteria

Using Validation Operators

Validation operators are used within InfoPath to build criteria that is used to validate data entered on to a form—most of the operators work in a similar fashion to operators you may be familiar with from other applications, including Microsoft Excel. Keep in mind that in addition to using these operators by themselves, you can also combine them with And or Or statements to create complex validation rules.

Performing Comparisons

The most basic type of operators are used for comparison:

■ Is Equal To, Is Not Equal To

■ Is Less Than, Is Less Than or Equal To

■ Is Greater Than, Is Greater Than or Equal To

You are probably familiar with how these comparison operators work—if the comparison is true, then the condition is met and an error message will be displayed. You have seen a couple of these comparison operators in action in the previous example. To use these operators in your own validation rules, right-click the data entry control that you want to work with and select Properties. In the Properties dialog box that opens, click the Data Validation button on the Data tab. In the Data Validation dialog box that opens, click Add to open the blank dialog box shown in Figure 9-6.

9

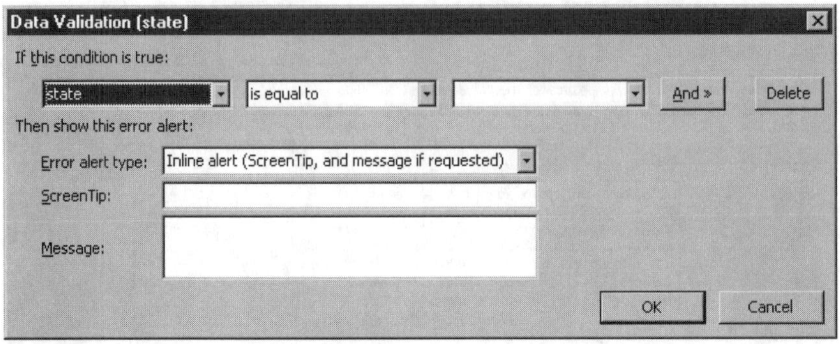

New data validation rule options

Using the leftmost drop-down list provided under If This Condition Is True, select the field or group you want to use for your comparison. By default, this is set to the field that is associated with the data entry control that you are working with, but you can change this to any valid field or group that you are using. Next, use the middle drop-down list to select the operator you want to use in your criteria.

Use the third drop-down list to select a comparison option. The items that appear in this list change depending on the data type of the object that you are working with. For example, if you are working with a text field, you'll have a number of different options for entering values to use in a comparison. You can type text, a number, a date, and so on, by using the options shown in Figure 9-7.

On the other hand, if your data entry control is tied to a numeric field, you will only be able to enter a number to be used in your comparison.

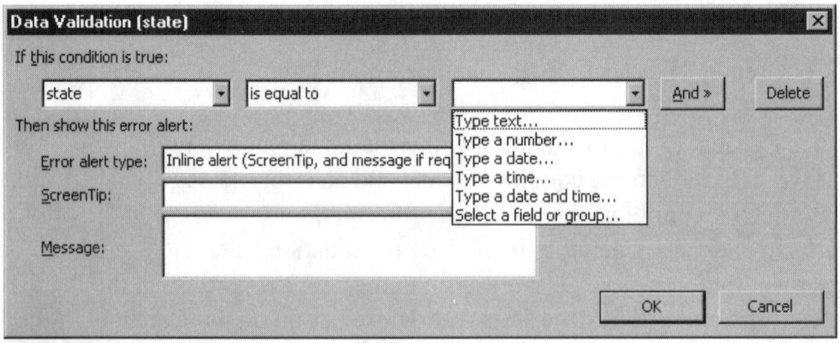

Comparison option

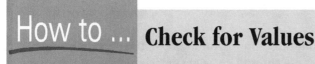

Check for Values

Another neat way to validate user input is to check that they have actually entered some values onto your form. To do this check, you have a special set of operators called Is Blank and Is Not Blank that you can use to check whether some data entry has occurred.

To use these operators, follow the same procedures as outlined previously to create a new validation rule and select this operator from the drop-down list provided. Notice in the illustration that the third (right) drop-down list is unavailable, because this operator isn't used to make a comparison against another entered or selected value—you are only checking whether the data entry object itself has some content.

Data Validation (state)						X
If this condition is true:						
state ▾	is blank ▾	▾	And »	Delete		
Then show this error alert:						
Error alert type:	Inline alert (ScreenTip, and message if requested) ▾					
ScreenTip:	This field cannot blank. Please enter a state.					
Message:	This field cannot be blank. Please enter a state.					
			OK	Cancel		

If the user is working with the form and skips a field, the Is Blank operator can be used to let them know, either with an inline message or dialog box, that they have skipped the field.

After you establish your validation rule criteria, you need to select what happens when that criteria is met. By default, validation rules are set to create inline alerts, where the data entry control is underlined in red, indicating that there is an error. Alternately, you could also have InfoPath pop up a dialog box with an error message—it's up to you. Make your selection from the drop-down list provided and then enter some text for the ScreenTip and message. InfoPath does not allow you to leave the ScreenTip blank, and if you have selected to use a dialog box, you have to enter some text for this as well.

Using Pattern Matching

Pattern matching within validation rules allows you to create patterns that can be used to search through values that are entered into data entry controls. Unlike the comparison operators, such as Equals To, for which you need an exact match, the pattern-matching operators (Contains, Begins With, and so on) can be used to match even part of a value.

There are two different types of pattern-matching operators available—the first is Contains/Does Not Contain, which can be used to search through data that has been entered into a data entry control to find a particular value. For example, if you have a form in which you don't want users to enter special characters (like an asterisk) in the Company Name field, you could use the Contains operator to trigger an error message when it encounters any of these special characters, as shown in Figure 9-8.

This operator works regardless of where the special character is within the text. In addition to single characters, you can check for entire phrases (for example, Contains "USA").

The other pattern-matching operator is Begins With/Does Not Begin With, which is used to compare a value against the beginning characters of a value entered. For example, you could create a validation rule for a Phone Number field such that for all numbers entered starting with 828, an error message would appear reminding the user to check for a changed area code, as in the example shown in Figure 9-9.

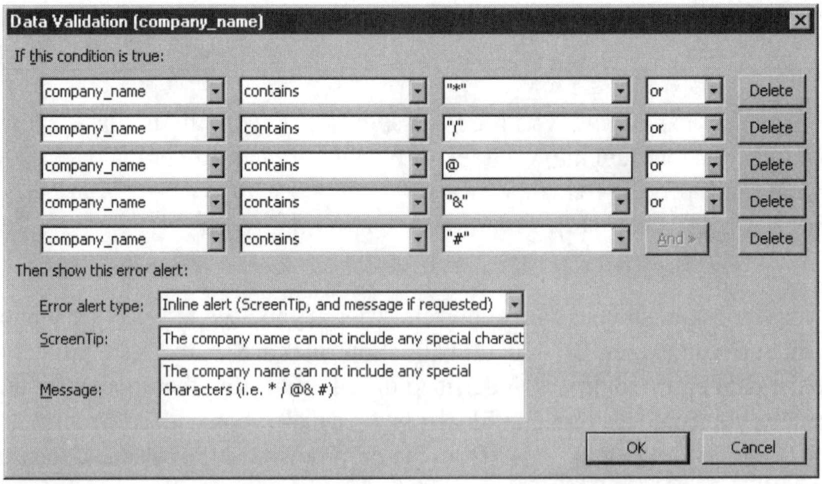

FIGURE 9-8   An example of the Contains operator in use

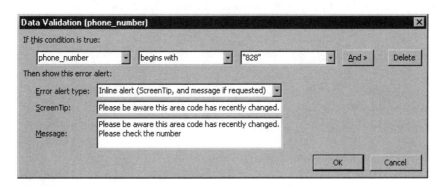

FIGURE 9-9   An example of the Begins With operator in use

Working with Expressions

XPath expressions were introduced in Chapter 7, in the discussion of expression boxes. As you probably remember, XPath is a reference and query language for XML documents and can be used to address different parts of XML schemas so that you can select the specific part that you want. In addition to referencing parts of an XML document, XPath also provides functions and operators for working with the data held in these elements.

To create an XPath expression for validation, you need to select the operator of "the expression" when creating your validation rule. This changes the data validation dialog box to show a text box that you can use to enter your expression. By default, your expression is shown as:

```
. = ""
```

The period stands for the field that you are currently working with; the equal sign and quotes have been placed there as a starting point for you to build your own expression. For example, if you want to check a Country field to see whether a value of USA has been passed, your expression would look like this:

```
. = "USA"
```

In addition to referencing a single field, you can also refer to other fields that appear on your form by using the fully qualified name. For example, if your form contains a field for ZIP code, you could check the value of this field and display an error related to your original field:

```
../my:zipcode = 28720
```

You can also use the XPath operators to perform calculations that you can use for validation. In the following example, the expression has been written to calculate a 10 percent tax rate and display an alert if this amount is greater than $100:

```
../my:ordertotal * .10 > 100
```

A key point about working with expressions is that not all the operators and functions described in Chapter 7 are valid for use with validation expressions. If you find yourself coming up against a brick wall and you can't find the operators or functions that you need using XPath, it may be time to consider using scripting to validate your form data, as described in the next section.

Working with Scripting

Now that you have been working with validation for a little while, you may have noticed that sometimes your criteria is a little more complex and can't be properly translated using the operators provided. If this is the case, you may want to consider using scripting to validate your form data. In this section, we'll look at that technique, but we may be getting a little ahead of ourselves. We haven't actually looked at scripting within InfoPath yet, but the next chapter covers it in depth, so you may need to flip back and forth between the next chapter and this section to make the most of this material.

TIP   *Alternately, put a bookmark in this section and come back to it after you have read Chapter 10.*

Script validation works on the basis of events—when a particular event fires, a snippet of JScript or VBScript can run, allowing you to validate the contents of a control and generate any error messages that are required. There are three different events that you can use for script validation: On Before Change, On Validate, and On After Change.

The difference between the three is that On Before Change is an event that fires when the user enters some data into a control, whereas On Validate fires when the validation rules are applied and On After Change fires after the user leaves a field.

How do you decide which to use? If you are using scripting validation in conjunction with the validation methods described earlier in the chapter, you will probably want to use the On Validate event so that your script will run when the validation occurs. You can then pass back an error message and allow the user to correct the error.

If you are not using the validation methods described earlier and are exclusively using scripting for validation, you can use any of these events to check your form for valid data, but if you want to catch errors when they are entered, use the On Before Change method.

Adding Scripting Validation

To add scripting validation to a data entry control that appears on your form, right-click the control and select Properties to open its Properties dialog box. Click the Data Validation button to open the dialog box shown here.

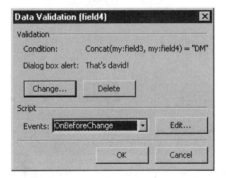

Using the Events drop-down list at the bottom of this dialog box, select the event you would like to use to validate your data (in this case, select OnBeforeChange) and then click the Edit button. This opens the Microsoft Script Editor, which is installed alongside InfoPath (see Figure 9-10). You will be entering into the Script Editor some script to be used for validation.

If this looks a bit daunting, don't worry—you are only going to enter a bit of code here; the remainder of scripting is left to Chapter 10. The Script Editor opens to a function that is related to the event that you selected, and the following line of code indicates where you need to enter your script for validation:

```
// Write your code here
```

In this example, you are going to look at the current value held within a text field used to hold the Country. If the content of this field is not USA, then you will display

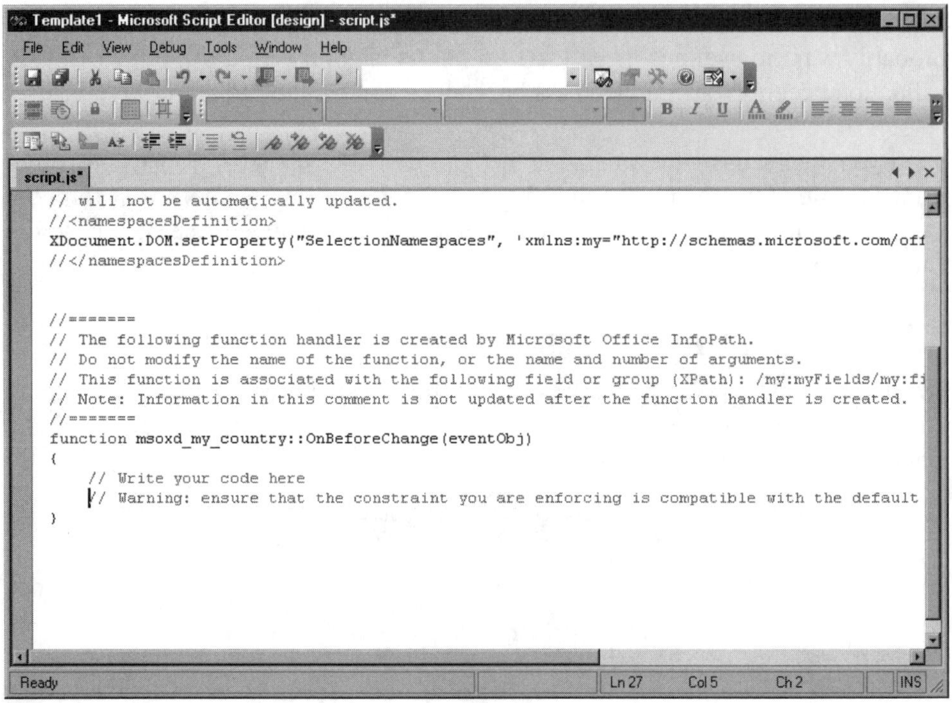

FIGURE 9-10   Microsoft Script Editor

an error message that states that this form can only be used for expenses in US dollars or the equivalent.

Within the Script Editor, you need to enter an If…then statement to check the value entered into the field. The easiest way to obtain the value entered into a field is to use a property called the nodeTypedValue. Once you have this value, you can check against a string literal that you have entered and then display an alert box, as shown here:

```
if (eventObj.Site.nodeTypedValue != "USA")
{
XDocument.UI.Alert("This form is only for expenses incurred in US Dollars");
}
```

This is a simple example of checking a value within a field. You have probably already noticed that this example introduced a number of concepts that are foreign to you at this point, like using scripting to access form data, showing alerts, and the like.

 *Again, this chapter focuses on working with simple scripting examples for the purposes of validation—for more detail on other, more advanced scripting topics, including other validation examples, see Chapter 10.*

You could also clear the values that have been entered immediately after displaying the error message by adding an assignment like the one shown here:

```
if (eventObj.Site.nodeTypedValue != "USA")
{
XDocument.UI.Alert("This form is only for expenses incurred in US Dollars");
eventObj.Site.nodeTypedValue = " ";
}
```

When creating scripts for validation, keep in mind that you may have three events to work with, but each of these events is tied to a function, and within that function you can perform multiple tasks. From the preceding example, not only could you check the contents of the field you are working with, but you also could look up an exchange rate, perform calculations, and so on, within the same function.

Summary

Now that you have had a look at how to create validation rules and are familiar with the operators that are available for use, you should be able to start creating your own validation rules. With the bit of scripting covered at the end of the chapter, you have a good lead-in to the next chapter, which is all about extending InfoPath and covers a wide range of programming topics, including scripting.

9

Chapter 10

Extend InfoPath

How to...

- Add scripting to a form
- Create custom task panes
- Use secondary data sources

Form design doesn't stop with data sources, controls, and formatting—InfoPath provides a robust set of tools that developers can use to meet complex user requirements. This chapter looks at these tools, starting with scripting. It also looks at how you can create your own custom task panes and use secondary data sources to look up information from other data sources. If you are looking to push the boundaries of InfoPath's functionality, this is definitely the chapter for you.

Working with Scripting

One of the key strengths of InfoPath is its capability to extend form functionality through scripting. InfoPath supports both JScript and VBScript and includes a built-in editor, Microsoft Script Editor (MSE) to create and edit scripts within your forms (MSE is a standard Microsoft script editor and is not built specifically for InfoPath).

Scripting can be used for a wide gamut of tasks, from validating data and performing simple calculations to connecting to secondary data sources, manipulating form data, and more. In the course of this chapter, you are going to learn some of the ways that you can use scripting in your own forms, but before you get started, you need to look at some of the options you have for working with scripting in InfoPath.

To start, you can create your forms in either VBScript or JScript. VBScript (short for Visual Basic, Scripting Edition) is based on Microsoft Visual Basic and was introduced to provide Visual Basic developers with an easy-to-write scripting language for the Web. JScript is Microsoft's implementation of JavaScript, a scripting language that is loosely related to the Java language. While JScript is Microsoft's own "flavor" of JavaScript, it is standards-based, so if you are familiar with JavaScript, you will have no problems here.

NOTE *During the course of this chapter, the scripting examples are in JScript exclusively. Appendix B provides a handy reference for some of the most commonly used declarations, methods, functions, and so on, that JScript provides. For more information on working with VBScript, check out http://msdn.microsoft.com/scripting/.*

If you are a scripting novice, you need to select which scripting language you want to use, a decision that is based on personal preference more than anything else. To set the default scripting language to be used each time you create a new form, select Tools | Options and then click the Design tab (which is available only while designing a form). There is a drop-down list box at the bottom of the dialog box that you can use to select the default scripting language that will be used for new forms.

> **TIP** *By default, your scripting language is JScript.*

So, with your default language set, you are ready to find out how you actually create scripts within your form, starting with a look at the Microsoft Script Editor.

Using the Microsoft Script Editor

The Microsoft Script Editor (MSE) is tightly integrated into InfoPath and provides a feature-rich environment you can use to create your own scripts. To launch MSE from within InfoPath, select Tools | Script | Microsoft Script Editor, which opens the window shown in Figure 10-1.

> **NOTE** *If you have worked with other web or application development tools from Microsoft, MSE may seem familiar to you—Microsoft distributes this editor with a number of other products.*

MSE opens in a separate window and you can switch between your form's design and MSE by using ALT-TAB. MSE's workspace is broken down into a number of different areas, with the main code window taking up the most real estate on the screen. The Document Outline, usually shown on the left, lets you jump to a specific section of code.

> **TIP** *To view MSE in full-screen mode, press SHIFT-ALT-ENTER.*

When creating and debugging your scripts, you need to save the script in MSE and then switch over to InfoPath to preview your form and test the script. This can be a bit cumbersome at first but you will soon get the hang of it! From within the preview of your form, all of your script will run; if there are any errors, an error dialog box will appear and you will have some debugging options that will allow you to return to MSE to correct the problem. Alternately, you could close the preview and use ALT-TAB to get back to MSE. It's up to you.

10

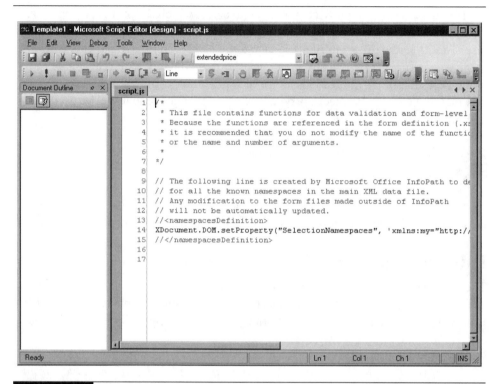

FIGURE 10-1   Microsoft Script Editor

    If you did a full install of Microsoft Office, you have the debugging tools installed. If you did a partial install or if the debugging tools are not installed, InfoPath will prompt you to install the tools the first time you start the Microsoft Script Editor.

Understanding the InfoPath Object Model

When you are working with scripting, there are a number of elements that have nothing to do with InfoPath. For example, if you are using JScript as your scripting language, there are a number of declarations, functions, methods, and so on, that are provided as part of the JScript language that are unrelated to InfoPath. As you start working with scripting, you will find out that the underlying scripting language simply provides the framework and basic structure for your scripts. For example, you are going to use standard JScript functionality to declare variables, perform calculations, and control scripting flow with if…then statements.

When you need to actually dig into your form to extract information about the form or your form data, you need to turn to the InfoPath object model. An easy way to think of an object model is to think of your InfoPath form as a house. An object model simply describes all the different components that make up the house and provides different methods for extracting information about the house and its contents. For example, you may want to describe to someone where you are going to have dinner—in your house object model, the reference may be DiningRoom.Table, where you are referring to both the room and the location within the room where you are going to eat.

Within InfoPath, the object model is used to describe the form itself and the data within the form. This object model has been broken down into a number of functional areas, as shown in Table 10-1.

You will find all of these areas broken down in the InfoPath Developer's Help file, which can be accessed from within MSE by selecting Help | Microsoft Script Editor Help and navigating to the folder named InfoPath Developer's Reference. There is also a diagram of the object model that demonstrates where everything fits.

As you work more and more with scripting, you will become more familiar with the object model and how it is used. When you first get started with scripting in InfoPath, you might spend a bit of time looking up where to find different properties and methods. For example, if you want to put a command button on your form to close the form, you would need to find where in the object model this functionality is provided (if at all).

By searching the developer's reference, you would find that you can close a form by using the Quit method, which is available from the application object, as shown here:

```
function CTRL13_5::OnClick(eventObj)
{
Application.Quit(false);
}
```

Object	Description
Application	The base of the object model, providing details about your InfoPath form, including the application name and version (for example, InfoPath 11.0.5531) and the other high-level information
ExternalApplication	Used to control InfoPath from external applications—can be used to open, close, and create forms, register form templates locally, and so on
XDocument	Used to reference the contents of a form, including form data fields and more through XDocument
Windows	Used to reference a form's Window objects (for example, command bars, and so on)
View	Used to reference views within a form

TABLE 10-1 InfoPath Object Model

The reference includes sample scripts and examples where you would use different properties or methods, and you can cut and paste these examples directly into your own forms. Throughout this chapter, you will be working with the most common areas of the object model and the properties, methods, and events associated with those different areas. But there is no way the entire object model can be covered in this chapter, so make sure that you keep that developer's reference handy, and don't be afraid to go look something up if you are unsure.

Working with Events

Before you can start writing your first script, you need to understand where you can use scripting in your form. There are two main areas where scripts are used—with command buttons and with events. Command buttons are controls that you can add to your form; when the user clicks the button, a script will fire. Creating and using command buttons is a simple and effective way of using scripting, but it doesn't cater to all the different ways you may want to use scripting in your form.

The majority of tasks that you likely want to accomplish will be attached to events within your InfoPath form. An event is some action that occurs. For instance, when you first open a form, an OnLoad event fires. Similarly, when a field is updated, there is another event that fires called OnAfterChange. (And to make it even more confusing, when you do use a command button on your form, there is a special OnClick event that is associated with the button.) Most of the scripts you will write will be attached to these events, so when the event fires, the script will be run. Table 10-2 lists some of the different events that you can associate with scripts.

So, if you want to display a dialog box whenever a form is opened, you can put a bit of script behind the OnLoad event so that when the event fires, a snippet of script is run to display the dialog box with your message.

Event	Description
OnLoad	Fires when a form is first loaded.
OnSwitchView	Fires when a user switches between two form views.
OnVersionUpgrade	Fires when a form template is upgraded.
OnSubmitRequest	Fires when a form is submitted.
OnBeforeChange	Fires when a particular field is changed, but is before the new value is actually committed.
OnValidate	Fires when a particular field is changed and gives the user the opportunity to change the field.
OnAfterChange	Fires when a particular field has been changed.
OnClick	Fires when a command button is clicked.

TABLE 10-2 InfoPath Events

To add some script to the OnLoad event, select Tools | Script | On Load Event to open MSE and place your cursor within the OnLoad event for your form, which should look something like this:

```
function XDocument::OnLoad(eventObj)
{
      // Write your code here
}
```

When working with events, always leave the function declaration alone—InfoPath generates this part for you and there is no need to change it. To add some script to run when the form loads, you would need to replace the placeholder text with your own script. In this example, you want to display a dialog box when the form loads. To do this, you can use an alert (more information about alerts is provided later in the chapter, in the section "Working with Alerts"). So, your code would look something like this:

```
function XDocument::OnLoad(eventObj)
{
      XDocument.UI.Alert("Your form has been loaded");
}
```

Make sure that after you enter this script, you save the script within MSE. To run this script, switch over to InfoPath and preview your form using File | Preview Form | Default; your dialog box should appear when the form loads.

You could use this same method to associate a script with the other events as well. For example, if you want to add some validation to a field and use the OnBeforeChange event, right-click a data-entry control on your form, select Properties, and then click the Data Validation button to open the Data Validation dialog box, shown here.

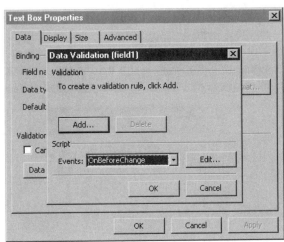

Use the Events drop-down list at the bottom of the dialog box to select the OnBeforeChange event and then click the Edit button to open MSE, which should open to a code snippet that looks something like this:

```
function msoxd__field1::OnBeforeChange(eventObj)
{
        // Write your code here
        // Warning: ensure that the constraint you are enforcing is
compatible with the default value you set for this XML node.
}
```

You could then add some code to validate the values entered into the field and display a warning message to the user, either through an alert or one of the validation error methods described earlier.

It is worth mentioning that these events (onBeforeChange, onValidate, and onAfterChange) may fire twice when a field is changed (once for deletion and the other time for insertion). To determine for which operation the event is being raised, check the eventObj.Operation property, as in the following example:

```
Function msoxd_my_field1::OnBeforeChange(eventObj)
{
            if (eventObj.Operation == "Insert")
            {
                <variables>
    XDocument.UI.Alert("inserted");
    <do stuff>
}
}
```

Working with Form Fields

Building upon your newfound knowledge of the InfoPath object model, this section explains how to control the content of controls that may appear on your form. To start, you are going to look at a simple example. On the form shown in the following illustration, you are going to place some script behind the command button so that when you click the button, the text box shown on the form will display "Hello World."

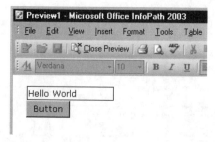

To use the "Hello World" code that follows, you need to create a new blank form and drag both a text box and a button control onto your form. Since you are creating the data source on-the-fly, there will be a field created in your data source named field1, which you will be using to display the text. To add some script behind your command button, right-click the button, select Button Properties, and then click the Microsoft Script Editor button. This opens MSE and positions your cursor in the OnClick function for your button.

So, to select the field that is displayed on your form, use the selectSingleNode method, as shown in the following script:

```
var myField
myField = XDocument.DOM.selectSingleNode("//my:field1");
myField.text = "Hello World";
```

Once you have selected this node, you can then set the Text property to display the text "Hello World" on your form. This is a very simple example, but you can use this same method to access all the data in your form.

If you have fields that are in a repeating group, you can use a similar method to retrieve the values stored in these fields by using the selectNodes method to select multiple nodes within your data source. In this example, you are going to look at an order form that is used to record an order made by a customer, as shown in Figure 10-2.

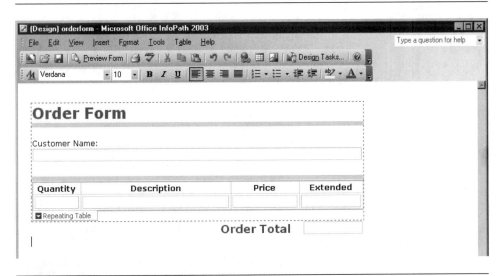

FIGURE 10-2   A typical form with a repeating table

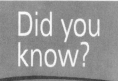

Did you know?

Expression Boxes vs. Scripting

You are probably experiencing a sense of déjà vu here. This is similar to the example that was used in Chapter 7 when creating XPath expressions in expression boxes. While expression boxes are easy to create, they are limited in what they can be used for. Scripting, on the other hand, provides a robust development environment for creating complex calculations that extend far beyond the capabilities found when using expression boxes.

The form itself has a simple header with fields for the customer name and a repeating table that is used to gather information about the items that the customer has ordered, including the quantity, description, price, and extended price (which is the quantity order multiplied by price). To demonstrate how to select multiple nodes, you are going to create script that sums the extended price column and displays the result in a total field at the bottom of the repeating table.

When working with the selectNodes method, it treats the node you select as an array, which you can reference using square brackets ([]). For example, the following script selects the extended price field and then loops through all the order lines to sum this value from each line:

```
var runningtotal = 0;
var orderlines =
XDocument.DOM.selectNodes("//order/items/item/extendedPrice");
     for (var i=0; i<orderlines.length; i++)
     {
     runningtotal +=
parseFloat(orderlines.item(i).nodeTypedValue);
     }
     var ordertotal = XDocument.DOM.selectSingleNode("//total");
     ordertotal.nodeTypedValue = runningtotal;
```

You'll notice that whenever you use the selectNodes method to select multiple nodes, you can access some of the same properties that are available when working with arrays. For example, in the preceding code, the selected node is called orderlines, which is then used to select all the extendedPrice fields. You can use the length property of orderlines to determine how many lines have been entered on the order form and then use the subscript to get a particular value for extendedPrice from one of those lines.

Another trick that you may pick up on is the use of the property nodeTypedValue, which can be used to return a value of a particular type. In this instance, you are working with decimal fields, so the parseFloat method is used to parse the value to a floating decimal point type.

Both of these techniques are not specific to InfoPath. You can find more information on using them from the JScript reference in Appendix B or by searching in the online help from the Microsoft Scripting Editor.

Working with Date Fields

When working with a form, chances are that you will want to date the form with the current date and time. Rather than have the user type this information in each time, it is much easier to let the scripting do the work. To work through the scripting examples for this section, you need to create a new blank form and drag a date picker control onto your form.

Because the goal is to keep things simple, the default name of the field, field1, will be used. If you like, you can put some text beside the field to label it (for example, Invoice Date), as this is the field where you are going to place the current date. Next, you need to open the OnLoad event so that your script will run whenever the form is first loaded. To view the OnLoad event, select Tools | Script | On Load Event to open MSE.

JScript provides a handy function that you can use to get the current date from the operating system, so in this example you are going to use this trick to get started. Since you have added a date picker control to your form, field1 is expecting a date field, so you need to do a little conversion on the current date to make it fit the format required by your control.

With date fields in JScript, a number of different methods are available that you can use to break the date apart into components. For example, the getMonth method can be used to get the current month from a date field, while getDays is used to return a number representing the current day of the month. You can find a complete listing of these date functions in Appendix B, but for now, you are going to use the getMonth and getDays methods along with getYears to strip apart the current date and put it back into a format that the control will like.

Putting all of these concepts together, the script for your form's OnLoad event would look something like this:

```
var CurrentDate = new Date();
var m = CurrentDate.getMonth() + 1;
var d = CurrentDate.getDate();
var y = CurrentDate.getFullYear();
```

10

```
       if (m < 10)
              m = "0" + m;
       if (d < 10)
              d = "0" + d;
var FormDate = XDocument.DOM.selectSingleNode("//my:field1");
FormDate.text = (y + "-" + m + "-" + d);
```

The preceding script uses the CurrentDate variable to retrieve the current date and then uses the variables m, d, and y to represent the month, day, and year.

Notice that the preceding script adds 1 to the month—the getMonth function is zero-based, so January is returned as 0, February as 1, and so on.

The next four lines in the preceding script check whether the month and day need a leading zero and, if so, add that to the front. The final two lines dimension a variable FormDate to hold the contents of field1 and then perform some simple concatenation.

Why so much trouble for a simple date field? Date fields within InfoPath have to be entered into a form in a specific format. You need to enter the year, month, and date with dashes or slashes in between, and you have some leeway regarding the order in which you enter these values, but the safest bet is to put it in the format YYYY-MM-DD.

If you are working with a text field, as opposed to a date field, you have a few more options available to you. When working with date fields, you can either use toDateString or toTimeString to get the string that represents the date you are working with. Returning to the earlier example, if field1 were a text field, your script would be much simpler and would look something like this:

```
var CurrentDate = new Date();
var FormDate = XDocument.DOM.selectSingleNode("//my:field1");
FormDate.text = CurrentDate.toDateString();
```

Regardless of which method you choose, you will probably want to put the script into a function that you can call throughout your form. This will come in handy if you ever need to use the date transformation techniques again.

For a look at how these functions might be created, modify the Issue Tracking sample form that is installed with InfoPath. There are two functions—getDateString and getTimeString—that demonstrate how to use functions to convert date values.

Working with Strings

Strings within your InfoPath scripts can be manipulated by using a number of simple operators—to start, you can concatenate two strings by using a simple + operator. In the following example, a form has three fields—a first name field, a last name field, and an e-mail address field. The script reads the first and last name from the form and then concatenates the two fields to make an e-mail address, following a pattern established by the company.

```
var first = XDocument.DOM.selectSingleNode("//my:first");
var last = XDocument.DOM.selectSingleNode("//my:last");
var email = XDocument.DOM.selectSingleNode("//my:email");
email.text = first.text + "." + last.text + "@widgets.com";
```

To take this example even further—the e-mail field in this example has been displayed using a text box, but you can right-click that text box and use the Change To menu to change it to a hyperlink. With a little more concatenation, you could add a mailto: link at the start of the e-mail address so that the form displays a live link that will launch the user's default e-mail client. The script for this technique looks like this:

```
var first = XDocument.DOM.selectSingleNode("//my:first");
var last = XDocument.DOM.selectSingleNode("//my:last");
var email = XDocument.DOM.selectSingleNode("//my:email");
email.text = "mailto:" + first.text + "." + last.text +
"@widgets.com";
```

In addition to concatenating strings, you can also pull them apart. JScript treats strings like arrays of characters, so you can reference any character in a string by using the charAt property and referencing the character with a subscript, as shown here:

```
"David".charAt(3);  //returns v
"InfoPath.charAt(5);  //returns p
```

You also have standard string functions like toUpperCase, toLowerCase, and length, as well as other supported JScript string functions.

NOTE *For a reference of even more string functions, check out Appendix B.*

Working with Alerts

Alerts are the most common method used to show critical information to a form user. If you read through Chapter 9, you have already had a brief look at working with alerts. An alert is a pop-up dialog box that can be shown with text that you enter to communicate with a form user, as shown here.

You can easily create alerts by using the UI (user interface) object that the InfoPath SDK provides. There is only one argument required for the Alert method and that is the text that you want to appear. So, to show an alert to a user concerning a customer credit limit, your script would look something like this:

```
XDocument.UI.Alert("This order exceeds the customer's credit limit");
```

If you want to create a multiline alert, you can add a carriage return to the text by adding /n escape code wherever you want to go to the next line. For example, the following script,

```
XDocument.UI.Alert("Please check the value/nentered and try again. /nValues
entered must be above 10,000");
```

would produce an alert similar to the one shown here.

NOTE   *For a list of escape codes, see the JScript reference in Appendix B.*

You can use alerts throughout your scripting to display information to the user. The downside of the ease of use is that you can't control the size, shape, or position of the alert dialog box. If you want more finite control or want to use an alternate dialog box to display information for the user's benefit, you need to consider creating your own HTML pages to display using the ShowModal method of the UI object.

TIP   *For more information on using the ShowModal method, check out the InfoPath Developer's Reference and search for UI.ShowModal.*

Controlling Script Flow

If you were to create a script that could run from the first line to the last straight through, you would be doing well—for the rest of us, a little flow control is required to make the most of scripting within InfoPath. Fortunately, there are a number of different control structures that you can use within InfoPath to control the flow of your script; the most popular seems to be the if…then statement.

To create an if…then statement in your script, you need to enclose the condition to be evaluated in parentheses and place the script that should be run if the condition is true in curly brackets, as shown in the following simple example:

```
if (InvoiceAmount > 10000)
 {
XDocument.UI.Alert("Please use a different form");
}
else
    XDocument.UI.Alert("This is the correct form");
```

You can use if…then statements on their own or add an else statement to the end. Since this is a function provided by the underlying JScript engine, you may not find documentation on it in the InfoPath Developer's Reference. However, the JScript reference within MSE has numerous examples.

TIP   *In addition to if…then statements, InfoPath also supports do…while and for loops and others for controlling the flow of your script.*

Catching Scripting Errors

Unless you are perfect, you are going to encounter some errors in your script. If you choose to not use any type of error trapping, these errors can cause your form to stop working or cause nasty error messages to appear.

A much easier way to deal with potential errors is to use a try…catch statement to determine how errors are handled. A try…catch statement, simply put, runs a section of script and, if it results in an error, processes a second section of script to "catch" and handle the error.

10

In the following example, a try...catch statement has been used in conjunction with a simple calculation. This script merely retrieves a value from a total field and multiplies it by 1.1 (which works for a tax rate of 10 percent):

```
try
        {
        var myTotal =
XDocument.DOM.selectSingleNode("//my:total");
        myTotal = myTotal * 1.1


        }
    catch (e)
        {
        XDocument.UI.Alert("Error:" + e.description);
        }
```

If you were to place this script in a form and run it, you would see immediately how a try...catch statement works. When referencing the myTotal field, the preceding script does not use the Text property, so the resulting script would throw an error. With catch statements, the error returned can be any variable you like (in this instance, it is named e) and you can obtain the properties of this error to determine the error number or description.

A complete list of JScript error codes and descriptions is included in Appendix B.

Once you have figured out what the problem is, you can correct it. The correct script for performing this calculation is listed here:

```
try
        {
        var myTotal =
XDocument.DOM.selectSingleNode("//my:total");
        myTotal.text = myTotal.text * 1.1
        }
    catch (e)
        {
        XDocument.UI.Alert("Error:" + e.description);
        }
```

Creating Custom Task Panes

Another easy way to extend InfoPath functionality is to create your own custom task pane. You can create task panes by using HTML and the web development tool of your choice. Custom task panes can be used to display help text or instructions for filling out a form, to display additional information the form user may need (for example, lookup tables), and even to interact with the form data. The following sections look at how to create a simple HTML page and display it in a custom task pane.

To start, you need to create your HTML page using the editor of your choice. The example in this section is a page of instructions on how to fill out a particular form. When the user fills out the form, they can view these instructions in the task pane when required. Once you have developed a web page to use in a custom task pane, preview it in Internet Explorer to make sure all the content looks right. Note the name and location of the HTML file.

Next, in your form's design, select Tools | Form Options to open the Form Options dialog box, and then click the Advanced tab, shown in Figure 10-3.

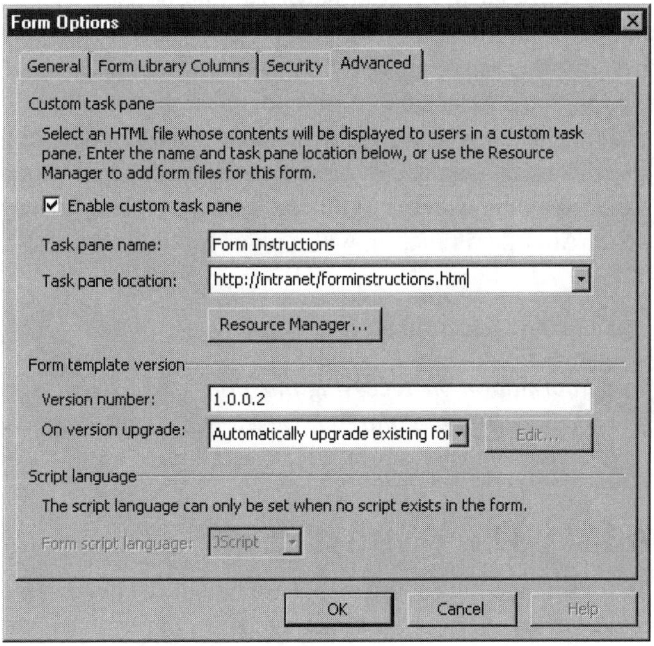

FIGURE 10-3   Advanced form options

Click the Enable Custom Task Pane check box and then enter a name for your pane. In this example, the pane is called Form Instructions. For the task pane location, type the location of your HTML file, including the full path.

Alternatively, you can add the HTML page that you created as a resource so that you can select it from the Task Pane Location drop-down list. Resources within an InfoPath form are additional files that are added to the form template file and can include script files, images, HTML pages, and so forth. To add your HTML page as a resource, click the Resource Manager button and browse to select the file. In addition to the HTML file, you also need to select any related files (graphics, style sheets, and so on).

 *When you add a resource file to a form, it is embedded into the form. If you need to edit a resource later, you need to export it from the Resource Manager to get the file back again.*

Once you have added your file to the Resource Manager, it should appear in the Task Pane Location drop-down list and you can select it from the list. Now, click OK to close the Form Options dialog box and return to your form's design. Whenever you preview your form, your new custom task pane will be available from the drop-down list at the top of the task pane, as shown in Figure 10-4.

In addition to displaying simple HTML pages, you can interact with your InfoPath form through the extension property of the task pane. To use this property within your task pane page, you need to declare your XDocument object first and then you can use the extension property to access functions and variables within your script. In the following example, you could have a link in your HTML page that called the SumAllOrders function within your InfoPath script:

```
myTaskPane = window.external.XDocument;
myTaskPane.Extension.SumAllOrders();
```

 *For more information on accessing functions and variables within your InfoPath scripts, open the InfoPath Developer's Guide and search for the keyword "extension."*

Using Secondary Data Sources

Secondary data sources are data sources that are outside of the data source that the form is connected to. For example, you may have an employee expense form that is attached to your accounting system and have the need to look up an employee's contact details from another database or system. By connecting to a secondary data source, you can retrieve this information and use it in your own form.

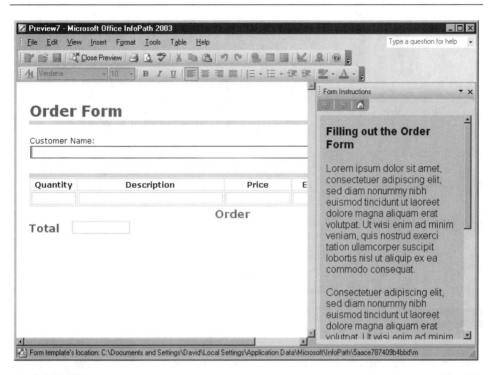

FIGURE 10-4   A custom task pane

Creating a form that accesses a secondary data source is a two-step process: create a connection to the data source, and bind a control to that data source. In this example, you are going to look up a customer number from a secondary data source and populate a drop-down list on a form.

To connect to a secondary data source, select Tools | Secondary Data Sources and click the Add button to open the Data Source Setup Wizard. In this example, you are going to walk through the process of creating a secondary data source from a SQL Server database, but the process is similar if you are connecting to an XML file or web service.

On the opening wizard page, select the Database option and then click Next to continue to the next wizard page, shown in Figure 10-5, where you can select the SQL server to connect to to retrieve your secondary data.

Next, click the Select Database button to choose your data source using a standard File | Open dialog box. You can select your connection from the list of available ODC files or create a new one.

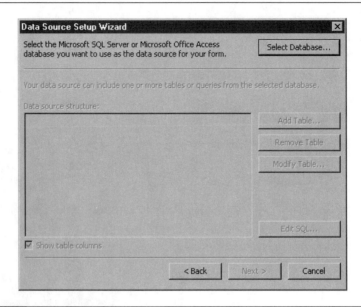

FIGURE 10-5 Data Source Setup Wizard

For more information on creating an ODC file, refer to Chapter 5.

Once you have selected your data source, a list of available tables will appear and allow you to select the tables you want to use in your secondary data source.

If you want to connect to an Access database and want to connect directly to the database, you can use the Select Data Source dialog box to browse and select your Access (MDB) database file.

You are now ready to start working with the secondary data source you have just created—the Data Source Setup Wizard should now appear again, as shown in Figure 10-6, and show your database details as well as any tables you may have selected earlier.

Using this wizard page, you can add multiple tables to your data source and specify the relationship between them. To add an additional table to your data source, click the Add Table button to select a table from a list. The next step in the process is to specify the relationship between the two tables, which is also sometimes called a "join type" because it details how the tables are joined back together. To add a relationship between two tables, click the Add Relationship button.

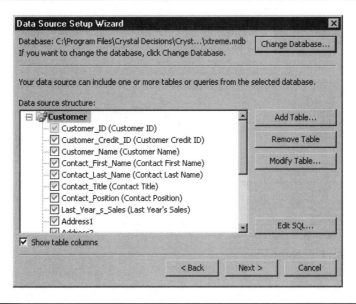

FIGURE 10-6   Database details

This opens another dialog box that allows you to select the field in each table that will be used to define the relationship. After you select the fields, click the Add Relationship button to add this join. You can specify multiple relationships based on fields within your tables or remove them using the Remove buttons. When you are finished, click Finish to return to the Data Source Setup Wizard.

TIP   *You can use the Remove Table and Modify Table buttons to remove tables or modify the relationships between tables. You can also click the Edit SQL button to use SQL to write your own queries.*

The final step of the Data Source Setup Wizard is used to enter a name for your secondary data source and instructions on when to connect to this source. Next, you need to add a control to your form and bind the secondary data source to this control. In this instance, you are going to add a drop-down control to your form using the techniques we covered earlier in the book. Normally with a drop-down list, you could enter the values to appear, but in this case you are going to let the secondary data source do all the hard work for you.

Once you have added the drop-down control to your form, right-click the control and select Properties. In the Drop-Down List Box Properties dialog box, shown in Figure 10-7, in the List Box Entries area, select the Look Up in a Database, Web Service, or File radio button.

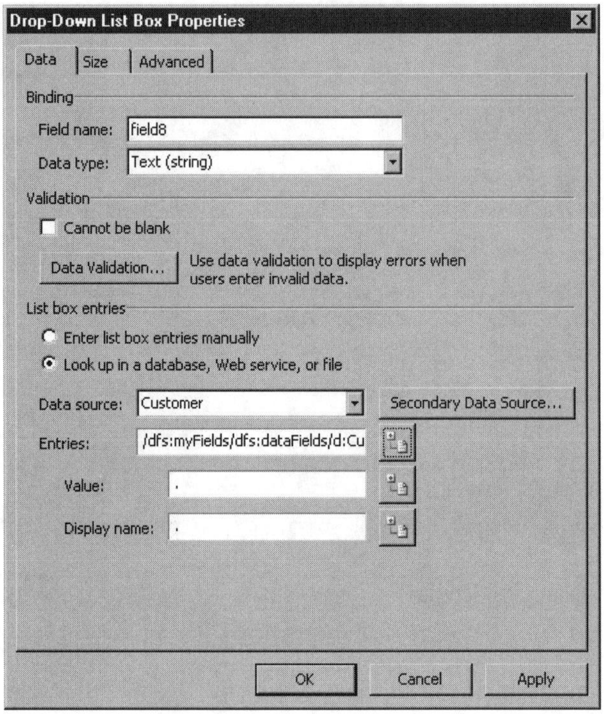

FIGURE 10-7 List box properties

Use the Data Source drop-down list to select the secondary data source you just created. Next, click the icon beside the Entries text box to select the field you want to display in the drop-down list. Once you click OK and preview your form, the drop-down list will be populated from the secondary data source and field you selected. This information will be stored with your form and submitted to the XML file or database when you submit or save your form.

Summary

There are many ways you can extend your InfoPath forms, and this chapter introduced most of them. Whether you are adding features to a form by using scripting or adding your own task pane or database lookups, InfoPath is a robust, feature-rich platform for developing electronic form solutions. But what would a form be if you couldn't get it out to the users? That is where the next chapter picks up, which presents the options that are available for distributing forms.

Part IV

Distribute Forms

Chapter 11

Publishing Overview

How to…

- Save your form
- Modify existing forms
- Extract form files
- Select a publishing method

Now that you have tackled some of the more complex form design tasks, it is time to look at one of the final steps in the form design process—distributing your forms to users. This chapter looks at a number of different issues with regard to publishing your forms, including saving your forms during development, modifying existing forms, and extracting all the different files that make up a form.

The second half of the chapter looks at the different publishing methods that you can use to publish your form to end users; that discussion serves as an introduction to the following chapters, in which you will be looking at these publishing methods in detail. So, whether you need to distribute your form to one user or one hundred, it all starts here.

Saving Your Form

As you have been working through the previous chapters and developing your own forms, you have probably been saving your form template as you went along. You can save the form at any time by selecting File | Save, which opens the dialog box shown in the following illustration with the option to either Publish or Save your form.

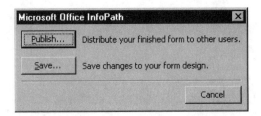

If you are still working on your form's design, or if you want to save a copy of the form locally, select the Save option, which opens a standard Windows Save As dialog box (shown in Figure 11-1) and allows you to save your form locally as an XSN file.

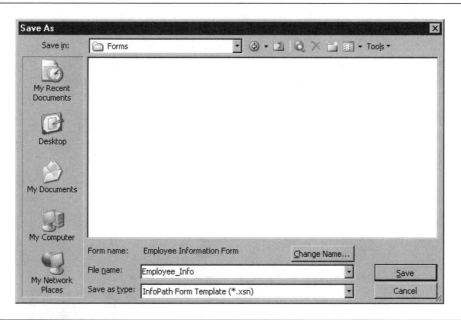

FIGURE 11-1   Options for saving your forms

Your form file will be saved as a form template with an .xsn file extension. You can use the Change Name button to change the title of the form that will appear to users when they are filling out the form.

It is always a good idea to save a copy of the form file locally as you are working on it—when you have finished testing the form and are ready to publish it, you can publish the final form to the appropriate server or shared location.

If you would like to keep track of versioning while you are designing your form, select Tools | Form Options and then click the Advanced tab to view the dialog box shown in Figure 11-2. By default, InfoPath starts with version 1.0.0.0 and automatically increments the last part of the version number with each change you make to the form (1.0.0.1 to 1.0.0.2, and so on).

If you want to enter your own version number, you can do so by using the text box provided on the Advanced tab, as long as the version number conforms to the convention of 9999-9999-9999-9999. If you do choose to enter your own version numbers, InfoPath will no longer automatically increment the version number, so you will have to update this information each time.

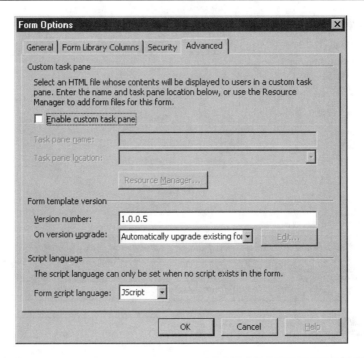

FIGURE 11-2 Form options

 *Manually setting your own version number may cause problems when you upgrade existing forms, causing form data to be lost. Unless you absolutely need to do it yourself, let InfoPath handle the versioning, to eliminate some headaches later.*

Modifying Forms

After you have saved the form template, you can later open it in InfoPath by selecting File | Open in design mode and continue working with the form's design. You can save or publish the form as often as required, incorporating any changes you need to make.

NOTE *An important concept when modifying forms is that any forms that need to be modified need to be saved to the same location when you are finished with the modifications. Otherwise, you may end up breaking the link between the form and any existing XML files created from an earlier version of the form.*

As you put InfoPath forms into production, you will need to change these forms from time to time to cater to additional requirements, enhancements, and so on. To help alleviate problems when upgrading and maintaining forms, InfoPath can upgrade existing forms to bring them up to the current version.

For example, if you had created a form that collected Employee details, including the employee's name, address, social security number, and so forth, and put it into production, you could have hundreds of XML files from where the form was used to collect this information. If you were to change the form template and delete the social security number, for example, the default settings within InfoPath would automatically upgrade the form to use the new form template. In this case, it would mean that the Social Security Number field would be deleted and that that information would be lost. It also would eliminate any errors that the user may have received if they had tried to open the old form with the new form template.

Upgrading existing forms is set by default within each form on the Advanced tab of the Form Options dialog box (refer to Figure 11-3). The On Version Upgrade option is set to automatically upgrade existing forms, but there are actually three choices presented in the drop-down list:

- **Do Nothing**   Leaves the existing forms as is, which may cause the form template not to work.

- **Use Script Event**   Allows you to use the Edit button to invoke the Microsoft Script Editor and enter some JScript or VBScript that should be run when the OnVersionUpgrade event is triggered.

- **Automatically Upgrade Existing Forms**   Default setting used to upgrade existing forms to the design of the new form template.

TIP *For a refresher on working with scripting and creating alerts, refer to Chapter 10.*

11

Losing Data

Keep in mind that when you upgrade a form, you may also lose existing form data—in the example posed earlier, the data in the Social Security Number field in the data source was deleted, because the new form template did not include this field. There are some other specific cases in which existing form data will be deleted—including when a field or group is deleted, moved, or renamed or when a repeating field or group is changed to a nonrepeating group. You may also experience problems when converting a rich text field to another data type.

With these limitations in mind, it is probably a good idea to test any forms that you have updated prior to publishing them. One easy way to do this is to save an "audit trail" of your form design by getting into the practice of testing each version of a form template by filling out the form and saving the data. You can then use the data from these form files to test the upgrade process and ensure that your users will enjoy a seamless upgrade.

Extracting Form Files

InfoPath form templates are saved as XSN files that encapsulate all the different components of an InfoPath form, including the form's design, styling, and scripting. While having a single file makes it easy to develop and distribute InfoPath forms, sometimes you will want to view or edit the individual files that make up an InfoPath form. In order to separate these files, you need to extract the form files from your XSN file.

To extract the form files from an existing form, open the form in design mode and then select File | Extract Form Files to open the dialog box shown in the following illustration.

You can use this dialog box to select a folder in which the extracted form files will be saved or you can click the Make New Folder button in the lower-left corner to create a new folder to hold the form files. An InfoPath form can be made up of a number of different types of files. For example, Table 11-1 lists and describes the files that were used to create the sample Employee Details form.

In addition to the files listed in Table 11-1, you can also have other types of files, depending on the complexity of your form. For example, if you use graphics or clip art in your form, those files (JPG, GIF, and so on) would also be extracted.

Also, referring to Chapter 10, in which you looked at scripting, if you are using scripting in your form, you may also have JS or VBS files, which hold either JScript or VBScript code. In addition, you may also have dynamic link libraries (DLLs) or executables (EXEs) that are used to extend InfoPath functionality.

11

Filename	Description
Manifest.xsf	A manifest file generated by InfoPath that contains information about the different components that make up an InfoPath form
Myschema.xsd	The XML Schema for the form you have created
Sampledata.xml	An XML file containing the sample data to be used with your form
Template.xml	An XML file containing the template for the default data to be displayed when you create a new form
View1.xsl	The style sheet that will be used to transform the data to create View1 within the form

TABLE 11-1 A Set of Files Extracted from a Typical Form

Your form can also contain other schema files, auxiliary DOM configuration files, and user-added files in the resource manager (such as HTML files for the Task Pane, other image files, and so forth).

Publishing Your Form

After you are finished designing and testing your form, it is time to publish it to the users who will be filling out your form. This section looks at the different methods that are available for publishing your InfoPath forms. The goal of this part of the chapter is to introduce you to the different publishing methods and give you an introduction to each—the following chapters will be drilling down into the specifics of how each of these publishing methods works and how you can use each of them to distribute your forms to users.

Publishing to a Shared Folder

One of the easiest methods you can use to publish forms to users is to publish them to a shared folder. This shared location could be a folder on your own computer or a folder on your network that has been shared by your network administrator. This enables other users to access files saved to that folder, including InfoPath forms. If you are working in an environment where you have common network drives already established, this is an easy way to distribute your forms because no additional setup is required. You just need to advertise the location of the forms and ensure that the users have the appropriate rights to access the folder where you have saved your forms.

With this ease of use comes a trade-off—this publishing method does not provide an easy way to organize forms or form data. Another disadvantage of this publishing method is that forms deployed to a shared location will not be able to take advantage of all the features InfoPath provides.

In Chapter 10, you had a look at the different types of security levels that you can use within your forms and the advantages/disadvantages of each. When you deploy a form using the shared location method, the form itself is not secure and will not have access to resources on the local computer where the user is filling out the form. If you are creating simple data-entry forms, this may not be an issue, but complex forms that connect to external data sources and access other software applications may not run correctly (if at all).

 To successfully deploy fully trusted forms, you need to actually install the form on a user's computer, which is discussed a little later in this chapter.

Publishing to a SharePoint Form Library

Like the other Office 2003 applications, InfoPath is tightly integrated with SharePoint Portal Server 2003, so you can use SharePoint as a central repository for your forms and form data. Using InfoPath, you can create *form libraries* to organize your forms, so that when users want to fill out a form, they can simply open the form from the library, as shown here.

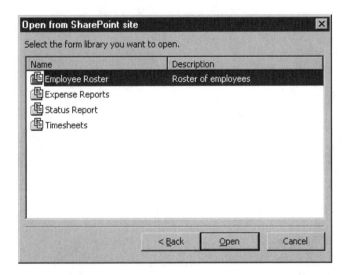

After the user has finished filling out a form, they can save the form results back to the SharePoint form library. This information then can be consolidated into a datasheet, like the one shown in Figure 11-3.

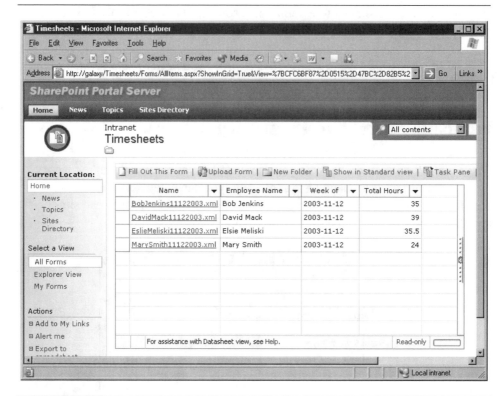

FIGURE 11-3 A datasheet within a form library in SharePoint

You can then export the form data to Excel for further analysis or you can print the results, create charts and pivot tables using Excel, or even link or export the data to a Microsoft Access database and report off of the same. For organizations that are looking for a data capture and consolidation solution, the combination of InfoPath and SharePoint Portal Server can meet most requirements.

 *For more information on using InfoPath with SharePoint Portal Server, flip ahead to Chapter 12.*

Publishing to a Web Server

Another method that you can use to publish your forms to users is to publish them to a web server. This publishing method would allow you to use an existing web site as a location for storing your InfoPath forms. If you are looking for an easy way to deploy forms to users outside of your organization, this is probably the easiest method and doesn't require any additional setup, other than installing and configuring a web server somewhere within your network.

You could even create your own web pages with links to the different forms that are available, but you would need to manually maintain this "front end" to your forms, which still does not provide a way to consolidate and/or display the data being collected.

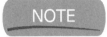 *If you need an easier way to manage your forms and form data, you may want to consider publishing your form to your intranet or web site using SharePoint Portal Server 2003.*

Installing Custom Forms Locally

Another option for installing InfoPath forms is to install them locally on the user's machine. This method of form distribution allows you to create fully trusted forms that can access all the resources available on your local machine. Forms that have been installed using this method are sometimes also called custom-installed forms, because they appear on the Custom Installed Forms tab of the Forms dialog box when opening a form to fill out, as shown in Figure 11-4.

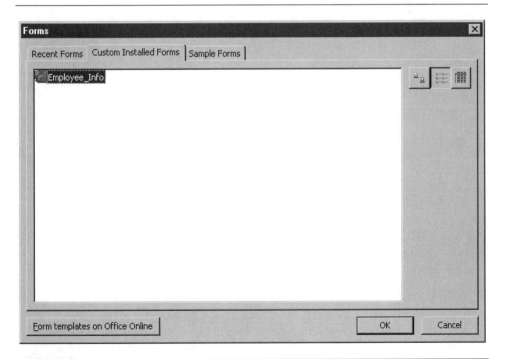

FIGURE 11-4   Custom-installed forms

To install custom forms on a user's computer, you can either modify the form files manually or use the RegForm utility provided by Microsoft to create a custom setup program to install the form for you. Of the two methods, the RegForm utility is the easiest and less prone to error, but both methods are covered in the following chapter.

Summary

Regardless of your organizational infrastructure, there is a way to deploy InfoPath forms to your users, whether it is through installed forms on each desktop, SharePoint form libraries, or other methods. In the chapters that follow, we are going to drill-down into the details of how these different publishing methods can be utilized and some of the pros and cons for each. Whichever method you choose, it all starts here.

Chapter 12

Work with Form Libraries

How to…

- Use form libraries
- Create a form library
- Publish a form to a form library
- Modify a form in a form library
- Analyze form data from within SharePoint

Chapter 11 looked at the different methods that you can use to publish forms to users inside and outside of your organization. One of the methods introduced is to publish forms as form libraries in SharePoint Portal Server. This chapter looks in detail at how to create and maintain these libraries, as well as how to use features within SharePoint to further consolidate and analyze form data.

By the end of the chapter, you should have all the information that you need to start using SharePoint as a distribution framework for your InfoPath forms. This chapter begins by looking at how to create and modify form libraries. Then, it describes how end users work with these libraries.

Working with Form Libraries

To understand what a form library is, it's best to first take a look at the underlying server technology that makes form libraries possible. Microsoft SharePoint Portal Server is a server-based portal environment for sharing information between users. Organizations use SharePoint to create web sites, share documents, and build web applications in a secure, robust environment that can be integrated with existing business processes and applications, including InfoPath.

From within InfoPath you can create form libraries that reside on a SharePoint server. Each of these libraries is associated with a single form, and users can fill out a form directly from the library itself. After the user fills out the form and saves it, the form data is then available from within the form library and is consolidated into a summary view.

NOTE   *You may see SharePoint referred to as "SharePoint Portal Server" or "SharePoint Services." The difference between the two is that SharePoint Portal Server is the stand-alone portal server, whereas SharePoint Services is a scaled-down version of SharePoint technology that ships with Windows Server 2003. Throughout this chapter, these two servers both are referred to as "SharePoint," as they are two versions of the product built on the same technology. For more information on SharePoint, visit www.microsoft.com/ sharepoint.*

A typical usage scenario would be for a Time Sheet form, used to collect the time worked from multiple employees. Users could fill out this form from the form library and then save their results to the same library. The timesheet information is then available in a summarized format, allowing someone from the payroll department to use the functionality within SharePoint to export this information to Excel or Access or perform further analysis or consolidation.

Creating a Form Library

Before you can actually start to create a form library, you need to check with your SharePoint administrator to verify that you have permission to publish content to your SharePoint server. You can verify that you have the appropriate rights by visiting the SharePoint server and selecting Start | Programs | SharePoint Portal Server | SharePoint Central Administration, which will open the dialog box shown in Figure 12-1.

If you haven't done so already, you need to create at least one portal site and ensure that you have at least Web Designer rights so that you will be able to create your form libraries. Once you have verified that you have the correct administrative rights, you can then start to create your first form library.

NOTE   *For more information on administering SharePoint Portal Server or SharePoint Team Services, check out www.microsoft.com/sharepoint.*

To create a new form library, select File | Publish to open the Publishing Wizard and then click Next to open the wizard page shown in Figure 12-2.

Select the option to publish To a SharePoint Form Library and click Next to continue to the wizard page shown in Figure 12-3.

12

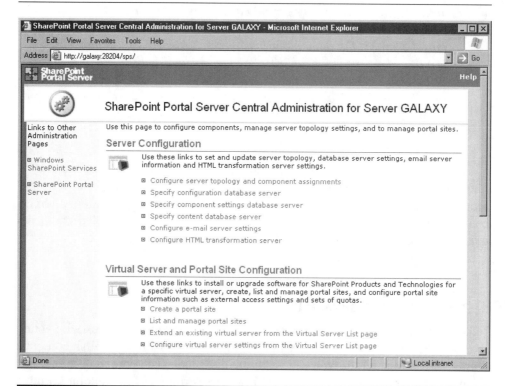

FIGURE 12-1   SharePoint portal administration

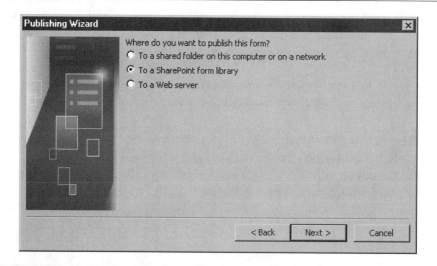

FIGURE 12-2   The Publishing Wizard

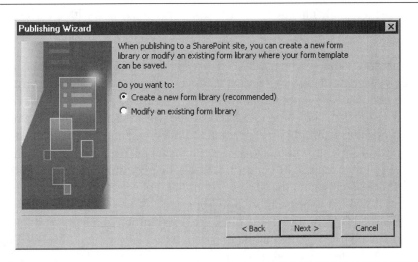

FIGURE 12-3   Form library options

Since this is the first time you are publishing this form, select the Create a New Form Library option and click Next to continue. This opens the wizard page shown in Figure 12-4, which prompts you for the location of your SharePoint server.

Enter the complete URL for the server where SharePoint is installed, including the http:// prefix, and click Next. You may be prompted to log on to your SharePoint

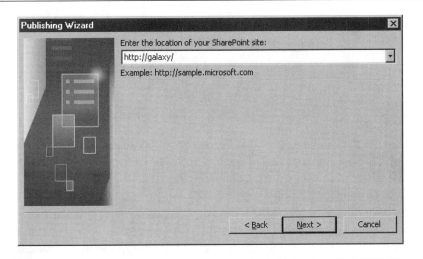

FIGURE 12-4   Connecting to your SharePoint server

server. When the authentication is finished, you are presented with a wizard page like the one shown in Figure 12-5.

Use this page to enter a name and description for your form library. It is important to note that this name will be used when determining the URL that will be used to reference your form library, so it is always a good idea to use underscores instead of spaces to eliminate any ambiguity in the URL. When you are finished entering a name and description, click Next to continue to the wizard page shown in Figure 12-6.

When creating a form library for the first time, you need to select which fields from your InfoPath form will be shown as columns within the form library. Remember that these columns are used to consolidate and display information entered onto forms that are saved within the library—if you do not select a particular field from your form, it will not appear in the form library.

To select fields from your form, click the Add button, which opens a standard data source dialog box (shown in the illustration) that allows you to select a field or group of fields to be used as a column.

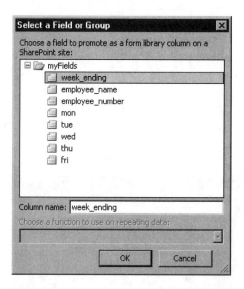

You can use the Column Name text box at the bottom of the dialog box to change the name of the column as it will appear within your form library. This does not change the underlying data source field name; it just changes the way a column is labeled within your form library.

If you have selected a group of fields that is repeating data, you can also use the drop-down list at the bottom of this dialog box to select a summary operator to be applied to this data. For example, if you have a repeating field that is used to enter expenses for an expense report, you could use the drop-down list to select a summary

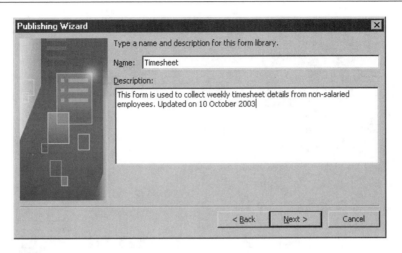

FIGURE 12-5   Form library options

function to be used to summarize this data for display in a column within your form library.

When you have finished specifying your columns and any summary operators that you may want to use, click Finish to complete the Publishing Wizard and create your form library. When the creation process is finished, you will be presented with a summary wizard page similar to the one shown in Figure 12-7 that will verify that

12

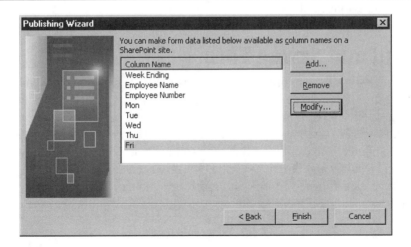

FIGURE 12-6   Selecting fields

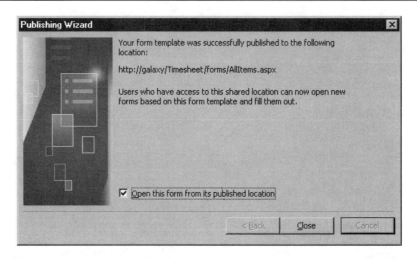

FIGURE 12-7   Finishing up the Publishing Wizard

the form has been published and give you the URL for users to access this form directly.

 *In this example, the URL is http://galaxy/Timesheet/forms/AllItems.aspx.*

You can now distribute this URL to users who may need to fill out the form, which is the next task to look at.

Filling Out and Saving Forms

The easiest way to fill out a form stored in a form library is to open your web browser and, using the URL provided when you created the library, visit the form library's home page, which looks something like the page shown in Figure 12-8.

Clicking the Fill Out This Form button opens the form associated with the library on your computer. You can then fill out the form as you normally would, with all of the same features and functionality that you are accustomed to.

When you are finished filling out your form, you can then select File | Save, which opens a standard Save As dialog box with the form library as the default

FIGURE 12-8   A typical form library home page

location. Enter a unique name for your completed form and then click the Save button to save the form.

If you visit the default home page for your form library, you should now see your form listed, and marked as a new item. In addition, the data in the form fields that you marked as columns should appear in the columns beside the field name, as shown in Figure 12-9.

You can now view the data from your form, use the datasheet view to analyze the data, and more. But before you get too far into working with a form library from an end-user's perspective, you need to look at how to modify the structure and display settings of the library itself, which is what the next section discusses.

FIGURE 12-9   Form library columns

Modifying a Form Library

One of the most important features within SharePoint is the ability to customize the content to suit your own use. In the preceding sections, you used InfoPath to create a form library to store both your forms and form data, but you created that form library by using the default settings, giving it a standard "look and feel." This section discusses how you, as an administrator, can customize your form library and change the look and feel of the content.

> **TIP**
>
> *A little later in this chapter, you'll look at how end users work with a form library, but the information in this section deals exclusively with customizing the form library from an administrator's perspective, as end users will probably not have access to the tools used here.*

A good place to start the discussion of modifying form libraries is with columns. You may have noticed that, by default, SharePoint displays a number of "standard" columns in addition to the columns you have specified from your form. These columns include

■ **Type**   An icon showing the InfoPath icon

■ **Name**   The name of the XML data file

■ **Modified**   The date and time the file was last modified

■ **Modified By**   The name of the user who last modified the form

■ **Checked Out To**   If the form is checked out, who it is checked out to

While this information may be relevant to the forms stored within your form library, it makes it difficult to view the form data, because you have to scroll over to the right to see the columns generated from your form data.

Fortunately, SharePoint provides a wide degree of customization and you can actually modify this page to suit your preferences. To customize this page, click the Modify Settings and Columns link in the lower-left corner of the page. This opens a Customize page like the one shown in Figure 12-10.

The Customize page can be used to change general form library settings (like the name and description) as well as to delete a form library or add a form library to a category, but the settings that you want to change are actually located at the bottom of the page in the Views section. Find this section and click the All Forms link to edit the default view for your form library. This opens the dialog box shown in Figure 12-11, in which you can customize the default view (including which columns are shown) for your form library.

> TIP
>
> *Keep in mind as you are editing the All Forms view that you can use these same techniques to create your own unique views to display your form data.*

The following sections look at how to customize this view, including selecting the columns that appear, specifying the column order, grouping, sorting, and more.

Changing Column Settings

All the columns that are available for use with your form library are listed in the Columns section of the Edit View page. There are two different controls related to

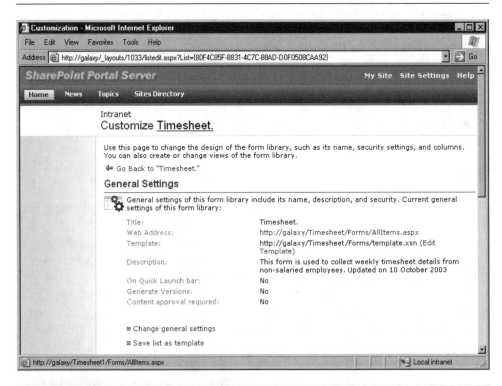

FIGURE 12-10 Customization options

each column. The first control is marked Display and is used to determine which columns appear on your view. All the form columns that you specified during the publishing process are listed here, as well as the default columns that are available through SharePoint. Standard columns include the following:

- Type (icon linked to document)
- Name (linked to document with edit menu)
- Modified
- Modified By
- Checked Out To
- ID
- Created By

- Created

- Name (for use in forms)

- Name (linked to document)

- Edit (link to edit item)

- File Size

- Title

The second control, to the right of the column name, is used to control the order in which the columns appear on the view. A drop-down list has been provided for you to specify the order in which the fields should appear—as you select a number (for example, making the Name field position 1), the order associated with the other columns automatically adjusts (for instance, the column in position 1 becomes 2, and so on).

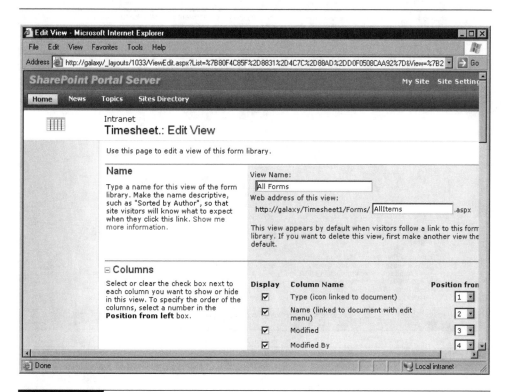

FIGURE 12-11   Edit View options

Sorting Column Data

In addition to controlling which columns are to appear on the view, you can also control the sort order of the data within these columns. By default, InfoPath sorts the data in the order in which it was saved to the form library. You can change this sort order on the Edit View page by expanding the Sort options, shown in Figure 12-12.

Using the drop-down lists provided, you can select a primary and secondary sort order for your view from the available columns for this view. Once you have selected a column to use when sorting, you can also select the sort order by using the radio buttons immediately below the drop-down list.

 *You don't actually have to display a column on your view to use the column for sorting.*

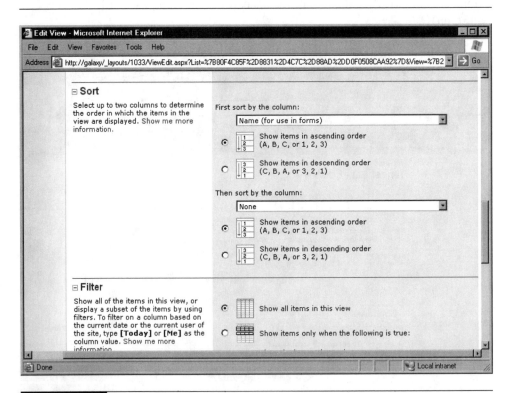

FIGURE 12-12   Sort options

Filtering Column Data

If you don't want to display all the data within your view, you can filter the data by using the settings found when you expand the Filter options in the middle of the Edit View page. By default, this view is set to Show All Items in This View, but you can enter some criteria to be used to filter the data shown in your view.

Setting up a filter is a three-part process. First, you need to select the field that you are going to use in your filter from the drop-down list provided. This can be a field that appears on your form or a field that is not displayed—it doesn't matter. Once you have selected the field to use, the next step is to pick a filter operator from the drop-down list provided. There are eight different operators you can select from:

- Is Equal To

- Is Not Equal To

- Is Greater Than

- Is Less Than

- Is Greater Than or Equal To

- Is Less Than or Equal To

- Begins With

- Contains

You need to enter some value to compare against. For example, if you want to show only timesheets from employee number 224, you could set your criteria to employee_number Is Equal To and enter 224 in the text box provided.

In addition to strings and numbers, you can also use placeholders as the value to compare against. For example, if you want to filter the view to only show forms that were updated today, you could set your criteria to modified, Is Equal To, and the variable [Today], which would return today's date.

TIP *There is also another placeholder, [Me], that would return the current user.*

When setting up filtering, you can create a filter with multiple criteria by clicking the Show More Columns link. This adds a set of radio buttons immediately below the criteria you are working with that lets you choose either an And or Or relationship;

12

immediately below that will appear another set of fields that you can use to enter a second (third, and so on) criteria.

Grouping Column Data

In addition to controlling which columns are to appear on the view, you can also control the sort order of the data within these columns. By default, InfoPath sorts the data in the order in which it was saved to the form library. You can change this sort order by expanding the Group By options shown in Figure 12-13.

Using the drop-down lists provided, you can select a primary and secondary sort order for your view from the available columns for this view. Once you have selected a column to use when sorting, you can also select the sort order by using the radio buttons immediately below the drop-down list. This will cause the data shown in your view to be grouped by a particular field, in the order specified. This can be a handy way to display large amounts of data, as shown in the view in Figure 12-14, where the form data has been grouped by a week_ending field.

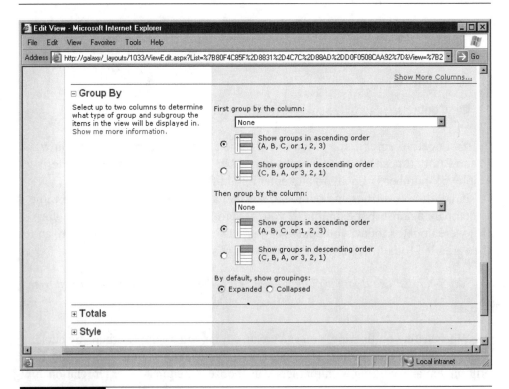

FIGURE 12-13   Grouping options

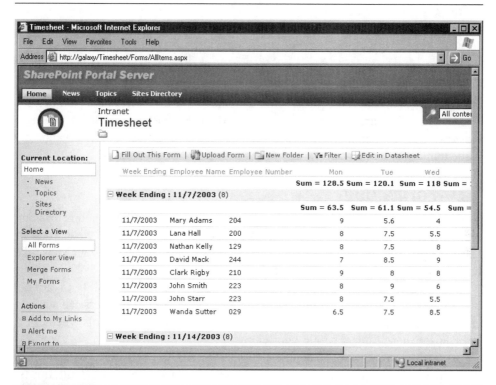

FIGURE 12-14   Grouped data

Totaling Column Data

To analyze form data directly on your view, you can also add totals to the data columns that appear in your view. If you expand the Totals options on the Edit View page, you get a list of all the different columns displayed on your view, along with a drop-down list to the right of the column name that you can use to select a summary function. Seven different summary functions are available:

- Count
- Average
- Minimum
- Maximum

■   Sum

■   Std Deviation

■   Variance

You may notice that all of these summary functions are not available for all fields. The functions that are available are determined by the type of the column you are working with. Text columns, for example, only have the Count operator available, while numeric columns can use any of the summary operators listed.

View Formatting

At the bottom of the Edit View page is a hodge-podge of formatting options for your view, starting with different Style options that you can apply to your view. You can select a style from the available list to apply formatting attributes to your view, like basic table formatting, shading, and so on.

The Folders options near the bottom of the page offer you the ability to turn on or off folder display within your view. As you will see a little later, users can actually create folders to help organize their form data, and this setting controls whether or not you see those folders within your view.

At the bottom of the page are the settings for Item Limits, where you can select the number of items that you want to appear on your view page. By default, this is set to 100 items, but you can increase or decrease this number depending on your preferences. As always, once you have made any changes to the formatting options previously mentioned, click OK to accept your changes and return to the Customize settings page.

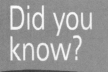

Using Summary Operators

If you find that you want to use summary operators on a field that is a string (but should have been numeric), you need to go back to your form's design in InfoPath and change the type of the field in the underlying data source and then republish your form. If you have already published form data to your form library, you may also receive an error when you attempt to update the form with the new numeric data types. In this instance, it is probably better to publish your form to a new form library and migrate the old form data across manually.

Working with Form Libraries

Now that you have created your form library and understand how to fill out and modify forms, you are ready to look at some of the other techniques that you need to know to work with form libraries and the form data that is collected. The following sections look from an end user's perspective at the features within SharePoint that you can use to customize your form library and analyze form data, starting with uploading forms.

Uploading Forms

If all of your users have access to a SharePoint server, form distribution and collation is easy. As you saw earlier, all they need to do is visit the home page for your form library and click the Fill Out This Form button and then save the results back to the library. But if your users do not have access to the SharePoint site or if you have a number of forms that have already been completed offline and saved to a form file, you can also upload these forms into your form library.

To upload a form to a form library, click the Upload Form button on the main page of your form library, which opens a dialog box with a Browse button that allows you to browse your computer for a file to upload. Alternately, you can click the Upload Multiple Files link, which opens the dialog box shown in Figure 12-15.

You can use the file browser to select all the form files to be uploaded. When you are finished selecting the form files, click the Save and Close button at the top of the page to upload these forms into your form library.

NOTE *Make sure that all the forms that you are uploading have been created using the form that your form library is based on—otherwise, you may receive an error message when the form that you upload and the form library are incompatible.*

Sorting and Filtering Form Data

You may have already noticed that the columns within your form library appear as hyperlinks—clicking these links sorts your form data by the column you have selected. When viewing your form library, you can tell what sort order is applied by looking for a small up or down arrow beside the column name, indicating ascending or descending order.

TIP *To change the order, click the column heading a second time.*

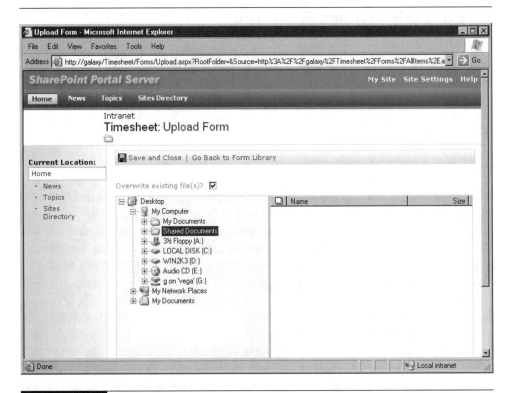

FIGURE 12-15   Uploading options

You can also filter the data within your columns based on the contents of a column. From the main page of your form library, click the Filter button to display a drop-down list on the top of each column. You can then use these drop-down lists to select a field to filter by and click Hide Filter Choices to return to viewing all the forms within your form library.

Working with Form Library Data

Now that you have had some experience working with your form library, you are ready to dig a little deeper and look at how to analyze all of that form data that you have been collecting. Up until now, you have been looking at your form data through a standard view, in which all the form data is shown in a table.

To analyze data, SharePoint also provides a datasheet view that allows you to view and edit the data in a spreadsheet-like interface with rows and columns of data.

In addition to being an easier interface to navigate, the datasheet view also provides the ability to export and link data to other Microsoft Office products, including Excel and Access, for further analysis and reporting.

The following sections describe how to use the datasheet view and related Office tools to analyze your form data and turn this data into decision-making information, starting with a look at the datasheet itself.

Editing in a Datasheet

To invoke the datasheet view of your form library data, click the Edit in Data Sheet button, which changes the display of your data, as shown in Figure 12-16.

Notice that the columns are exactly the same as in the standard view and that each column has a drop-down list shown on top of the column heading. You can use these drop-down lists to select the sort order for the sheet, as well as to filter the sheet contents.

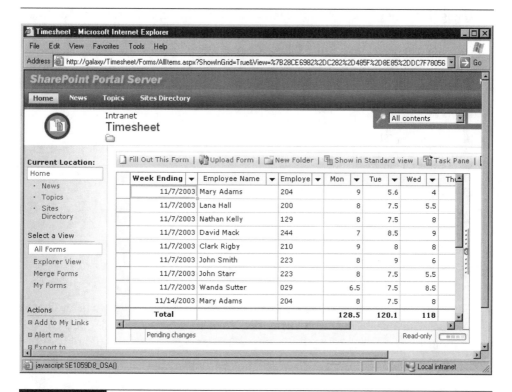

| FIGURE 12-16 | Datasheet view |

To create a filter to narrow the data shown in the datasheet, use the drop-down list above the column you want to use in your filter to select the Custom Filter option. This opens the Custom Filter dialog box, shown in the following illustration, which allows you to enter the criteria to be used when filtering this view.

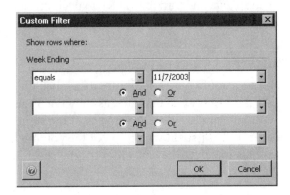

Using this dialog box, you can enter up to three different criteria based on this field, with either an And or Or operator between them. You can use the drop-down lists provided to select one of the following operators:

- Is Equal To

- Is Not Equal To

- Is Greater Than

- Is Less Than

- Is Greater Than or Equal To

- Is Less Than or Equal To

- Begins With

- Contains

Then, you can use the drop-down list on the right to select a value to be evaluated or you can type a value in the box provided. When you are finished, click OK to accept your filter criteria and return to the datasheet view, which should now only show the rows of data that meet the criteria you entered.

 *To show all the records again, select Show All from the drop-down list at the top of the column.*

From within the datasheet, you can also edit the underlying InfoPath forms that provided the data shown. To edit form data, right-click within the datasheet and, from the right-click menu, select Document | Edit Document. This launches InfoPath on your computer and allows you to edit the form data. When finished, click the Save button within InfoPath to save your form data back to the form library.

Analyzing Form Library Data with Excel

In addition to controlling how your form data will appear, the datasheet also provides a powerful set of tools for analyzing form data, including links to Office programs, such as Excel. Using the features found within the datasheet, you can export form library data to Excel and use Excel spreadsheets to print form data, creating charts and graphs, and analyze form data using pivot tables. The following sections cover how to do these tasks and more.

Viewing and Printing

Excel's strength lies in the ability it provides to analyze large amounts of information. And a tight integration with SharePoint makes it easy to extract form library information. To export your form library data, navigate to the main page of your form library (which, in this chapter's running example, is http://servername/Timesheet/Forms/AllItems.aspx) and make sure you are in the datasheet view. Next, click the Task Pane button in the toolbar above the datasheet to open the task pane to the right of the datasheet.

To export your form library data to a linked Excel spreadsheet, use the down arrow at the bottom of the task pane to scroll down to the Export and Link to Excel link. When you click this link, a separate process will launch and open Excel on your computer and display your form library data in a new spreadsheet as a list, like the spreadsheet shown in Figure 12-17.

TIP   *You may receive a warning message about linking to external data and another warning message about linking to SharePoint. In both cases, click Open or OK to proceed, because the export process is a relatively low security risk.*

You'll find that because the information is linked to your form library data, you won't be able to change any of the values presented, but you can use the data as you would with any other spreadsheet and apply formulas, formatting, and so on, as required.

12

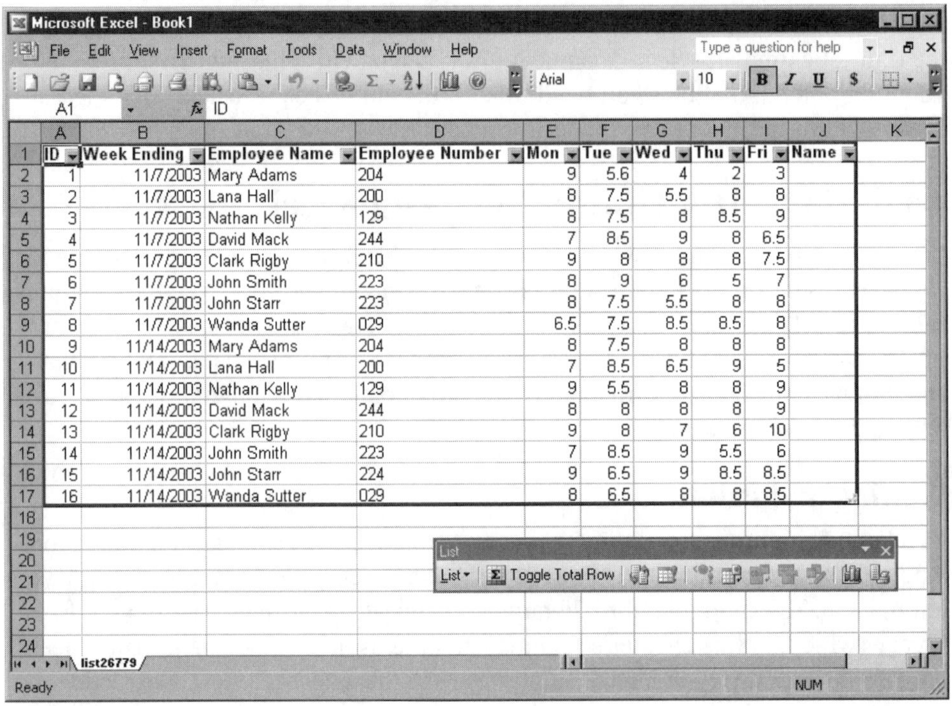

ID	Week Ending	Employee Name	Employee Number	Mon	Tue	Wed	Thu	Fri	Name
1	11/7/2003	Mary Adams	204	9	5.6	4	2	3	
2	11/7/2003	Lana Hall	200	8	7.5	5.5	8	8	
3	11/7/2003	Nathan Kelly	129	8	7.5	8	8.5	9	
4	11/7/2003	David Mack	244	7	8.5	9	8	6.5	
5	11/7/2003	Clark Rigby	210	9	8	8	8	7.5	
6	11/7/2003	John Smith	223	8	9	6	5	7	
7	11/7/2003	John Starr	223	8	7.5	5.5	8	8	
8	11/7/2003	Wanda Sutter	029	6.5	7.5	8.5	8.5	8	
9	11/14/2003	Mary Adams	204	8	7.5	8	8	8	
10	11/14/2003	Lana Hall	200	7	8.5	6.5	9	5	
11	11/14/2003	Nathan Kelly	129	9	5.5	8	8	9	
12	11/14/2003	David Mack	244	8	8	8	8	9	
13	11/14/2003	Clark Rigby	210	9	8	7	6	10	
14	11/14/2003	John Smith	223	7	8.5	9	5.5	6	
15	11/14/2003	John Starr	224	9	6.5	9	8.5	8.5	
16	11/14/2003	Wanda Sutter	029	8	6.5	8	8	8.5	

FIGURE 12-17 A spreadsheet with exported and linked form data

NOTE *In addition to exporting and linking to Excel, the datasheet view also enables you to print form library data directly through Excel. This feature uses the same process just described, except that when the Excel spreadsheet is generated, the Print dialog box is immediately called and will print the spreadsheet.*

Charting and Graphing

If you want to perform some quick graphical analysis on your form library data, nothing beats a chart or graph to get the point across. From the datasheet view, you can directly invoke the graphing engine within Excel to create charts and graphs from your form library data.

To create a chart or graph from your form library data, make sure you are in the datasheet view and then use the down arrow at the bottom of the task pane to scroll down to the Chart with Excel link. When you click this link, a separate process will launch and open Excel on your computer, display your form library data in a new spreadsheet as a list, and invoke the Chart Wizard, shown in Figure 12-18.

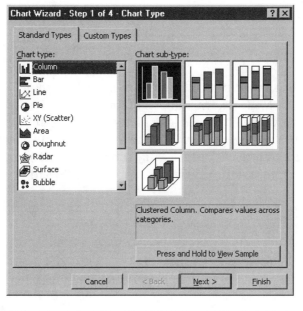

FIGURE 12-18   Chart types

In the first step of the Chart Wizard, you need to select a chart type to be created. There are a number of different chart and graph types available:

■ Column

■ Bar

■ Line

■ Pie

■ XY (Scatter)

■ Area

■ Doughnut

■ Radar

■ Surface

■ Bubble

■ Stock

12

- Cylinder

- Cone

- Pyramid

Once you select a chart type, the right half of the dialog box displays a number of subtypes that are available, with different formatting options, orientation, and so on. To see what your chart would look like, select a subtype and then click the Press and Hold to View Sample button to display a preview of your chart. When you are happy with the results, click to select the subtype that you want to create and then click Next to proceed to the next step in the Chart Wizard.

TIP *If you don't see the chart type you want, you can always click the Custom Types tab to create your own custom chart type.*

The next step of the wizard (illustrated in Figure 12-19) is used to select the data that will be used for your chart. By default, your form library data from your spreadsheet

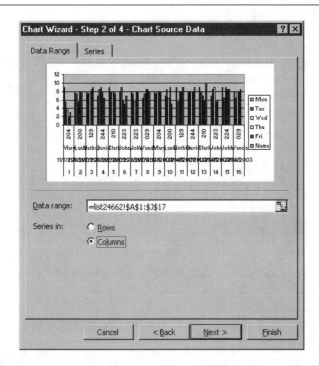

FIGURE 12-19   Data options

will be selected but you can narrow or increase this selection by entering a cell range in the text box provided or by using the selector to grab a range of values.

When you are finished selecting your data range, click Next to proceed to the next step of the wizard (shown in Figure 12-20, labeled Chart Options).

This dialog box enables you to change different chart attributes, including the chart title and options for the chart's axes, gridlines, legend, and more.

> **TIP** *All of these formatting options and attributes are also available after your chart has been created, so if you don't know exactly what you want, you can always come back later and change these options or attributes.*

When you are finished changing these settings, click Next to proceed to the last step in the Chart Wizard, where you can select the chart location. You can place the chart either as a new sheet within your workbook or as an object in an existing workbook. To finish the Chart Wizard, click the Finish button to add your chart or graph to the location you have specified. It couldn't be easier! You can now format the chart as you normally would within Excel, adding titles, gridlines, and so on, to suit your needs.

Analyzing Form Library Data with Access

Another popular method of analyzing form library data is to use Microsoft Access to create queries and reports to transform data into decision-making information.

12

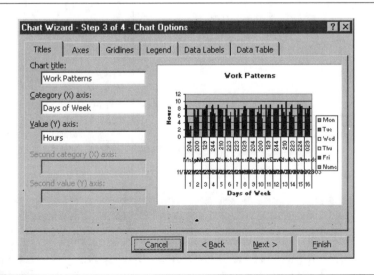

FIGURE 12-20   Chart options

How to ... Create Pivot Tables

Last, but certainly not least, in the bag of Excel tricks is the pivot table. If you haven't worked with pivot tables before in Excel, they are a special formatting structure that allows you to calculate and show summary values by specifying rows, columns, and fields to be calculated.

Pivot tables are a great way to display form library data because they can be used to summarize thousands of rows of data into a succinct summary format. To create an Excel pivot table from your form library data, make sure you are in the datasheet view and then use the down arrow at the bottom of the task pane to scroll down to the Create Excel Pivot Table Report link.

When you click this link, a separate process will launch and open Excel on your computer, display your form library data in a new spreadsheet as a list, and invoke the pivot table dialog box, shown here.

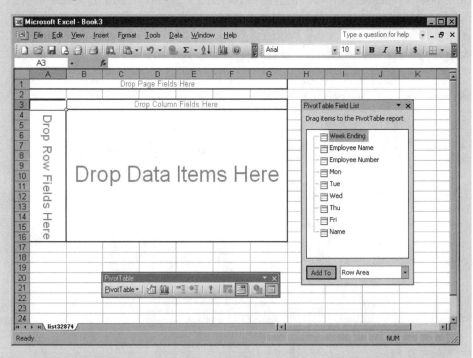

To create your pivot table report, drag fields from the field list to the areas marked Drop Row Fields Here, Drop Column Fields Here, and so on. As you drag rows, columns, and data items, Excel will crunch your form library data and display a summary based on the rows and columns you have selected.

The following sections look at how you can export form library data to Access, create tables that are linked to your form library, and create queries and reports from your data. The first section looks at the easiest method that you can use to analyze form data—do a one-off export of the data to an Access database.

Exporting Form Library Data

If you need to quickly analyze form library data as a one-off task or collate the data in a format that you can share with users outside your organization, exporting the form library data to Access is an easy method you can use. When you export the form data to Access, you are creating a separate copy of the data that you can then analyze and send to users outside your organization, as opposed to creating a "linked" table that remains tied into your form library and is automatically updated. (Creating linked tables is described in the next section.)

To export your form library data, navigate to the main page of your form library (http://servername/Timesheet/Forms/AllItems.aspx in the example) and click the Edit in Datasheet button to open your form library data in a datasheet view. Next, click the Task Pane button in the toolbar above the datasheet to open the task pane to the right of the datasheet, like the one shown in Figure 12-21.

To export your form library data to Access, use the down arrow at the bottom of the task pane to scroll down to the Export to Access link. When you click this link, the task pane changes and prompts you for the location to which you want to export your form library data. You can either select the option to use an existing database or create a new database for your exported data. Once you have made your selection, click OK to either select a database to use or to select the name and location for the database to be created.

During the export process, a new table will be created and named based on the view you are working with (the table in the example is named Timesheet:All Forms) and the data from your form library columns will be placed in this table, as shown next.

ID	Edit	Week Ending	Employee Name	Employee Num	Mon	Tue
3	[...]	11/7/2003	Mary Adams	204	9	5.6
5	[...]	11/7/2003	Lana Hall	200	8	7.5
7	[...]	11/7/2003	Nathan Kelly	129	8	7.5
1	[...]	11/7/2003	David Mack	244	7	8.5
6	[...]	11/7/2003	Clark Rigby	210	9	8
2	[...]	11/7/2003	John Smith	223	8	9
4	[...]	11/7/2003	John Starr	223	8	7.5
8	[...]	11/7/2003	Wanda Sutter	029	6.5	7.5
10	[...]	11/14/2003	Mary Adams	204	8	7.5
11	[...]	11/14/2003	Lana Hall	200	7	8.5
12	[...]	11/14/2003	Nathan Kelly	129	9	5.5
13	[...]	11/14/2003	David Mack	244	8	8
14	[...]	11/14/2003	Clark Rigby	210	9	9

Timesheet : All Forms : Table

Record: 1 of 16

12

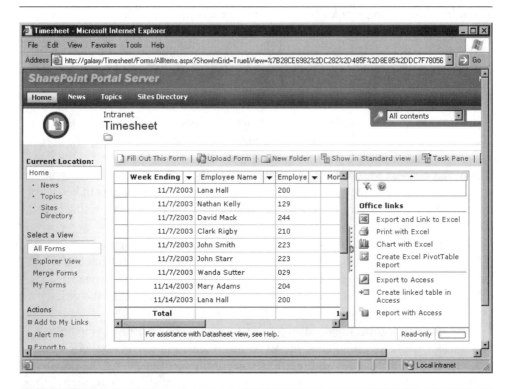

FIGURE 12-21   Task pane options

Access automatically adds an ID field as a unique key for your table and another field marked Type that contains the value XML. There is also an Edit field that contains a hyperlink to the underlying form. You can click this link to open the form from SharePoint and then click the Edit in Microsoft InfoPath button to edit the form content.

 *Since you are working with a one-off export of the data, you would need to export the data again after you modified the form and saved it back to your form library.*

Once the data has been exported to a table within your Access database, you can use this data as you would with any other Access database, including running queries or reports across the data, exporting to other formats, and so on.

Since this table was exported from your form library and is not tied into any back-end systems, you can edit the table's structure and design to suit your own use (including deleting the extra Edit and Type columns that were added during the export process).

Linking Form Library Data

Although exporting data to Access may be the simplest method you can use to analyze form library data, what happens when you enter a few more forms and want to analyze the data again? You would need to export the data again and rerun your reports, queries, and so forth. A much easier solution if you need to analyze data periodically is to link an Access table to your form library data. Linked tables are updated automatically and ensure that whenever you run a query or report, you are getting the most current information available.

To link your form library data to an Access table, use the down arrow at the bottom of the task pane to scroll down to the Created Linked Table in Access link. When you click this link, the task pane will change and prompt you for the location where you want to create the linked table. You can either select the option to use an existing database or create a new database for your exported data; once you have made your selection, click OK.

During the linking process, a new table will be created and named based on the view you are working with (for example, Timesheet:All Forms) and this table will be linked to your form library data.

> **TIP** *A linked table will appear within Access with a small arrow on the left side of the table icon.*

Since the table is linked to your form library data, you won't need to export the data each time you want to run a query or report. Whenever you open the linked table, the data in the table is read directly from your form library data. And since the table is linked to your form library data, you won't be able to change the design of the table to add or delete fields.

> **NOTE** *If you do need to add additional fields, consider creating another table within Access and then specifying a relationship between the two tables.*

A linked table within Access can be used just like regular tables. You can use this data in your own queries, from simple select queries to complex queries involving multiple tables and other criteria. You will not be able to perform update queries on this table (because the table data is linked directly to your SharePoint form library) but you can use this table for reporting or export the data to other database or spreadsheet formats.

12

Creating Reports

If you want to take your analysis a step further and create presentation-quality reports from your form library data, you can use the built-in report writer within Access to quickly create reports that you can customize as required.

To create a report from your form library data, use the down arrow at the bottom of the task pane to scroll down to the Report with Access link. When you click this link, the task pane will change and prompt you for the location where you want to create your report. You can either select the option to use an existing database or create a new database for your exported data—once you have made your selection, click OK.

During the report creation process, a new table is created and named based on the view you are working with (for instance, Timesheet:All Forms) and this table will be linked to your form library data. Once the linked table has been established, Access creates a report from the linked data using a columnar style, which places all the fields from your table in a single column in the report, as shown in Figure 12-22.

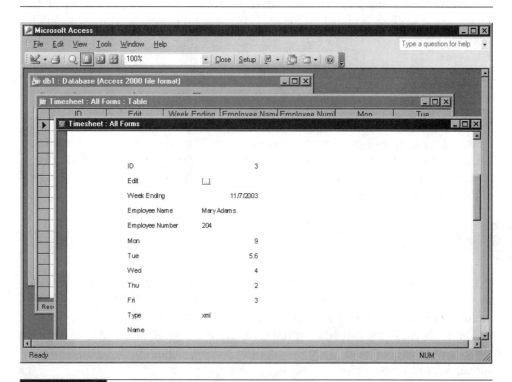

FIGURE 12-22 A typical report created from form library data

While this may not suit every application, it provides a starting point for your own report design. You can see the design of the report that was created by selecting View | Design View. You can then change the order and position of fields, add grouping, add sorting, and so on, as you would with any other Access report.

 *For more information on creating and modifying reports with Access 2003, check out* How to Do Everything with Microsoft Office Access 2003, *by Virginia Andersen (McGraw-Hill/Osborne, 2003).*

Summary

Throughout this chapter, you have seen the benefits of using SharePoint and form libraries to distribute your forms and collect form data. Whether you are a small organization just getting started with electronic forms or a large multinational company that processes thousands of forms a day, form libraries provide a host of features that will cut down on manual intervention and allow you to quickly extract and analyze form data with a minimum of effort.

If you don't use SharePoint or are looking for another way to publish forms or form data, don't despair! The next chapter looks at some of the other methods that you can use to publish form templates and resulting form data that don't require SharePoint Portal Server.

12

Chapter 13

Install Custom Forms

How to...

- Create trusted forms using the RegForm utility

- Create a script to install a form

- Create an MSI file to install a form

- Manually create a trusted form

- Install a custom form

Chapter 10 described how the security model works within InfoPath and explained that to utilize the full functionality of the InfoPath SDK and access system and external resources, you need to create trusted forms.

This chapter looks at how to create and distribute trusted forms to users, starting with an introduction to RegForm, one of the tools provided in the InfoPath Software Developers Kit (SDK). You'll discover how to create trusted forms from a command-line utility and how to create installation programs using scripting and Windows Installer packages. You'll also find out how to customize the installation programs that you create, as well as how to manually create and distribute trusted forms.

By the end of this chapter, you should be able to use your newfound skills to create and deploy fully trusted forms in a wide variety of situations.

Installation Overview

There are a couple of different ways you can create fully trusted forms for use with InfoPath—the most popular method is to use a utility called RegForm to make the necessary changes to your form and create an installation script that you can use to install the form on a user's computer. When you run this script, it will register the form on the user's computer and add it to the list of Custom Installed Forms.

Alternately, instead of using the utility to make your form fully trusted, you could manually change the form files within your InfoPath form and distribute the form using your own custom script or installation tool.

Regardless of which method you use, the process behind the scenes is the same. First, you must change the form itself so that it is based on a Uniform Resource Name (URN) instead of a Uniform Resource Locator (URL). This involves manually changing two of the form files to include a "name" attribute with a URN that usually includes the name of the form and your company for identification.

Did you know?

What's the Difference?

The difference between a URL and a URN is that a URL is used to point to a specific resource (for example, www.microsoft.com/) whereas a URN is used to refer to a resource with a name (for instance, *mycompany:myform*) that has "persistent significance" such that anyone who sees the URN should be able to work out where to find the resource. In this case, by combining the form name with your company name, this URN refers to a specific form in use at a specific company.

You will be looking at how to make these changes in detail a little later in the chapter, but the basic process involves extracting the form files from within InfoPath and then using an XML or text editor (like Notepad) to modify the form definition file (XSF) and form template file (XML).

The second step to make a form fully trusted is to change the requireFullTrust attribute to "yes" in the form definition file. Once you have made the changes to these two attributes, you can then reassemble your InfoPath form from the extracted files.

Once you have created your fully trusted form, you can then use functionality found within the InfoPath object model to install and register your form. Regardless

Did you know?

Creating CAB Files

It is important to note that you need to reassemble your form files manually, using a utility or application that can create CAB (cabinet) files. As you saw in Chapter 2, an InfoPath form uses this file format to encapsulate all the different types of files that make up an InfoPath form. Microsoft has a few different command-line utilities that you can use to create CAB files, but the easiest method is to use one of the Zip utilities that can generate CAB files (for example, ACDZip) and then rename the file to change the file extension back to .xsn. Microsoft also recommends that you place the manifest file first in the cabinet file.

13

of the method you choose to use to install your form, you need to use the InfoPath SDK and, specifically, the RegisterSolution method to register your form in InfoPath. This will enable users to see and choose the form under Custom Installed Forms.

For more information on extending InfoPath or the InfoPath object model, check out Chapter 10.

The easiest way to use this method is through a bit of JScript or VBScript that runs through the Windows Scripting Host, but you can also use this method from the installation setup or a program of your choice.

You'll find out how to both automatically and manually create this type of installation script a little later in this chapter.

Working with the RegForm Utility

As promised earlier, you are going to start your detailed lesson of how to create fully trusted forms by learning how to work with the RegForm utility, which does most of the hard work for you. Before you can start learning about it, you need to obtain a copy of the InfoPath SDK (if you don't already have one), which is available for download at www.microsoft.com/downloads/ (search for "infopath sdk") or from the MSDN web site at http://msdn.microsoft.com/InfoPath/.

The InfoPath SDK itself is a collection of forms and developer samples that demonstrates different ways to use InfoPath and integrate it into existing systems and databases. Once you have downloaded and installed the SDK, the RegForm utility, by default, will be available in the C:\Program Files\Microsoft Office 2003 Developer Resources\Microsoft Office InfoPath 2003 SDK\Tools\ folder.

The utility itself is a command-line tool that doesn't have a graphical user interface—you need to run it from a command prompt with a number of switches to convert a form into a fully trusted form that can be installed on a client computer.

Since you are going to use this utility often, you may want to move it to a more convenient location (for instance, C:\InfoPathTools\).

When you create a trusted form using the RegForm utility, you have the option to create an installation script or (if you have Visual Studio .NET installed on your computer) a basic Microsoft Installer (MSI) file that you can use to install the trusted form on the client's computer. The following sections look at both of these installation methods.

Creating a Trusted Form and Installing Using Scripting

The easiest method to create and install a trusted form is to use the scripting method, which is the default method used by the RegForm utility. This process converts your form to a fully trusted form and creates an installation script (written in JScript) that you can use to install your form.

To get started, you need to have a fully tested InfoPath form that is ready to be distributed. To use the RegForm utility on this form, open a command prompt from the Start menu: select Start | Run, type **CMD** in the Run dialog box, and then click OK to open a Windows Command Prompt. Navigate to the directory where you have installed the RegForm utility—by default, this is C:\Program Files\Microsoft Office 2003 Developer Resources\Microsoft Office InfoPath 2003 SDK\Tools\.

The basic input required for the utility is the path and filename of the form you want to make fully trusted and the /t switch set to YES, which is used to specify whether the form is fully trusted or not. So, if you were running the utility on a form named employee.xsn that is stored locally, your command would look like this:

```
RegForm employee.xsn /t YES
```

The RegForm utility will make a backup of your form and save it with a .bak extension in the same location as the original. Next, it will change the form files to make them fully trusted and create an installation script using JScript, as shown in Figure 13-1.

13

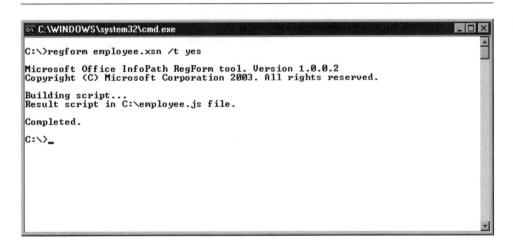

FIGURE 13-1   The completed RegForm utility

After the utility has finished running, you should have three files in your directory:

```
Employee.xsn
Employee.bak
Employee.js
```

You can now use the JScript file provided to install your trusted form.

Installing Your Trusted Form

To install your form, all you need to do is run the script file that was generated by the RegForm utility. You can run this file from a command prompt or by simply double-clicking it from within Windows. A dialog box similar to the following appears and asks if you want to register the form template.

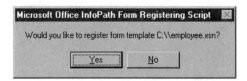

Click Yes to continue. A new dialog box displays the status of the registration process—click OK to continue.

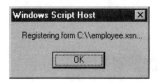

When the form has been properly registered, you will receive a confirmation message. Click OK.

You can also run your installation script in "silent" mode by running the script with a /silent switch at the end (for example, employee.js /silent).

Open InfoPath and your new fully trusted form will be available as a custom installed form. To fill out your form, select File | Fill Out a Form, which opens a task pane on the right side of the workspace. Locate and click the link for More Forms and then click the Custom Installed Forms tab, as shown in Figure 13-2.

You can now fill out your form as you normally would—since the form is fully trusted, it will be able to access all the required resources on your computer. When you are finished filling out your form, you can save or submit it just like usual.

Installing a Form from a Different Location

Another common scenario you may encounter when installing forms using the scripting method is that the actual form file itself may be in a different location than your installation script. You can use the /d switch with your installation script to specify where to find the InfoPath form you want to install. For example, if you have a network drive (for example, F:) on which you store all of your InfoPath forms, you could install your form with a command similar to the following:

```
employee.js /d f:\forms\employee.xsn
```

As long as the computer on which you are installing your form has appropriate access to that drive, you will be able to install your form from the specified location.

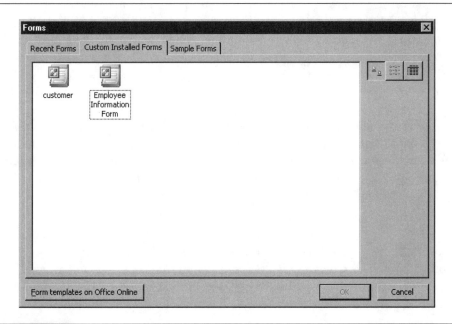

FIGURE 13-2   Custom Installed Forms

Creating an Installation Using an MSI File

While the scripting method is the easiest way to convert and install your forms, the RegForm utility also enables you to create simple Windows Installer (MSI) files that you can use to install your trusted forms.

 *Don't forget! To use this functionality, you must also have Visual Studio .NET installed on your computer, because the utility uses the .NET development environment.*

In addition to providing additional options not offered using the scripting method, using MSI files allows you to deploy forms using "push" technology, such

 **Remove a Form**

If you ever need to remove a trusted form that you have installed on your computer, you can use the same script that was originally created with the RegForm utility. The script has an /uninstall switch that will remove the form, as shown here:

```
employee.js /uninstall
```

You may run into a problem if you haven't kept the original installation script but still need to remove the form. You could delete the form template file itself, but that would still not remove it from the list of Custom Installed Forms within InfoPath. To manually remove a form from this dialog box, you need to delete a key within the Registry.

CAUTION *If you are not familiar with working with the Windows registry, please make a backup of your Registry before you get started by selecting File | Export and picking the option to export All. Keep this backup in a safe place in case you make a mistake later and want to return to a "good" copy of the Registry.*

Open the Registry by selecting Run from the Start menu and type **REGEDIT**. Navigate through the Registry to find the keys under HKEY_LOCAL_MACHINE\ SOFTWARE\Microsoft\Office\11.0\InfoPath\SolutionsCatalog\, which should look something like the keys shown here.

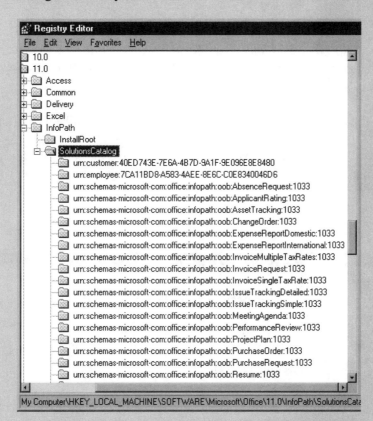

There is one key in this folder for each InfoPath form that is installed on your computer, listed by URN. To manually remove a form from InfoPath, click to select its key and then press the DELETE key to remove it. When you open InfoPath, this form will no longer appear on the Custom Installed Forms tab.

as Microsoft's System Management Server. Using this installation method also means that the forms you install are shown in the Add/Remove Programs listing and thus can be easily removed or repaired if required.

13

To convert a form to be fully trusted and create an MSI file to install it, use the RegForm utility with an /MSI switch as follows (no further information is required to create the MSI file):

```
regform employee.xsn /t YES /MSI
```

 If you are using Visual Studio .NET 2003, during the conversion process, you may receive a blank error message with the title "The project you are trying to open was saved with a previous version of Visual Studio…" Click No and then OK to continue.

When the process is finished, the utility displays a screen like the one shown in Figure 13-3.

Your MSI file has been placed in the same location as the converted form, along with a backup of the original form file. You can now use this file to install your form onto other computers.

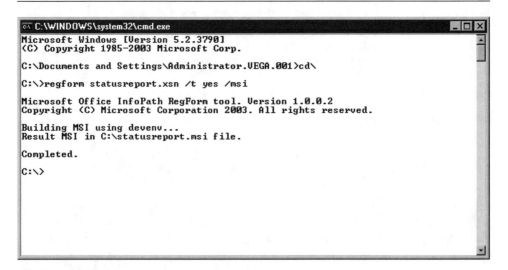

FIGURE 13-3   The completed RegForm utility

Installing Your Form

To install your form, simply locate and double-click the MSI file that was generated in the last step. This launches the Windows Installer service and starts the setup program that the RegForm utility created. Click Next on the Welcome screen.

 *Most computers already have the Windows Installer service installed and configured. (If yours does not, you can download a copy of the service from the Microsoft web site.)*

The first step in your setup program, shown in Figure 13-4, is to select where you want to install your form. By default, this location is set to C:\Program Files\InfoPath Form Templates\, but you can change to it wherever you like.

Also, make sure that you select the option at the bottom of the dialog box to make this installation for Everyone, and then click the Next button to continue.

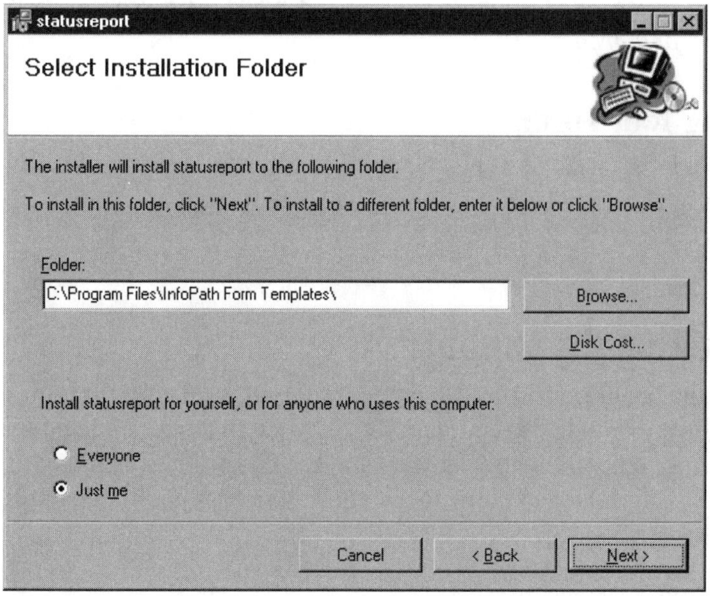

13

statusreport

Select Installation Folder

The installer will install statusreport to the following folder.

To install in this folder, click "Next". To install to a different folder, enter it below or click "Browse".

Folder:

C:\Program Files\InfoPath Form Templates\   Browse...

Disk Cost...

Install statusreport for yourself, or for anyone who uses this computer:

○ Everyone

◉ Just me

Cancel   < Back   Next >

FIGURE 13-4 Installation folder options

When the Confirm Installation screen appears, click Next to begin the installation process. A progress screen appears immediately to keep you updated on the installation process. When the installation has finished, an Installation Complete summary screen appears. Click Close to exit the setup program.

If all of those installation steps seem a bit much to you, you can always use the switches available for MSI files to change the way the setup behaves. For example, if you want to display a progress dialog box during the installation (but none of the other options), you could use the /qr switch:

```
employee.msi /qr
```

Likewise, if you want a completely "silent" install with no progress dialog boxes or indicators, you could run the MSI file using the /qb switch:

```
employee.msi /qb
```

 *For a complete list of standard Windows Installer switches to use with MSI files, check out http://msdn.microsoft.com/library/enus/msi/setup/command_ line_options.asp.*

Removing Your Form

To remove a form installed using an MSI file, you can locate the form in the Add/ Remove Programs section of the Control Panel or simply rerun the MSI file, both of which will open the dialog box shown in Figure 13-5 and allow you to remove the form.

Customizing the Output

In both of the scripting and MSI methods we used the RegForm utility with the default settings (with the exception of the /t switch to create a trusted form). There are a number of other switches that you can use to control the output of the RegForm utility. This section looks at how to use those switches and the features that they provide.

Changing the URN

As you saw earlier in the chapter ("Did you know? What's the Difference?" sidebar), when modifying a form to make it fully trusted, you are changing it from being URL-based to being URN-based. By default, when you don't specify a URN, the RegForm utility automatically creates a URN based on the form template and your

FIGURE 13-5   Remove options

company name. You can specify these values by using the /FT and /C switches, respectively. For example, if your form name is EmployeeInformation and your company name is Avantis, you could pass these values to the utility:

```
regform employee.xsn /t yes /ft employeeinformation /c avantis
```

If you don't specify the form and company name, the utility generates and assigns a generic GUID to your form. While this may seem like the easiest answer, a GUID is a generated string of characters and numbers. Earlier, when you looked at manually deleting a form from InfoPath's Custom Installed Forms, you saw that you had to delete a Registry key. If you choose to let the RegForm utility generate a GUID for the URN, it is almost impossible to determine which form is which without cracking open the underlying form files.

So, if you don't want to use the form and company name and don't want the utility to generate a GUID, you can specify your own URN by using the /U switch of the RegForm utility, as shown here:

```
regform employee.xsn /t YES /u urn:EmployeeInfo:Avantis
```

13

A URN usually consists of the form name and your company name, but you can create any type of URN you want. The structure of your URN must include two parts after the "urn" designation, separated by a colon, and the total length of the URN can't exceed 255 characters.

The "urn" must be in lowercase letters; otherwise, the utility will give you an error message.

Changing the Version Number

In addition to specifying a custom URN, you can specify the version number for the form you are converting. InfoPath forms have an internal version number that is automatically incremented each time the form is saved. To view the version number of a form, open the form design in InfoPath, select Tools | Form Options, and click the Advanced tab, shown in Figure 13-6.

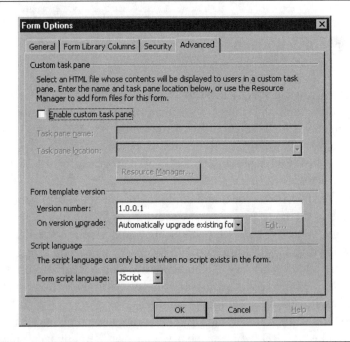

FIGURE 13-6 Advanced options

You can also use this dialog box to specify your own version number, but if you do so, InfoPath will not automatically update the version number from that point on.

When distributing forms, you can override the version number by using the /v switch of the RegForm utility to specify a new number. Version numbers follow the pattern of 9999.9999.9999.9999, so to pass a version number using this switch, your command line would look something like this:

```
regform employee.xsn /t YES /v 2.5.0.1
```

This only changes the version number of your new, fully trusted form. The backup of the form (employee.bak) will still have the old version number.

Changing the Output File and Location

The final set of switches available for the RegForm utility are used to control the output filename and location. If you have specified that you want to create an installation script (which is the default behavior), this switch can be used to change the filename and location of your JS script. Likewise, if you are creating a Windows Installer setup, the switch can be used to change the name of your MSI file, as shown here:

```
regForm employee.xsn /t YES /MSI /O c:\installs\installform.msi
```

Manually Creating Trusted Forms

If you don't want to use the RegForm utility or if you want to use another installation method, you can always use the manual method to create a trusted form. To manually convert your form, open the form within InfoPath and select File | Extract Form Files to extract the files to a directory. Next, locate the manifest.xsf file and open it for editing using Notepad or the XML editor of your choice—you won't be making too many changes to the file, so Notepad will be fine.

Within Notepad, select Edit | Find and locate the element marked xDocumentClass. To convert your form to be fully trusted, you need to add two attributes to this element, as follows (using the earlier example form and company names):

```
requireFullTrust="yes
name="urn:EmployeeInformation:Avantis"
```

13

Save this file back with its original name and extension and then open your XML template (template.xml) using the same method. You need to locate the tag marked mso-infoPathSolution and change the href reference within that tag to be the URN you specified before:

```
<?mso-infoPathSolution solutionVersion="1.0.0.2"
href="urn:EmployeeInformation:Avantis" productVersion="11.0.5329"
PIVersion="1.0.0.0" ?>
```

 *You can also change the solutionVersion attribute to specify the version of the form you are converting. This is the equivalent of using the /v switch with the RegForm utility.*

You need to repackage all the form files you extract back into an XSN file. You can use the MAKECAB utility that ships with Windows (which is also available for download from Microsoft.com), but, as described earlier, the easiest method is to use one of the Zip utilities that can generate CAB files (for example, ACDZip) and then change the file extension back to .xsn.

Installing Your Form

To install your form, you need to use either JScript or VBScript to register your form within InfoPath. The following is a JScript sample:

```
ExternalApplication = new
ActiveXObject("InfoPath.ExternalApplication");
ExternalApplication.RegisterSolution("C:\\employee.xsn");
ExternalApplication.Quit();
ExternalApplication = null;
```

You could also create your own custom installation program using Visual Studio .NET or the tool of your choice (InstallShield, WiseInstall, and so forth) but you would need to run this snippet of code from within your setup program to properly register your form within InfoPath.

Removing Your Form

To remove a form from InfoPath, you can use the same snippet of script—only this time, instead of registering your form, you would be unregistering the form:

```
ExternalApplication = new ActiveXObject("InfoPath.ExternalApplication");
ExternalApplication.UnregisterSolution("urn:EmployeeInformation:Avantis");
ExternalApplication.Quit();
ExternalApplication = null;
```

Keep in mind that this removes the form from the Custom Installed Forms listing, but it does not actually delete the underlying form file. You would need to add your own code if you wanted to delete the form field as well.

Summary

You now should have everything that you need to start distributing fully trusted forms, regardless of which method you choose. Chapter 14 looks at all the additional publishing methods (for example, those not covered in the preceding two chapters) that you can use to distribute your forms to users. Chapter 14 also is the last chapter of the book (and you didn't think you'd make it, did you?).

13

Chapter 14

Other Publishing Methods

How to...

- Publish forms to a web server
- Publish forms to a shared location
- Send forms via e-mail
- Export a form to HTML
- View a form template using a style sheet

Now that you have had a look at installing forms and using SharePoint form libraries, you are ready to look at some of the alternate methods of distributing forms and form data. All the methods used in this chapter don't require any further software or installations (other than the InfoPath Software Development Kit for some utilities) and provide simple solutions for distributing forms and form data.

As an added bonus, this chapter also covers how users who don't have InfoPath installed can still view form templates and form data through a handy command-line utility and some XML style sheets. So even if you have decided to use one of the other distribution methods mentioned in previous chapters, there are still a few items in this chapter that you may find interesting and some techniques that may come in handy.

This chapter's look at all of these different publishing methods and utilities begins with a discussion of publishing your form templates to a web server.

Publishing to a Web Server

One of the easiest methods of publishing a form is to publish it to a web server, so that users within your organization can access these forms from a central location. Since an InfoPath form remains tied to its original form template, you will want to pick a web server that form users will have access to and that will not change frequently. You will also want to make sure that you have the appropriate rights to publish to this web server before you get started.

To publish an InfoPath form template to a web server, design your form as you normally would and, when you are happy with the form's design and function, select File | Publish to open the Publishing Wizard. In the first step of the Publishing Wizard, click Next. In the next step, select the option to publish your form To a Web Server and then click Next. This opens the wizard page shown in Figure 14-1, which prompts you for the web URL and filename for your form, as well as the form name.

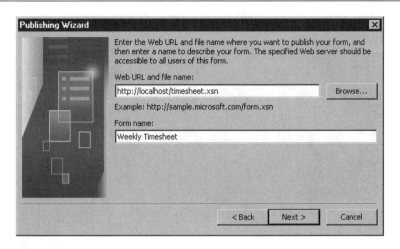

FIGURE 14-1   The Publishing Wizard

When you specify the web URL and filename, you need to enter the complete path and filename for your form, including the .xsn file extension.

TIP   *Just to make sure that you have access to the publishing location, you may want to go to My Network Places and add the web server as a network place before you start this process. If you don't have access to the web server, you may need to ask your system administrator to increase your rights.*

After you have entered a form name, click Next to continue to the wizard page shown in Figure 14-2, where you can enter the URL that end users need to use to open this file. Click Finish, which opens a confirmation page. If everything looks correct, click Finish to complete the publishing process.

For users to be able to fill out the forms you have published, they need to set this web server up in their own My Network Places and, from within InfoPath, use File | Open to open the form from the web server. They can then fill out the form as they normally would and, when finished, save or submit their form data according to the form's design.

NOTE   *This method uses forms that are URL based, which are "sandboxed" and thus do not have access to local system resources. If you do need to distribute forms that are fully trusted, you may want to consider using the RegForm utility and installing these forms locally on each user's computer.*

14

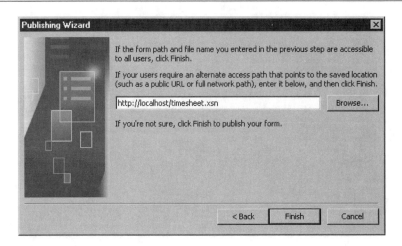

FIGURE 14-2   Publishing options

Publishing to a Shared Location

Another quick and easy method you can use to publish form templates is to publish them to a shared location on your organization's network. A shared location could be a shared drive that your system or network administrator has created for you or it could be a file share on a file server that everyone in the organization has access to. Regardless of which type of shared location you set up, the publishing process is the same and relatively trouble-free.

To publish an InfoPath form template to a shared location, open your form in design mode and select File | Publish to open the Publishing Wizard. Click Next, select the To a Shared Folder option, and then click Next. This opens a wizard page similar to the one shown previously in Figure 14-1 for publishing to a web server, again prompting you for the path and filename for your form, as well as the form name. When you specify the path and filename, you need to enter the complete network path and filename for your form, including the .xsn file extension.

After you enter the requested information, click Next to continue to the next wizard page, where you enter the URL that end users need to use to open this file. Like before, click Finish to open a confirmation page; click Finish again to complete the publishing process.

For users to be able to fill out the forms you have published, they need to open the form from within InfoPath. Use File | Open to open the form from the shared location. They can then fill out the form as they normally would and, when finished, save or submit their form data according to the form's design.

The same security principle applies here—create a fully trusted form if the form needs to access local system resources.

Sending Forms via E-Mail

In addition to publishing forms on a web server or shared location, you also may need to send forms via e-mail from time to time. This method is most effective when you need to share form data between users; it is not a preferred method of publishing or distributing forms to be filled out. Remember that when you fill out a form, it is tied to either a URL or URN, so it is not a good practice to distribute InfoPath form templates through e-mail.

But if you do need to send form data—as either a partially or fully filled out form—via e-mail, InfoPath features a tight integration with Outlook 2003 that allows you to send an InfoPath form as the body of an e-mail message, with the InfoPath form file attached. The recipient can see the InfoPath form in the e-mail, and if they have InfoPath installed, they can open and work with the attached form file.

To send your form, select File | Send to Mail Recipient. In the dialog box that appears, enter the e-mail address or alias of the recipient, a subject for your e-mail message, and an introduction, which can include instructions on what to do with the form (for example, "Please review and send back with comments") or can simply be notes that you want to pass along with the form. When you are finished entering this information, click the Send button to send your form.

Sending a form via e-mail may disconnect the form from back-end systems. For example, you may send a form to a user outside of your organization who does not have access to resources that may be used in the form, so the form may not work properly.

14

Viewing and Publishing Forms as HTML

Another easy method you can use to publish or distribute form data is to export it to HTML. There are two different methods you can use to publish your form, depending on your requirements. If you want to export a form to HTML from within InfoPath, there is a simple export process that you can use from the File menu to export your form, which can then be viewed in a web browser, posted to a web site, and so on.

If you need to convert a large number of forms or if you are sending the form to a user who does not have InfoPath and may need to view the form, there is also a "downlevel" tool provided in the InfoPath SDK (Software Development Kit) that can be used to convert the form so that it can be viewed using your web browser.

The following sections examine both of these methods and describe how they can be used with your forms, starting with the export method.

Exporting a Form to HTML

In order to export a form to HTML, you need to have an InfoPath form that has been filled out, like the one shown in Figure 14-3.

To export your form from within InfoPath, open the Form View you would like to export and select File | Export To | Web. This opens a standard Save As dialog box that enables you to enter a filename and location for your exported form. When you are finished, click OK to export your form.

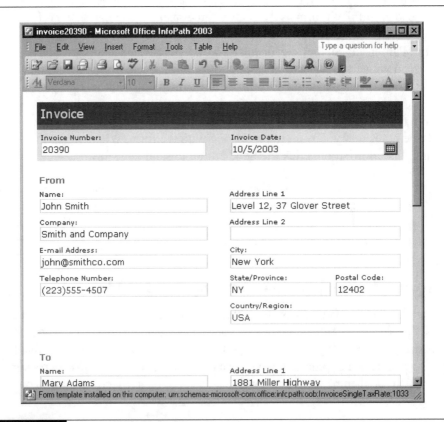

FIGURE 14-3   A typical InfoPath form

You'll notice that when InfoPath exports your form and data, it doesn't use a standard HTML file format. The file format that InfoPath uses instead is MHT, which is an abbreviation for MHTML (MIME Encapsulation of Aggregate HTML Documents). MHTML is an Internet standard that was originally defined as a method of sending complete web pages in the body of an e-mail message. Since this file format was introduced, it has been adapted for a variety of other uses, such as to archive web pages and publish HTML documents using a single file structure.

TIP *In fact, from any Microsoft Office application, you can select File | Save As to save the document as an MHT file.*

An MHTML file can contain multiple web pages and all the required images, scripts, and other external files that are required to make the pages appear as normal. Once you have exported your form to this format, you can then open it using your web browser, as shown in Figure 14-4.

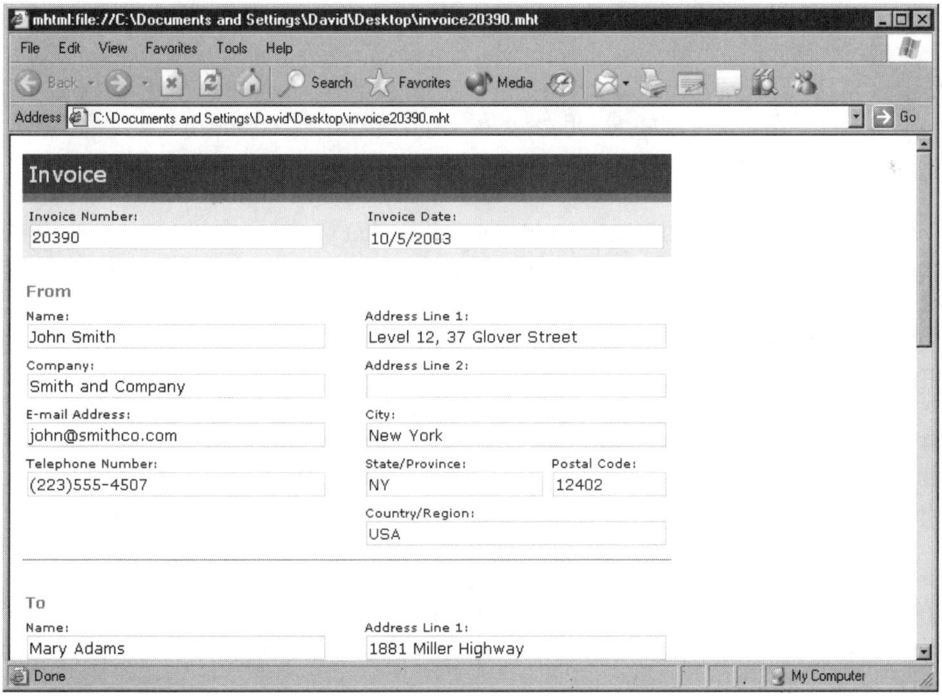

14

FIGURE 14-4   An exported form

You can also open an MHT file in any application that supports opening and editing MHT files, including Microsoft Word. The following are a few points to remember when working with the MHT file that InfoPath generates:

- Your exported form is static, so if you update the form data and want to update your web pages, you need to go through the export process again.

- If you choose to edit the MHT file, the form design may not be as precise as the design you created on the form. Since MHT files are made up of HTML files, and different editors handle HTML in different ways, you may end up with mixed results.

Using the Downlevel Tool

If you need to convert a large number of forms to HTML or if you do not have InfoPath installed, you may want to consider using the "downlevel" tool provided in the InfoPath SDK to take an InfoPath form and generate a downlevel view that can be viewed through a standard web browser.

If you haven't done so already, you need to download and install the InfoPath SDK to perform the tasks listed in this section. You can find a link to the SDK and related documentation from the main InfoPath web site at www.microsoft .com/infopath.

The downlevel tool is a command-line utility that you can use to convert a single form or to write batch scripts to convert large numbers of forms. The good news is that you don't need to have InfoPath installed to use the utility, so it is a good solution for users who may need to view forms but don't have InfoPath installed locally.

The utility creates this downlevel view by creating a style sheet that is used to display the form in a web browser. This style sheet is similar to the style sheets that you looked at in Chapter 2 that are used to define InfoPath views, but this style sheet has been created specifically for viewing the form in a web browser.

To use the downlevel tool, you need to have the InfoPath SDK installed. By default, the tool is located in C:\Program Files\Microsoft Office 2003 Developer Resources\Microsoft Office InfoPath 2003 SDK\Tools\XDown\ (although you may want to move the xdown.exe file to a more convenient location).

Creating a Downlevel View of a Form Template

The first use of the downlevel tool that you'll look at is to create a downlevel style sheet for a form template (XSN), which will allow users to view the structure of the form template using a standard web browser.

To use the downlevel tool, you need to pass a number of command-line switches, including the name of the form template, as well as a destination for the transformed files. Suppose that you have a form like the one shown in Figure 14-5, named invoice.xsn, and you want to create a downlevel style sheet and place all the required files in a directory called C:\Myforms\. The command line might look something like this:

```
XDown /d invoice.xsn c:\myforms\
```

The /d switch is required whenever you use the utility. It indicates that you want to create a downlevel view—the source form and target location follow afterwards.

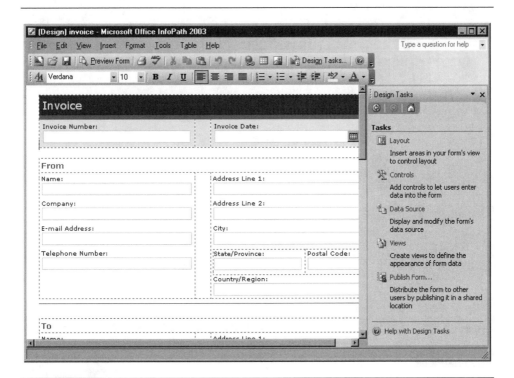

FIGURE 14-5   A sample invoice form

If you are using the downlevel utility on a computer that has InfoPath already installed, you also need to add the /C switch at the end of the command line. Otherwise, when you go to look at the downlevel form, it will be opened in InfoPath instead of your web browser.

If you were to look in the C:\Myforms\ directory, you would see that the downlevel utility actually separated the InfoPath form into its component files and that you can now view the form by viewing the template.xml file that was generated. Your form should appear something like the form shown in Figure 14-6.

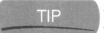
If you open your form and an application other than Internet Explorer or Netscape opens, you may need to change your file associations, because another application has the XML file format associated with it. Alternately, you could also open this file from within your web browser.

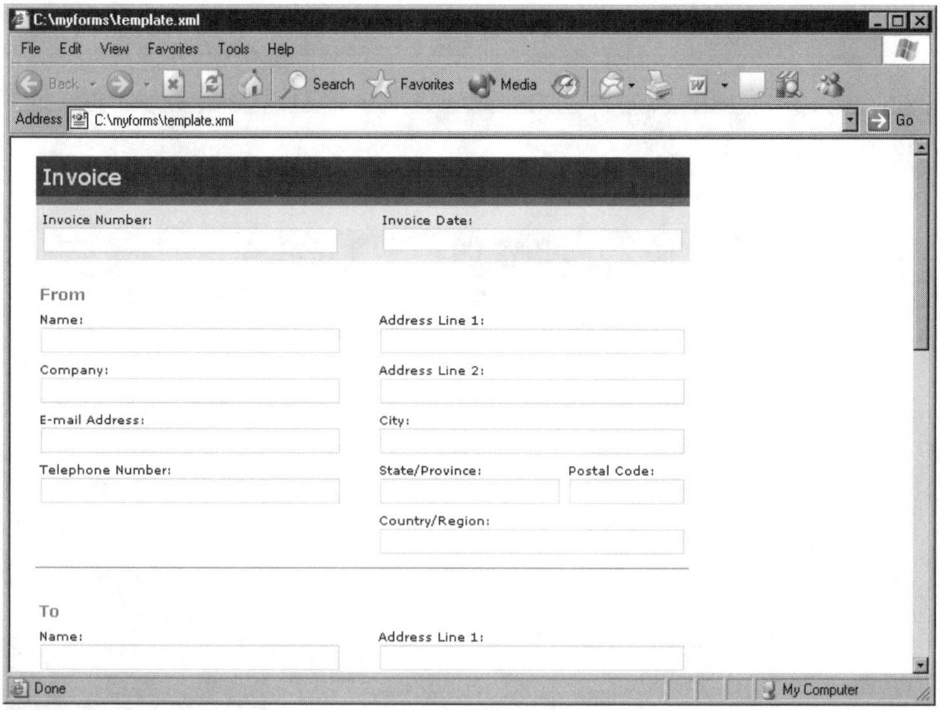

FIGURE 14-6 A downlevel view of the form

Creating a Downlevel View of a Form with Data

Once you have created the downlevel style sheet for your form template, you can then use that style sheet to view InfoPath forms you have filled out. This will enable users to see the XML data file in the form itself without having InfoPath installed on their computer.

First, locate the style sheet that was created in the previous step—it will have an .xsl extension and will be located in the same directory as the other expanded files. Next, you need to locate the XML file that was created when you saved your form after filling it out. From the example in this chapter, the Invoice form we have been working with has been filled out and saved as invoice20390.xml.

If you were to view this file as it is in Internet Explorer or a web development tool like Dreamweaver, it would look something like the screen shot shown in Figure 14-7 (not very pretty!).

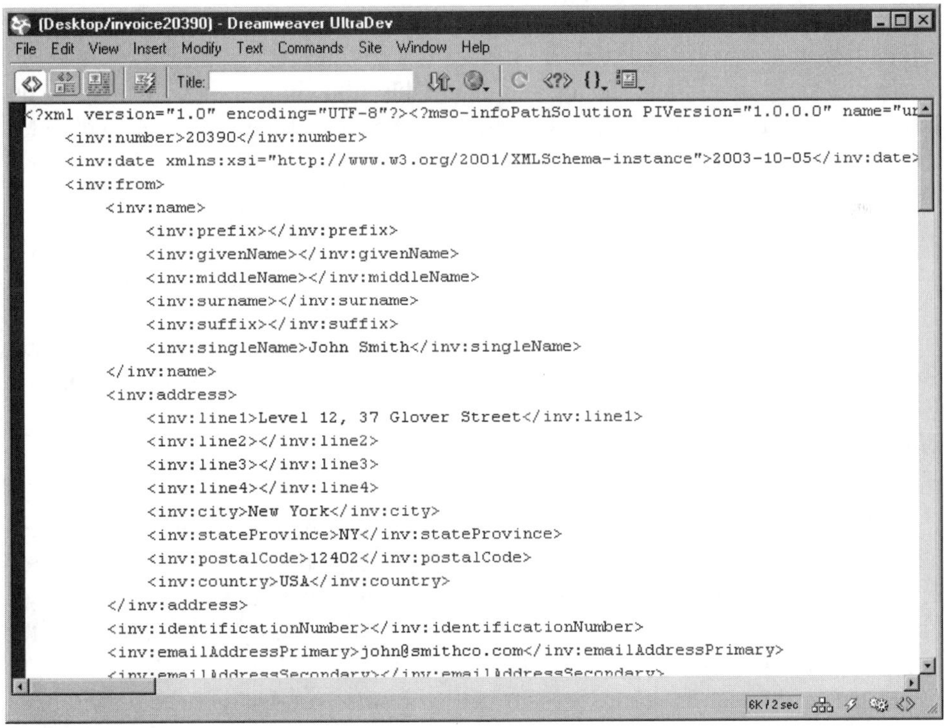

FIGURE 14-7   An XML file viewed in Dreamweaver

To apply the downlevel style sheet to this XML file, you need to edit the XML file itself. You can edit this file in Notepad if you like, or if you use a special XML tool (like XMLSpy) or web editor (FrontPage, Dreamweaver, and so on), you can use these tools as well; just make sure that you save the file back with an .xml extension. At the start of your XML file will be a section marked:

```
<?xml version="1.0" encoding="UTF-8"?>
```

Immediately after this section, you want to add a reference that tells your XML file to use the downlevel style sheet that was created earlier from your form template. To do so, insert the following element immediately after the preceding text:

```
<?xml-stylesheet type="text/xsl" href="default.xsl"?>
```

Remember to substitute the name and location of the style sheet you have generated earlier—in this example, the style sheet is just called default.xsl. If you want to view this XML file in your web browser on a computer that already has InfoPath installed, you need to do a little further editing.

On the same line of text, locate and delete the following—this will "break" the association with InfoPath so that you can view the XML file in Internet Explorer, instead of opening the form in InfoPath:

```
<?mso-application progid="InfoPath.Document"?>
<?mso-infoPathSolution solutionVersion="1.0.0.3" productVersion="11.0.5531"
PIVersion="1.0.0.0" href="file:///C:\xdown\invoice.xsn" ?>
```

You should now be able to open the form within Internet Explorer and it should look similar to the original form and display the form data in all the correct places.

Working with Views

By default, when you are working with the downlevel tool, it creates a downlevel style sheet that allows you to view the form's default view. But forms can have many views and often there will be a print version of a view that you may want to display. By using the command-line switches provided with the downlevel utility, you can retrieve a list of the views in use within a form and then alter the XML file to use a downlevel style sheet created from this view.

To list all the views that are present within a form, you can use the /l switch, as shown in the following command line:

```
Xdown /l invoice.xsn
```

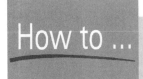 **Update Downlevel Files**

If you change your form template file, you may also need to update the style sheet and other files that are generated through the downlevel tool. The easiest way to do that is to use the tool's update flag to update the required files. But before you decide to update the files, it is always a good idea to look at which files would be updated or changed in the process. The downlevel utility provides the functionality through the /f switch, so to list all the files that would be changed, use the following command line:

```
XDown /d invoice.xsn c:\myforms\ /f
```

This produces a list of files that tells you which files are going to be changed or updated. You can then decide if you want to proceed with the update—if you decide to proceed, you can update these files using the /! switch. So, from the earlier example if the Invoice form had been changed, you would need to use the following command line to update all the related form files:

```
XDown /d invoice.xsn c:\myforms\ /!
```

This switch should enable you to integrate the output from the utility with other applications and systems—by updating the files instead of writing new filenames or other schemes, you can ensure that any processes or applications you hang off of these files won't be broken when you update the form template.

You don't need to specify a destination directory when using the switch, because you are not actually doing any transformations at this point—you are only getting a list of views that appear in the form, so the contents of the list depends on the views that are present in the form you are working with.

Once you have identified the name of the view, you can then use either the view name or the XSL filename with the /t switch to transform your XML file to include this style sheet. So, following through on the example used previously in this chapter, the Invoice form has a view called Print that has an associated style sheet named print.xsl. To create a downlevel style sheet from this view, the command line would look like this:

```
XDown /d invoice.xsn c:\myforms\ /t:print.xsl
```

14

This would place the reference to the style sheet in your XML file, so that when you later view the file, the downlevel style sheet for this view would be used, displaying the preferred print view used in your form.

 Be careful when specifying different views, because the view that you select may not have the same fields, which will cause an error when you try to view the form using an incompatible style sheet.

Additional Command-Line Options

As you have been using the downlevel tool, you may have noticed that it generates a lot of status messages while it is running. If you have a large number of templates to convert or if you are running this utility as part of a script or batch process, you may want to hide this commentary. The /v switch can be used to control how verbose the utility is when running. You can specify a value from 0 to 4, which ranges from no comments at all (0) to becoming a chatterbox. So, if you want to create a downlevel style sheet with no comments at all, your command line would look something like this:

```
XDown /d invoice.xsn c:\myforms\ /v:0
```

You may have also noticed that when the downlevel utility runs, it expands your XSN file and copies all the internal files to the destination directory you specified. This is the equivalent of using the Extract Form Files option within InfoPath, for one exception—the scripting files are not copied with the other form files. You can use the /a switch to copy all the form files, including any scripting files, to your destination directory. To copy all the form files using the first example with the Invoice form, the command line would look something like this:

```
XDown /d invoice.xsn c:\myforms\ /v:0
```

Summary

Regardless of your organization's environment, there is always an available method that you can use to publish InfoPath forms and data. This chapter first looked at simple publishing methods, such as publishing to a web server or file share, and then moved on to distributing forms by e-mail and publishing forms using HTML through exporting or style sheets. These topics bring you to the end of the book and your look at InfoPath. I hope you have enjoyed reading through this book and that you will enjoy designing forms and working with InfoPath as much as I do.

Part V

Appendixes

Appendix A
Sample Forms

InfoPath includes a number of sample forms that you can use straight out of the box or use as a starting point for your own development. This appendix incorporates a listing of all of the different sample forms that are available, as well as a brief description and listing of features that demonstrate different InfoPath features. And since you are probably going to use one (or more) of these forms as a starting point for your own development, the second half of the appendix will show you how to incorporate these forms into your own applications and systems, including how to view the underlying XML schema that has a sample schema for you to look through.

When customizing these sample forms, there are some limitations that you should be aware of—first, you will not be able to automatically create the data source "on-the-fly" when adding new controls to your form. You will need to bind these controls to an existing field or group within the data source you are working with. Second, you will not be able to modify the existing fields or groups within the data source and you may not be able to add fields or groups depending on the form and the data source in use.

In this scenario, you will need to identify if the form itself can be modified to meet your needs and if the underlying data schema needs extending. If you need additional fields and are unable to add them when customizing the form, you may need to consider using the form's underlying XML schema as the source for your own schema development or consider re-creating the data source and form using the sample form as a guide.

Sample Forms

InfoPath includes a number of sample forms of every shape, size, and description. The following section gives a brief summary of each of the sample forms, as well as key information you will need when considering customizing any of these forms.

> **TIP** *To customize a sample form for your own use, choose File / Design a Form and select the option in the Task Pane to "Customize a Sample." A list of available Sample Forms will appear; select a form and click OK to create a blank form based on that sample. You can then modify the form as you normally would.*

Absence Request

The Absence Request form is a single-view form that can be used to request an absence from work. The form provides fields for the date and time of the request, along with contact details for both the employee and manager. There is a repeating table to collect the details of the requested absence, including a start and end date, and the type of absence request (paid vacation, sick leave, and so on).

There are also two optional sections on the form for calculating absence available and this section could be used to track entitlements (vacation days left, and so forth) as the form was used over a period of time. There are also optional sections for business and personal contacts while away, as well as a notes section. All of the optional sections on this form are shown by default but can be deleted if not required.

Behind the scenes, scripting is used to automatically fill in the time and date that the form was completed and the functions to update the balances in the optional sections provide a good example of updating multiple values on a form.

Applicant Rating

The Applicant Rating form is a single-view form that has been designed to collect information about a potential new hire. The form can be used to collect information about the applicant and position they are applying for, as well as contact details for the interviewer and the date/time of the interview.

There is a large section of the form that has radio buttons for rating an applicant on different criteria with a Job Experience and Interview Preparation section shown by default and optional sections for Clerical, Management, and Technical Skills. At the bottom of the form there is also a section for comments and a recommendation for hiring.

The scripting in use within the form demonstrates how to calculate both simple and weighted averages and is an excellent example of calculating summaries across a range of different fields.

Asset Tracking

The Asset Tracking form can be used to collect information about assets within a company or department and is a great example of creating summary and detail views. There are three views within the form for a Summary List, Detailed List, and Individual Asset Details.

You can use the form to track assets by their make, model, serial number, and so forth, and you can enter detailed owner information, including names, addresses, and contact details.

The data source for this form is necessarily complex, so if you are using this form with an existing application or data source of your own, you may need to massage the form data to fit your own data structures.

Change Order

The Change Order form is a single-view form that can be used to request changes to a manufactured product but can easily be modified (by deleting the Parts section) to fit change requests for software development or generic requests.

The form includes an optional section where you can break down the cost of the change to be made and collect a comprehensive set of details about the change, who requested it, the vendor who will fulfill the request and the nature and cost of the change. The underlying data source is straightforward and it should be easy to integrate this form (or a variant thereof) into your existing project management processes.

Expense Report (Domestic and International)

One of the most popular InfoPath forms, the Expense Report form includes both a domestic and International version in two separate forms. The International version of the form allows for multiple currencies and can be a real time-saver when working with more than just US dollars.

The form includes fields you can use to enter employee and manager details, as well as itemized expenses, including a number of pre-set categories in a drop-down list. You can easily edit these categories for your own use by selecting the drop-down list's properties and manually editing the categories.

Invoice (Multiple Tax Rates and Single Tax Rate)

Another popular form is the Invoice form, which is a single-view form that comes in both a Single and Multiple Tax Rate version. The Invoice forms include sections for entering "To" and "From" details, although you may want to customize this form to always display your own details. This could easily be accomplished by deleting the "From" fields and entering your own company information using plain text.

This form also includes a section for an itemized list of items that are being billed for and includes the ability to specify a discount and tax rate for each item. You can also use fields at the bottom of the form to enter your terms; but again, if you are using this form often, you may want to delete this section and type your own fixed terms at the bottom.

The underlying data source is simple and easy to understand and should mean that you can integrate this form into most any system.

Issue Tracking (Simple and Detailed)

The Issue Tracking forms include a Simple and Detailed version, both featuring a single view. Both of these forms can be used to track a wide range of issues as well as track the priority and status of issues, including action items related to this issue.

At the bottom of the form there is a button marked "Send as E-mail" that you can use to create a simple work-flow application, sending the form data to another user for review. The scripting behind this button is an excellent example of programmatically sending a form via e-mail. You can peek behind the scenes and copy this script to use this technique in your own forms.

The data sources behind these forms is complex and could require some massaging before you could use it in existing project management systems or other applications. Still, for a simple issue tracking and workflow application, these forms are very handy.

Meeting Agenda

If only every meeting had an agenda! The Meeting Agenda form actually serves double duty, as the form features two different views. One view is for the Meeting Agenda, to be sent around before the meeting and the second view is for the Meeting Minutes to be distributed after the meeting is finished.

This form includes areas for entering agenda items, guest speakers, action items, materials provided, what to bring to the meeting, attendee details and more. Considering that the same form data is used to build the Meeting Minutes view, taking minutes for even the longest meeting is a snap.

It is recommended that if you do choose to use this form as part of a SharePoint form library that you limit the fields that the user can see within SharePoint, as there are a large number of fields within the form's data source. Another way to use the form data would be to export the form to HTML to distribute to users, which could be effective if you are sending minutes to users who do not have InfoPath installed or for users outside of your organization.

Performance Review

The Performance Review form is a single-view form that can be used to evaluate an employee's current or past performance. Using an objective and skill-based platform, the form collects information about the employee's current objectives and allows both the employee and manager to rate and comment on the success of these objectives.

The form provides an excellent primer in the use of radio buttons, with a large "skills table" that makes extensive use of radio buttons to allow the employee and manager to rate a number of different competencies.

The one downside to customizing this form is that the competencies are hard-coded within the data source, so if you change the label on the form, you will NOT be changing the underlying data. For example, changing "Problem solving" to "Solves large problems" on the form will not change the underlying data source, which will still read as a group named "problemSolving."

Still, this form is an excellent example of what can be done with InfoPath and can be used as-is if you are willing to use the competencies listed in the form (as opposed to your own).

A

Project Plan

Planning is key to any project and the Project Planning form should go a long way to keeping your work on track. This two-view form includes views for entering information about project contacts, as well as the project plan itself.

The Plan View allows you to enter information about the different phases of the project, including work items that need to be completed and budget figures for the project, such as expenses and income. The form includes a drop-down list for selecting the currency for the expenses and income, but can only be selected globally (that is, it can't be done for each expense), which may be a problem with projects that span two or more international sites.

Still, when integrated with a SharePoint form library, you can select the columns that are related to tasks and filter the tasks for only those that are incomplete, providing a powerful project management feature. With a large number of work items, the form can be hard to read, but exporting the data to Excel also provides an easy way to analyze project data.

Purchase Order and Purchase Request

The Purchase Order is a single-view form that can be used to internally request the purchase of a number of items. The form includes areas to enter the submitter, vendor, and shipping information and the itemized list includes the ability to enter individual discounts on items and tax rates. (The Purchase Request form is similar, but includes a section for a "Suggested Supplier" instead of a specific vendor's details.)

The data source behind both forms is well structured and while it does not comply with EDI standards, you should be able to use the resulting form data with external vendors and other applications and systems.

Resume

The Resume form is a single-view form that includes sections for entering your personal information, objectives, work experience, education, affiliations, skills, experience, and so on, in a simple layout.

The form includes a number of different views that you can use to create a formatted version of your resume, including a "contemporary" and "text only" versions. This form demonstrates the use of print views and can be used to collect information from prospective applicants to build up a database of resumes.

Sales Report

The Sales Report form is a simple single-view form that is used to track sales on a monthly basis using an itemized list (similar to the Invoice forms we looked at earlier). Using this form you can specify a number of different categories and then indicate what items from that category were sold, how much was charged, and so on.

The report then displays a summary at the bottom of the form by category. While this form is not very complex, it does do a good job of demonstrating how to display summary values on the same form as detailed values. To see the scripting behind the scenes that does all the work, select Tools | Script | Microsoft Script Editor and look for the "Update" functions (in other words, UpdateItemTotal).

Service Request

The Service Quest form is a single-view form that you can use to request services to be rendered (including everything from computer-related requests to building maintenance requests). The form's design is simple and effective and demonstrates the use of multiple drop-down boxes working in tandem—when you select an item from the first drop-down list for a particular service, the second drop-down list is filtered to show only those problems that are related to the service. For example, if you select "Carpeting and Flooring," you only see problems related to that service.

This functionality is accomplished through the use of a secondary data source, which you can see by selecting Tools | Secondary Data Source. You can use this technique in your own forms or use File | Extract Form Files to extract and edit the secondary data source if you like the form as it is and just want to add a few entries of your own.

Status Report

The Status Report form is a single-view form that can be used to generate and distribute status reports on projects, including bulleted lists for tasks accomplished last period, this period, and any outstanding issues.

There is a section at the bottom of the form for entering employee time-card information, but this form is not as complex as the Time Card forms that are coming up next. Use this form where you want a combined Status Report and simple timesheet; otherwise, delete the timesheet section of the form and use a separate form created especially for this purpose.

There is also a budget section at the bottom of the form for detailing the amount budgeted and spent, but in practice this can be cumbersome as there is no way to automatically carry over values from one status report to another. Again, if you are looking for a simple way to track expenses and don't mind repetitive data entry each time you use the form, this may suit you.

Time Card (Simple and Detailed)

The Time Card forms are another popular set of forms that most developers will have a look at, even if they end up creating their own. The timesheets are set up on

A

a weekly basis and provide two sets of fields for time in/out for each day. The detailed version of the form also includes a section to track absences, but you may find it easier to use the simple version of the form. There is also a section at the bottom of the page for entering and calculating payroll information; the form itself is well designed.

If you are looking for a timecard solution to track multiple projects, this is not it. The sections for attendance reporting only track hours overall and can't be broken down by a particular project or division. Still, with that said, both of these forms could easily slot into existing payroll processes and applications and save some data-entry time.

Travel Itinerary

The Travel Itinerary form has been designed to capture travel information, including appointments, hotels, air, and group transportation arrangements and display it in a clear, concise format. This form has been well-designed and was created to be printed. For a harried traveler, this form should alleviate confusion although the data entry may be a bit cumbersome.

In terms of integrating this form with existing systems, the potential is low—this form has been designed to capture and present information, as opposed to enter data into a back-end database or system, so the data source is very complex.

Travel Request

The Travel Request form is a single-view form that is used to request travel from a travel or booking agent and includes fields to enter detailed information about the travel that is intended. The form itself is well-organized and captures the majority of information someone would need to book or arrange flights, hotels, and so on, for a traveler.

Again, this form was designed to capture and display information, so integrating the underlying data to a back-end application or system may not be that useful. With some work from a database administrator or developer you could import this information into separate tables for use with a corporate expense application or other system. But given that this is just a travel request, this form will usually be printed and the form data discarded.

Vendor Information

And finally, our last sample form is the Vendor Information form, which can be used to collect information about potential or current vendors. The form includes sections for capturing contact details, as well as products or services the vendor offers, and ratings. (Of special interest is the use of a custom task pane to build the list of vendor products and services.)

The underlying data source for this form is well-structured and could be used to build a database of vendor information that could easily be used in other applications or systems.

Viewing the Underlying XML Schema

An important part of customizing the sample forms is understanding the underlying XML schema and the fields it contains. Understanding what data fields are being collected from the form will help you map this form to your existing processes, applications, and database systems. The process of mapping these data structures to an existing data source is called "semantic mapping" and will help you identify where you need to modify existing processes or import routines to fit your own use.

To see the underlying XML schema that is in use behind a form, open the form in design mode and then select File | Extract Form Files. Another dialog will open and prompt you where to save your form files—you can select a location on your computer or you can use the New Folder button at the bottom of the dialog to create a new folder to hold your form files. When you have selected a location for your files, click OK to extract the form files to the location you specified.

Next, browse to the location where you extracted the form files—you should see all of the different files that make up an .XSN form, including .XML, .XSL .JS and other file types. Locate the schema file (.XSD) and open this file using Notepad or the text editor of your choice. This schema file contains information about the underlying data source for your form and can be used to match the fields in the form to fields in an existing application or database you may use.

If you are just getting started setting up applications and systems, you can use this schema as a template for a new table or database to hold the form data. An example of an XML schema for the sample Absence Request form is shown next for your reference:

```
<?xml version="1.0" encoding="UTF-8"?>
<xs:schema
targetNamespace="http://schemas.microsoft.com/office/infopath/2003/sample/AbsenceReques
t" xmlns:ar="http://schemas.microsoft.com/office/infopath/2003/sample/AbsenceRequest"
xmlns:xs="http://www.w3.org/2001/XMLSchema" elementFormDefault="qualified"
attributeFormDefault="unqualified">

<xs:element name="absenceRequest">
        <xs:complexType>
                <xs:sequence>
                        <xs:element name="date" type="xs:date" nillable="true"/>
                        <xs:element name="time" type="xs:time" nillable="true"/>
                        <xs:element name="purpose" type="xs:string"/>
                        <xs:element name="contact" type="ar:contactType"/>
                        <xs:element name="manager" type="ar:contactType"/>
                        <xs:element name="awayContact" minOccurs="0">
```

A

```
                                    <xs:complexType>
                                        <xs:sequence>
                                            <xs:element name="business"
type="ar:contactType"/>
                                            <xs:element name="personal"
type="ar:contactType"/>
                                            <xs:any namespace="##other"
processContents="lax" minOccurs="0" maxOccurs="unbounded"/>
                                        </xs:sequence>
                                    </xs:complexType>
                                </xs:element>
                                <xs:element name="leaves">
                                    <xs:complexType>
                                        <xs:sequence>
                                            <xs:element name="leave"
maxOccurs="unbounded">
                                                <xs:complexType>
                                                    <xs:sequence>
                                                        <xs:element name="startDate"
type="xs:date" nillable="true"/>
                                                        <xs:element
name="returnDate" type="xs:date" nillable="true"/>
                                                        <xs:element name="hours"
type="xs:double"/>
                                                        <xs:element name="leaveCode"
type="xs:string"/>
                                                        <xs:any namespace="##other"
processContents="lax" minOccurs="0" maxOccurs="unbounded"/>
                                                    </xs:sequence>
                                                </xs:complexType>
                                            </xs:element>
                                            <xs:element name="totalLeaveThisRequest"
type="xs:double"/>
                                            <xs:any namespace="##other"
processContents="lax" minOccurs="0" maxOccurs="unbounded"/>
                                        </xs:sequence>
                                    </xs:complexType>
                                </xs:element>
                                <xs:element name="balances" minOccurs="0">
                                    <xs:complexType>
                                        <xs:sequence>
                                            <xs:element name="paidVacation"
type="ar:balanceType"/>
                                            <xs:element name="sickLeave"
type="ar:balanceType"/>
                                            <xs:element name="floatingHoliday"
type="ar:balanceType"/>
                                            <xs:element name="unpaidLeave"
type="ar:balanceType"/>
                                            <xs:element name="bereavement"
type="ar:balanceType"/>
                                            <xs:element name="other"
type="ar:balanceType"/>
                                            <xs:element name="newLeaveBalance"
type="xs:double"/>
                                            <xs:any namespace="##other"
processContents="lax" minOccurs="0" maxOccurs="unbounded"/>
```

```
                                        </xs:sequence>
                                    </xs:complexType>
                            </xs:element>
                            <xs:element name="notes" type="ar:xhtml" minOccurs="0"/>
                            <xs:element name="items">
                                    <xs:complexType>
                                            <xs:sequence>
                                                    <xs:element name="item" maxOccurs="unbounded">
                                                            <xs:complexType>
                                                                    <xs:sequence>
                                                                            <xs:element name="date"
type="xs:date" nillable="true"/>
                                                                            <xs:element
name="description" type="xs:string"/>
                                                                            <xs:element name="amount"
type="xs:double"/>
                                                                            <xs:element name="category"
type="xs:string"/>
                                                                            <xs:any namespace="##other"
processContents="lax" minOccurs="0" maxOccurs="unbounded"/>
                                                                    </xs:sequence>
                                                            </xs:complexType>
                                                    </xs:element>
                                            </xs:sequence>
                                    </xs:complexType>
                            </xs:element>
                            <xs:element name="list">
                                    <xs:complexType>
                                            <xs:sequence>
                                                    <xs:element name="listItem" type="xs:string"
maxOccurs="unbounded"/>
                                                    <xs:any namespace="##other"
processContents="lax" minOccurs="0" maxOccurs="unbounded"/>
                                            </xs:sequence>
                                    </xs:complexType>
                            </xs:element>
                            <xs:element name="signatures" type="ar:digitalSignaturesType"/>
                            <xs:any namespace="##other" processContents="lax" minOccurs="0"
maxOccurs="unbounded"/>
                    </xs:sequence>
                    <xs:anyAttribute namespace="http://www.w3.org/XML/1998/namespace"
processContents="lax"/>
            </xs:complexType>
    </xs:element>
    <xs:complexType name="balanceType">
            <xs:sequence>
                    <xs:element name="previousBalance" type="xs:double"/>
                    <xs:element name="totalThisRequest" type="xs:double"/>
                    <xs:element name="newBalance" type="xs:double"/>
                    <xs:any namespace="##other" processContents="lax" minOccurs="0"
maxOccurs="unbounded"/>
            </xs:sequence>
    </xs:complexType>
    <xs:complexType name="addressType">
            <xs:sequence>
                    <xs:element name="line1" type="xs:string"/>
                    <xs:element name="line2" type="xs:string"/>
```

A

```
                <xs:element name="line3" type="xs:string"/>
                <xs:element name="line4" type="xs:string"/>
                <xs:element name="city" type="xs:string"/>
                <xs:element name="stateProvince" type="xs:string"/>
                <xs:element name="postalCode" type="xs:string"/>
                <xs:element name="country" type="xs:string"/>
                <xs:any namespace="##other" processContents="lax" minOccurs="0"
maxOccurs="unbounded"/>
            </xs:sequence>
        </xs:complexType>
        <xs:complexType name="companyType">
            <xs:sequence>
                <xs:element name="name" type="xs:string" minOccurs="0"/>
                <xs:element name="address" type="ar:addressType" minOccurs="0"/>
                <xs:element name="identificationNumber" type="xs:string"
minOccurs="0"/>
                <xs:element name="telephoneNumber" type="xs:string" minOccurs="0"/>
                <xs:element name="faxNumber" type="xs:string" minOccurs="0"/>
                <xs:element name="emailAddressPrimary" type="xs:string"
minOccurs="0"/>
                <xs:element name="webSite" type="xs:anyURI" minOccurs="0"/>
                <xs:element name="ftpSite" type="xs:anyURI" minOccurs="0"/>
                <xs:element name="telex" type="xs:string" minOccurs="0"/>
                <xs:any namespace="##other" processContents="lax" minOccurs="0"
maxOccurs="unbounded"/>
            </xs:sequence>
        </xs:complexType>
        <xs:complexType name="companyWithContactType">
            <xs:complexContent>
                <xs:extension base="ar:companyType">
                    <xs:sequence>
                        <xs:element name="contact" type="ar:contactType"/>
                        <xs:any namespace="##other" processContents="lax"
minOccurs="0" maxOccurs="unbounded"/>
                    </xs:sequence>
                </xs:extension>
            </xs:complexContent>
        </xs:complexType>
        <xs:complexType name="contactType">
            <xs:sequence>
                <xs:element name="name" type="ar:nameType" minOccurs="0"/>
                <xs:element name="address" type="ar:addressType" minOccurs="0"/>
                <xs:element name="identificationNumber" type="xs:string"
minOccurs="0"/>
                <xs:element name="emailAddressPrimary" type="xs:string"
minOccurs="0"/>
                <xs:element name="emailAddressSecondary" type="xs:string"
minOccurs="0"/>
                <xs:element name="telephoneNumberWork" type="xs:string"
minOccurs="0"/>
                <xs:element name="telephoneNumberHome" type="xs:string"
minOccurs="0"/>
                <xs:element name="telephoneNumberCell" type="xs:string"
minOccurs="0"/>
                <xs:element name="telephoneNumberPager" type="xs:string"
minOccurs="0"/>
                <xs:element name="faxNumber" type="xs:string" minOccurs="0"/>
```

```xml
                <xs:element name="jobTitle" type="xs:string" minOccurs="0"/>
                <xs:element name="officeLocation" type="xs:string" minOccurs="0"/>
                <xs:element name="department" type="xs:string" minOccurs="0"/>
                <xs:element name="webSite" type="xs:anyURI" minOccurs="0"/>
                <xs:element name="ftpSite" type="xs:anyURI" minOccurs="0"/>
                <xs:any namespace="##other" processContents="lax" minOccurs="0"
maxOccurs="unbounded"/>
            </xs:sequence>
        </xs:complexType>
        <xs:complexType name="contactWithCompanyType">
            <xs:complexContent>
                <xs:extension base="ar:contactType">
                    <xs:sequence>
                        <xs:element name="company" type="ar:companyType"/>
                        <xs:any namespace="##other" processContents="lax"
minOccurs="0" maxOccurs="unbounded"/>
                    </xs:sequence>
                </xs:extension>
            </xs:complexContent>
        </xs:complexType>
        <xs:complexType name="digitalSignaturesType">
            <xs:sequence>
                <xs:any namespace="http://www.w3.org/2000/09/xmldsig#"
processContents="lax" minOccurs="0" maxOccurs="unbounded"/>
            </xs:sequence>
        </xs:complexType>
        <xs:complexType name="nameType">
            <xs:sequence>
                <xs:element name="prefix" type="xs:string" minOccurs="0"/>
                <xs:element name="givenName" type="xs:string" minOccurs="0"/>
                <xs:element name="middleName" type="xs:string" minOccurs="0"/>
                <xs:element name="surname" type="xs:string" minOccurs="0"/>
                <xs:element name="suffix" type="xs:string" minOccurs="0"/>
                <xs:element name="singleName" type="xs:string"/>
                <xs:any namespace="##other" processContents="lax" minOccurs="0"
maxOccurs="unbounded"/>
            </xs:sequence>
        </xs:complexType>
        <xs:complexType name="currencyType">
            <xs:sequence>
                <xs:element name="name" type="xs:string"/>
                <xs:element name="symbol" type="xs:string"/>
                <xs:any namespace="##other" processContents="lax" minOccurs="0"
maxOccurs="unbounded"/>
            </xs:sequence>
        </xs:complexType>
        <xs:complexType name="xhtml" mixed="true">
            <xs:sequence>
                <xs:any namespace="http://www.w3.org/1999/xhtml"
processContents="lax" minOccurs="0" maxOccurs="unbounded"/>
            </xs:sequence>
        </xs:complexType>
</xs:schema>
```

A

Appendix B JScript Reference

Scripting is a vital tool that developers can use to extend InfoPath functionality. The following material documenting JScript (one of the scripting languages that InfoPath supports) has been included in this appendix to make this book a "one-stop" reference for InfoPath.

For more information on using scripting in your own forms, turn back to Chapter 10 for everything you ever wanted to know about scripting with InfoPath.

This appendix is not designed to be an exhaustive reference on JScript but it does cover the most commonly used parts of the JScript scripting language.

A Few Words about Syntax

JScript is case sensitive, so you need to be careful when working with variable or function names. In addition, each line of JScript needs to finish with a semicolon:

```
XDocument.UI.Alert("Hello World");
```

If you do have errors in your script or if the script simply does not run, double-check both the case and semicolons to see if they are used correctly.

Declarations

Declaring variables within JScript is pretty easy using a simple VAR statement with the name of the variable you want to declare. For example, to declare a variable called invoice_total, your declaration statement would look like this:

```
var invoice_total;
```

The name and case of your variable is important and is one of the main errors you will encounter when working with JScript. You can name variables using a mix of alphanumeric characters, underscores, and dollar signs, but the variable name has to begin with a letter, underscore, or dollar sign. In addition, you can't name a variable the same name as a reserved word (a list of reserved words in JScript is provided near the end of this appendix).

When working with variables, six different types can be associated with a variable:

- number
- string
- object
- Boolean
- null
- undefined

When a variable is first created and unassigned (in other words, there is no value assigned to it) it is considered to be undefined:

```
var sales_tax;
```

When an assignment is made to the variable, it then takes the type of the value assigned. For example:

```
var sales_tax = 10;    //Number
var sales_tax = "Not applicable";  //String
```

Comments

You can add comments to your JScript code either by using double slashes (//) for single lines or by using an opening and closing slash and asterisk (/* and */) to comment out multiple lines of text, as shown in the following examples:

```
// This is a single line comment and each line requires a double slash preceding.
/* Where this is a multi-line comment and all lines are commented out
between the opening and closing slash and asterisk */
```

Operators

JScript includes a number of different operators that you can use to perform calculations, make comparisons, make assignments, and more. This section presents the most commonly used JScript operators, organized by type: Table B-1 lists the mathematical operators; Table B-2 lists the comparison operators; and Table B-3 lists the assignment operators.

B

Operator	Description	Example Usage
*	Multiplication	`OrderTotal * 1.1;`
/	Division	`TotalItems / 2;`
%	Modulus arithmetic	`Quantity % 2;`
+	Addition	`OrderTotal + TaxTotal;`
−	Subtraction	`OrderTotal - Discount;`
++	Increment	`++k  // to increment a counter`
--	Decrement	`--k // to decrement a counter`

TABLE B-1　Mathematical Operators

Operator	Description
<	Less than
>	Greater than
<=	Less than or equal to
>=	Greater than or equal to
==	Equality
!=	Inequality

TABLE B-2　Comparison Operators

Operator	Description	Example Usage
=	Assignment	`SalesTaxRate = .06;`

TABLE B-3　Assignment Operators

Operator	Description	Example Usage
parseInt	For parsing other variable types to integer	`parseInt(Quantity);`
parseFloat	For parsing other variable types to a floating decimal point number	`parseFloat(OrderTotal);`

TABLE B-4   Conversion Functions

Methods and Functions

One of the strengths of JScript is that a lot of the difficult work has been done for you, with methods and functions covering a wide range of functionality. From performing calculations to manipulating dates and strings, JScript has a method or function to suit you.

Conversion Functions

Since JScript variables can be of many different types, there are a couple of conversion functions you will be using often if you want to ensure that a particular field value is either an integer or floating decimal point number. These conversion functions are listed in Table B-4.

String Functions

String functions within JScript treat strings like an array and can be used to find substrings within a string, change the case of a string, concatenate two strings, and more. Table B-5 lists and describes the string functions.

Function	Description	Usage

charAt	Used to return a character at a certain position within a string.	`String.charAt(position);`
		`MyString.charAt(2);`
		`"David".charAt(3);`
		Returns "v"

TABLE B-5   String Functions

B

Function	Description	Usage

indexOf	Used to return the position at which a substring exists within a string, searching from left to right. Can also specify a second argument as a starting point.	`String.indexOf(substring);`
		`MyString.indexOf("Sales");`
		`MyString.indexOf("al",2);`
		`"David".indexOf("vi");`
		Returns 3

lastIndexOf	Used to return the position at which a substring exists within a string, searching from right to left. Can also specify a second argument as a starting point.	`String.indexOf(substring);`
		
		`MyString.indexOf("Market");`
		`MyString.indexOf("ke",2);`
		`"Mack".indexOf("ack");`
		Returns 2

split	Can be used to split a string into substrings using a delimiter (spaces, and so on) and put the resulting substrings into an array.	`String.split(" ");`
		`MyString.split(",");`
		`"My old dog".split(" ");`

toLowerCase	Used to convert a string to lowercase.	`String.toLowerCase();`
		`MyString.toLowerCase();`
		`"David".toLowerCase();`

toUpperCase	User to convert a string to uppercase.	`String.toUpperCase();`
		`MyString.toUpperCase();`
		`"Mack".toUpperCase();`

length	Used to determine the length of a string.	`String.length;`
		`MyString.Length;`
		`"David Mack".Length;`

TABLE B-5   String Functions *(continued)*

Date and Time Functions

The date and time functions within JScript are easy to use and provide methods to pull apart a date and work with the components. All the examples in Table B-6, which lists the date and time functions, assume that the variable InvoiceDate is a date-time field with a value of 12/11/2003 8:10:57 AM.

Function	Description	Example Usage
getDate	Returns the day-of-month value (1 to 31) from a date field	`InvoiceDate.getDate()` Returns 11
getDay	Returns the day of the week, where: 0 = Sunday 1 = Monday 2 = Tuesday 3 = Wednesday 4 = Thursday 5 = Friday 6 = Saturday	`InvoiceDate.getDay()` Returns 4
getFullYear	Returns the full year from a date field	`InvoiceDate.getFullYear()` Returns 2003
getHours	Returns the hours value from a date field	`InvoiceDate.getHours()` Returns 8
getMinutes	Returns the minutes value from a date field	`InvoiceDate.getMinutes()` Returns 10
getMonth	Returns the month value from a date field, where: 0 = January 1= February 2 = March 3 = April 4 = May 5 = June 6 = July 7 = August 8 = September 9 = October 10 = November 11 = December	`InvoiceDate.getMonth()` Returns 11
getSeconds	Returns the seconds value from a date field	`InvoiceDate.getSeconds()` Returns 57
getTime	Returns an integer value representing the number of milliseconds between midnight, January 1, 1970 and the time value in the Date object	`InvoiceDate.getTime()` Returns 1071090659513
getYear	Returns the year value from a date field	`InvoiceDate.getYear()` Returns 2003

B

TABLE B-6   Date and Time Functions

Array Functions

Arrays can easily be created in JScript by a simple declaration. And then any array elements can be referenced using square brackets []. Arrays in JScript are zero-based, so the first element will always be 0, as shown in the following example:

```
var myArray = new Array();
for (i = 0; i < 10; i++)
    {
    myArray[i] = i;
    }
```

Control Structures

Control structures are used within JScript to control the flow and execution of your scripts. A number of different structures are available, including if…then…else, do…while, and try…catch statements.

If…Then…Else

If…then…else statements are constructed by placing the statement to be evaluated in parentheses, followed by the script that is to be executed if the statement is true, as shown in the following example:

```
if (InvoiceAmount > 10000)
    XDocument.UI.Alert("Please use a different form");
else
    XDocument.UI.Alert("This is the correct form");
```

If you have multiple lines that are to be executed on the true condition, then you can use curly braces to surround these lines, as shown here:

```
if (InvoiceAmount > 10000)
 {
XDocument.UI.Alert("Please use a different form");
    XDocument.UI.Alert("This is the wrong form");
 }
else
    XDocument.UI.Alert("This is the correct form");
```

Do...While

Another control structure used in JScript is the do...while loop, which will execute a section of script as long as the while condition is met. In the following example, a counter variable (i) is incremented by one and displayed each time through the loop until it reaches 5:

```
var i = 0;
while (i < 5)
{
  i++;
  XDocument.UI.Alert(i);
}
```

Try...Catch

Try...catch statements are designed to catch errors, with a section of code to "try" or run and then a section of code to be run when an exception occurs. In the following example, the try statement is trying to perform a calculation—if an error occurs in the calculation, an alert will be displayed with the text shown:

```
try { cost = totalprice/quantity }
catch(e)
{ XDocument.UI.Alert("There was an error!");}
```

> **NOTE** *For more information on other types of control structures within JScript, check out the JScript reference found in the Microsoft Script Editor by selecting Help | Microsoft Script Editor Help.*

Error Codes

While InfoPath provides descriptive error messages when something goes wrong with your JScript, it is still handy to understand the error that has been thrown. Table B-7 details the syntax errors that you may run across when working with JScript, and Table B-8 presents the runtime errors.

B

Error Number	Description
1001	Out of memory
1002	Syntax error
1003	Expected ':'
1004	Expected ';'
1005	Expected '('
1006	Expected ')'
1007	Expected ']'
1008	Expected '{'
1009	Expected '}'
1010	Expected identifier
1011	Expected '='
1012	Expected '/'
1013	Invalid number
1014	Invalid character
1015	String constant not terminated
1016	Comment not terminated
1018	'return' statement outside of function
1019	Can't have 'break' outside of loop
1020	Can't have 'continue' outside of loop
1023	Expected hex value
1024	Expected 'while'
1025	Label redefined
1026	Label not found
1027	'default' can only appear in a 'switch' statement
1028	Expected identifier or string
1029	Expected '@end'
1030	Conditional compilation turned off
1031	Expected constant
1032	Expected '@'
1033	Expected 'catch'
1034	Expected 'var'
1035	'throw' must be followed by an expression on the same source line

TABLE B-7   Syntax Error Codes

Error Number	Description
5	Invalid procedure call or argument
6	Overflow
7	Out of memory
9	Subscript out of range
10	This array is fixed or temporarily locked
11	Division by zero
13	Type mismatch
14	Out of string space
17	Can't perform requested operation
28	Out of stack space
35	Sub or Function not defined
48	Error in loading DLL
51	Internal error
52	Bad filename or number
53	File not found
54	Bad file mode
55	File already open
57	Device I/O error
58	File already exists
61	Disk full
62	Input past end of file
67	Too many files
68	Device unavailable
70	Permission denied
71	Disk not ready
74	Can't rename with different drive
75	Path/file access error
76	Path not found
91	Object variable or With block variable not set
92	For loop not initialized
94	Invalid use of Null
322	Can't create necessary temporary file
424	Object required

TABLE B-8   Runtime Errors

B

Error Number	Description
429	Automation server can't create object
430	Class doesn't support Automation
432	Filename or class name not found during Automation operation
438	Object doesn't support this property or method
440	Automation error
445	Object doesn't support this action
446	Object doesn't support named arguments
447	Object doesn't support current locale setting
448	Named argument not found
449	Argument not optional
450	Wrong number of arguments or invalid property assignment
451	Object not a collection
453	Specified DLL function not found
458	Variable uses an Automation type not supported in JScript
462	The remote server machine does not exist or is unavailable
501	Cannot assign to variable
502	Object not safe for scripting
503	Object not safe for initializing
504	Object not safe for creating
507	An exception occurred
5000	Cannot assign to 'this'
5001	Number expected
5002	Function expected
5003	Cannot assign to a function result
5004	Cannot index object
5005	String expected
5006	Date object expected
5007	Object expected
5008	Illegal assignment
5009	Undefined identifier
5010	Boolean expected
5011	Can't execute code from a freed script
5012	Object member expected

TABLE B-8   Runtime Errors *(continued)*

Error Number	Description
5013	VBArray expected
5014	JScript object expected
5015	Enumerator object expected
5016	Regular expression object expected
5017	Syntax error in regular expression
5018	Unexpected quantifier
5019	Expected ']' in regular expression
5020	Expected ')' in regular expression
5021	Invalid range in character set
5022	Exception thrown and not caught
5023	Function does not have a valid prototype object

TABLE B-8   Runtime Errors *(continued)*

Special Characters

There are a number of special characters within JScript that you may need
to use within strings in your code. The "escape characters" in Table B-9 can
be used in place of these special characters, eliminating any errors that may
have occurred.

Character	Represents
\b	Backspace
\f	Form feed
\n	Line feed (newline)
\r	Carriage return
\t	Horizontal tab (CTRL-I)
\'	Single quotation mark
\"	Double quotation mark
\\	Backslash

TABLE B-9   Special Characters

B

Reserved Words

Reserved words within JScript cannot be used for variable or function names. They are

- break
- case
- catch
- class
- const
- continue
- debugger
- default
- delete
- do
- else
- enum
- export
- extends
- false
- finally
- for
- function
- if
- import
- in
- new
- null
- return
- super 9
- switch
- this
- throw
- try
- typeof
- var
- void
- while
- with

Constants and Literals

Finally, there are some constants and literals that are used within JScript, which are listed in Table B-10.

Constant/Literal	Description
NaN	Not a Number
null	A null value
true, false	Boolean values
infinity	Infinite value
undefined	An undefined variable

TABLE B-10 Constants and Literals

Appendix C Troubleshooting

When you are having problems with your InfoPath development, where do you turn? That is what this appendix is all about—how to troubleshoot your InfoPath forms and find the resources you need in a hurry.

Resources

With the introduction of any new product or technology, users are always scrambling for resources, whether it is documentation, web sites, or just somewhere they can post a question to get some answers. InfoPath is a relatively new product, so the resources available aren't as comprehensive as those you might find for products that have been on the market for a number of years. To help you locate the resources that are available, this appendix provides a list of InfoPath resources, including everything from Microsoft's own documentation to web sites and news groups.

Production Documentation

InfoPath doesn't include a printed user manual but a number of online documents are available for use. The following sections summarize these documents and identify where you can find them.

InfoPath Help File

The InfoPath help file can be viewed by selecting Help | Microsoft InfoPath Help within the InfoPath designer or by pressing F1. This opens the InfoPath Help task pane, shown in Figure C-1, and allows you to search for a topic or navigate through the table of contents.

Using the help file in this method requires a connection to the Internet and can be quite slow. It may be easier to access the help file content directly. The help file is located by default in C:\Program Files\Microsoft Office\Office11\1033\ and the name of the main help file is infmain.chm. Locate and double-click this file to open the compressed help file for InfoPath, which provides a better user interface that you can use to search the help file or print individual or multiple topics.

InfoPath Developer Help File

If you are developing more complex InfoPath forms or require information about scripting, the document object model (DOM), or extending your forms using any of the developer technologies within InfoPath, you need to check out the InfoPath Developer help file. This help file is also available by selecting Help | Microsoft InfoPath Help within the InfoPath designer or by pressing F1. This opens the InfoPath

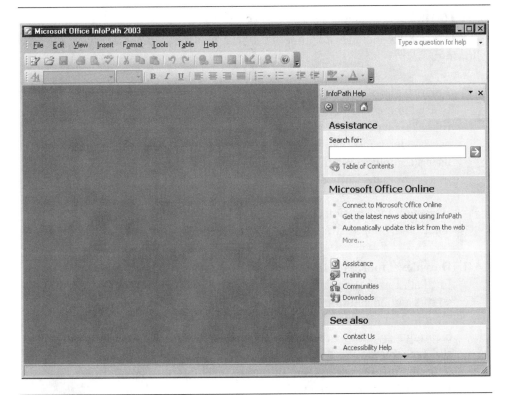

FIGURE C-1   InfoPath Help task pane

Help task pane, in which the InfoPath Developers Reference will be listed as the last node in the table of contents.

The Developer help file, named infref.chm, is located by default in C:\Program Files\Microsoft Office\Office11\1033\. Again, it may be easier to refer to this help file than to connect to the Internet to view the InfoPath help file contents.

InfoPath 2003 Software Development Kit

The InfoPath 2003 Software Development Kit (SDK) is available for download from http://download.microsoft.com (search terms: infopath sdk) and contains a number of sample forms, developer applications, tools, and utilities that you can use to extend InfoPath functionality and learn about key development technologies.

The following sections detail the tools that are available in the SDK, as well as the sample forms and applications that demonstrate InfoPath developer features.

C

SDK Tools

The InfoPath SDK includes a number of tools and utilities, including the following:

- **Form registration tool (regform.exe)**   This is a command-line utility that is used to create and distribute fully trusted forms. This utility can be used to make the necessary changes to your form to make it fully trusted and can create an installation script that you can use to install the form on a user's computer. When you run the script, it registers the form on the user's computer and adds it to the list of Custom Installed Forms.

NOTE   *For more information on creating and distributing fully trusted forms, check out Chapter 13.*

- **Downlevel tool**   This is a command-line utility that you can use to view InfoPath forms. You don't need to have InfoPath installed to use the utility, so it is a good solution for users who may need to view forms but don't have InfoPath installed locally. The utility creates a "downlevel" view by creating a style sheet that is used to display the form in a web browser. This style sheet is similar to the style sheets presented in Chapter 2 that are used to define InfoPath views, but this style sheet has been created specifically for viewing the form in a web browser.

NOTE   *For more information on using the downlevel tool, check out Chapter 14.*

- **HTML to XHTML conversion tool**   If you have existing HTML forms that you want to use as the basis on an InfoPath form, you can use this tool to convert regular HTML into XHTML that can be edited in an InfoPath form.

- **Processing instruction update tool**   This tool is used to update information that appears in the processing instructions of a form's XML document.

TIP   *For more information on how to use any of these tools, check out the documentation that ships with the InfoPath SDK, available after SDK installation from the Start menu, under Programs | Microsoft Office 2003 Developer Resources | Microsoft Office InfoPath 2003 SDK | InfoPath SDK Documentation.*

Sample Forms and Applications

The InfoPath SDK also includes a number of sample forms and applications that demonstrate InfoPath developer features or integration with other databases or applications. Some of these forms and components will work straight out of the box, but others require installation of both server and application components. For a list of the setup requirements for each of these applications shown in Table C-1, check out the InfoPath documentation at Programs | Microsoft Office 2003 Developer Resources | Microsoft Office InfoPath 2003 SDK | InfoPath SDK Getting Started.

Form Name	Description
ADO_CON	This sample form is used to demonstrate how to use ADO to connect to an Access database and includes a scaled-down version of the Northwind sample database to use.
Calc	This form demonstrates how to perform calculations using scripting and a number of simple arithmetic operators and functions. It includes examples of calculating minimums, maximums, averages, sums, and so on.
CLR	This form demonstrates integrating InfoPath with a Visual Studio .NET application. In this example, a C# program was written to create a Component Object Model (COM) object that can be called from an InfoPath form. The source code for the application is included, along with the necessary setup files to install the finished application.
DataInterop	This form demonstrates how to use active data objects (ADO) to connect to a SQL Server database and retrieve, view, and modify data. The form demonstrates advanced form design techniques, including retrieving data, master/detail views, and more.
DataSubmit	This form and related components demonstrate how to create a custom submission of InfoPath data.
Information Lookup	This form demonstrates how to perform a lookup from a secondary data source to populate lists of information within an InfoPath form.
MSForms	This form demonstrates how multiple forms can be merged into a single form, providing a summary file for further analysis.
PO_BizTalk	This form and related components demonstrate a simple workflow application with XML Web Services, BizTalk Server, SQL Server, and Outlook using a purchase order and approval process as an example.
PO_WebService	This form and related components demonstrate a simple workflow application with XML Web Services, SQL Server, and Outlook using a purchase order and approval process as an example.
WebSvc	This form demonstrates how to create a form based on an XML web service that can retrieve, modify, and submit information from the same.

TABLE C-1   Sample Forms

Web Resources

If you have been looking high and low on the Internet for InfoPath resources, your looking days are over! The following sections outline some of the best web resources from Microsoft and others, all designed to get you up to speed quickly on InfoPath and answer your technical questions.

Microsoft's Official InfoPath Web Site

www.microsoft.com/infopath

The official InfoPath web site features links to all the available resources from Microsoft, including product information, white papers, knowledge base articles, tutorials, how-to articles and links to newsgroups, and other related content. If you are looking for all things InfoPath from Microsoft, this is a great starting point.

InfoPath FAQ Web Site

www.infopathfaq.com

The InfoPath FAQ web site was one of the first independent web sites to emerge when InfoPath was first announced and remains one of the most popular. On this site, you will find links to InfoPath news articles, answers to common questions, FAQ documents, links to other InfoPath resources and downloads, a listing of InfoPath-related knowledge base articles, and links to other resources on the Web. The site includes a comprehensive search facility and is one of the best spots to find information on InfoPath.

InfoPath Group on Yahoo Groups

http://groups.yahoo.com/group/infopath/

If community is your thing, then you'll want to go to the InfoPath group on Yahoo Groups. This is the only independent newsgroup available for InfoPath developers, and you will find information posted here that is not shown anywhere else on the Web. There are candid discussions on InfoPath's strengths and weaknesses, tips and tricks from InfoPath developers, and "hacks" (and other unsupported methods), as well as tips on integrating InfoPath with non-Microsoft technologies.

Microsoft InfoPath Newsgroups

microsoft.public.infopath

The official InfoPath newsgroup from Microsoft is well supported and most queries are answered within a few days by MVPs or Microsoft staff. The newsgroup itself has been running since before the product was launched and often you will find information here that is not available anywhere else. You can read the newsgroup by using your favorite newsgroup reader or you can log on to the HTML version at http://communities.microsoft.com/newsgroups/default.asp?icp= Prod_officebeta&slcid=us.

Microsoft InfoPath Support Center

http://support.microsoft.com/default.aspx?scid=fh;EN-US;infopath2003

This is the official Microsoft Support site for InfoPath. Here you will find links to the most popular knowledge base articles and tutorials, as well as links to downloads and updates and other related content. This is a great place to stop by every once in a while just to see what's new or if there are any additional articles or updates you need to read.

MSDN InfoPath Developers Center

http://msdn.microsoft.com/Office/InfoPath

For a hard-core geek who is looking for all the developer-related information on InfoPath, MSDN is your one-stop shop for all things technical concerning InfoPath. On the InfoPath Developer's Center, you will find links to the InfoPath SDK and documentation, as well as tutorials and articles covering common development tasks and integration to other Microsoft technologies (not to mention sample forms and code!).

TIP   *You may also find InfoPath articles and topics from time to time on other XML-related web sites, such as www.xmlperfect.com or www.xml.com.*

Knowledge Base Articles

Microsoft has posted a number of knowledge base articles for InfoPath 2003, containing information on current bugs, fixes, and how-to information. A list of the InfoPath-related knowledge base articles at the time of this printing is provided in Table C-2. You can jump directly to any of these articles from http://support.microsoft.com/default.aspx?scid=fh;EN-US;KBJUMP or you can check for additional articles by visiting http://support.microsoft.com and searching with the keyword "InfoPath."

C

Article ID	Title
818233	Task Pane Key on a Microsoft Office Keyboard Does Not Always Operate As Expected
822020	Microsoft Office InfoPath Cannot Use a Web Service That Returns an ADO.NET DataSet
822024	Expression Box in InfoPath Gives Incorrect Results for Mathematical Expressions
822026	Data from a Large Table May Be Lost When the Data Is Pasted in an InfoPath Form
822030	InfoPath Caches the Solution Even When the XSL Does Not Load
822032	Create a Custom Validation Error Message That Contains the Name of the Control That Is Being Validated
823436	"Access Is Denied" Error Message When You Try to Open an InfoPath Form with the ExternalApplication Object
826989	InfoPath Cannot Automatically Submit Structured XML Data to a Web Service
826990	View Transformed InfoPath Form Data in Internet Explorer
826991	Install InfoPath to Access Features and Benefits
826992	Use Wildcard Characters in an InfoPath Form Query When Binding to an ADO Data Source
826993	Programmatically Submit an InfoPath Form to a SharePoint Team Services Document Library
826994	Dynamically Populate a Drop-Down List Box by Using a Web Service
826996	Bind a Rich Text Box Control to an Element That Is Returned from a Web Service
826997	Programmatically Change the Default View of a Microsoft Office InfoPath 2003 Form
826998	You Receive an Error Message If You Try to Programmatically Set the Text Value of an XML Node
826999	Handle Mixed Content Elements in XML Documents in InfoPath
827001	Distribute an InfoPath Form Template to Offline Users
827002	Debug a Script for a Microsoft Office InfoPath 2003 Form
827003	Change the URL of a Web Service in InfoPath
827004	Create a Required String Field for an InfoPath Data Source
827005	Use a Script to Transfer Data from a Secondary Data Source to InfoPath Fields

TABLE C-2 InfoPath Knowledge Base Articles

Article ID	Title
827006	Modify an External Schema for an InfoPath Form
827007	Display the Results of a Stored Procedure in an InfoPath Form
827008	Use a Script or a Secondary Data Source Field for Conditional Formatting
827009	Resize the Controls on a Microsoft Office InfoPath Form Based on the Width of the Form
827011	Add Page Numbers to a Microsoft Office InfoPath Form
827293	Activate a Product Trial Program License in Office 2003 Program
828853	Change the Script Language for Your InfoPath Form
831023	Convert a Microsoft Office 2003 Trial Edition to a Full Retail Edition

TABLE C-2   InfoPath Knowledge Base Articles *(continued)*

Troubleshooting FAQs

With any program, many things can go wrong (and sometimes all of them at the same time!). While it is impossible to foresee every problem that you may encounter, the following sections detail some of the most common problems or errors you may experience when designing and working with InfoPath forms.

I get an error message "InfoPath cannot create a new blank form"

One of the most common error messages when working with an InfoPath form is the following:

```
InfoPath cannot create a new blank form. You cannot fill out forms
based on this form template because the file has been moved or
copied from its published location.
```

C

One of the causes for this error message is that the form has been "disconnected" from the original form template. For example, if you are using a URL-based form that is not fully trusted, the original form location may have changed or may not be available, or if you have e-mailed a form to a user who does not have access to the original URL referenced in the form.

The best way to distribute fully trusted forms to users is to install the form locally on their machine using the regform.exe utility (or other methods demonstrated in Chapter 14). That way, you can be sure that the form templates are always available, even if it means a bit more administration to keep all the form versions up-to-date on different users' machines.

When designing a form, a control shows a binding error—how do I fix it?

Binding errors occur when a control is bound to an incorrect field or group of fields or when multiple controls have been bound to the same field. You can recognize binding errors by the icon that appears to the right of the control when you click it or hover your mouse over it:

- A green icon with an equal sign (=) to the right of a control indicates that the binding for that particular control is correct.

- A blue icon with an "i" indicates that the binding may be incorrect—right-click the control to view more information about the possible binding issue.

- A red icon with an exclamation point (!) indicates the binding is definitely bad, and the form may not function correctly until you correct the binding problem.

Most times, the problem will be self-evident—when you move your mouse over the control, the ToolTip text will appear (for example, "Control stores duplicate data") to give you information on the particular issue that needs to be corrected.

I get an error when I publish my form to a shared location or web server

Before you begin the publishing process, make sure that you have the appropriate rights to publish documents to the shared location or web server where you want to publish your InfoPath form. Check with your network or system administrator to ensure that you have the rights to read and write to the location that you want to publish to and then try the publish process again.

> **TIP** *To test that you have the rights required, set up the network location or web server using My Network Places on your computer and try saving a text file or other type of file to that location first before publishing your form. If this works, then you should be able to publish your form with no problems.*

My JScript doesn't work

There are two main areas where scripts go wrong—syntax and logic. On the syntax side, check the names of all of your variables, functions, declarations, and so on, to ensure that the names are consistent throughout your script and that the case is the same (because MyBalance is not the same as mybalance in JScript). Also check that you have properly terminated each line with a semicolon.

On the logic side of things, print out a copy of your script and walk through the logic to ensure that you are following a logical flow and that the script is producing the desired results. Next, use the tools within the Microsoft Windows Script Editor to walk through your code and observe the results of any calculations, variables in use, and so forth, to try to determine where potential errors exist.

Finally, as a last resort, start commenting out lines of code and get back to basics. Create the structure of your logic piece by piece and use tricks like alerts to ensure that the logical sequence is being followed. This can often help you determine problems where other methods fail (especially with complex nested loops or control structures).

I can't get the debugger to work when working with scripting

Whenever you installed InfoPath, you may not have installed the required files for debugging. Check out knowledge base article #826991 for more information on the correct installation procedure for installing all the InfoPath components (including debugging).

Where can I change the name of a form I am designing?

When you first save your form, you are presented with a standard Windows Save dialog box that has a Change Name button that allows you to enter the name of the form you have created. You could consider this the "title" of your form, as opposed to the XSN filename. To change the name of an existing form, select File | Save As and click the Change Name button again to specify a new name for the form.

With the outlines of the controls on my form, I can't see the fields clearly. Is there a way to change the default display?

By default, when you are creating a form, the borders of the control appear as a gray outline, which can be difficult to see. You can change the border around the

C

control by using the Borders and Shading settings, but you need to do this while you are designing the form, because there is no way to change the default settings.

 *Another easy option to make the fields more visible is to select View | Sample Data to show sample data in the controls on your form.*

Why can't I change the color of a horizontal line?

Horizontal lines in InfoPath are similar to the horizontal lines you would find when designing web pages. As such, they don't have a color property associated with them. You may have noticed that the sample forms include a number of different lines, of all sizes and shades. These lines are not actually horizontal lines at all, but rather the borders of tables that have had their color changed using the settings found in Borders and Shading.

As a workaround to add a horizontal line of any color, insert a layout table onto your form with one row and one column and then use the Borders and Shading settings to change the bottom of the row to display a border in the color of your choice.

The results of my expression box are wrong—how do I fix it?

There is a bug in InfoPath where the results of an expression box may be incorrect if decimal numbers are used in the calculation. This bug has been documented in knowledge base article #822024, available at http://support.microsoft.com, and there is no known work-around at this time, other than using scripting to perform the calculation and placing the results back in a control.

 For more information on working with scripting, check out Chapter 10.

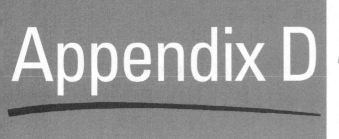

Appendix D

InfoPath Form Template XML Schema

In November 2003, Microsoft introduced an open and royalty-free license and documentation for the Microsoft Office 2003 XML Reference Schemas, including the InfoPath form template schema, listed here for your reference.

InfoPath Form Template XML Schema

```
<?xml version="1.0" encoding="UTF-8" ?>
<xsd:schema xmlns:xsd="http://www.w3.org/2001/XMLSchema"
xmlns:xsf="http://schemas.microsoft.com/office/infopath/2003/solutionDefinition"
targetNamespace="http://schemas.microsoft.com/office/infopath/2003/solutionDefinition"
elementFormDefault="qualified" attributeFormDefault="unqualified">
        <!-- xdTitle type -->
        <xsd:simpleType name="xdTitle">
                <xsd:restriction base="xsd:string">
                        <xsd:minLength value="1" />
                        <xsd:maxLength value="255" />
                        <xsd:pattern
value="([^\p{Z}\p{Cc}\p{Cf}\p{Cn}])(([^\p{Zl}\p{Zp}\p{Cc}])*([^\p{Z}\p{Cc}\p{Cf}\p{Cn}]
))?" />
                </xsd:restriction>
        </xsd:simpleType>
        <!-- xdViewName type -->
        <xsd:simpleType name="xdViewName">
                <xsd:restriction base="xsd:string">
                        <xsd:minLength value="1" />
                        <xsd:maxLength value="255" />
                        <xsd:pattern
value="([^\p{Z}\p{C}/\\#&amp;&quot;&gt;&lt;])(([^\p{Zl}\p{Zp}\p{C}/\\#&amp;&quot;&gt;&l
t;])*([^\p{Z}\p{C}/\\#&amp;&quot;&gt;&lt;]))?" />
                </xsd:restriction>
        </xsd:simpleType>
        <!-- xdYesNo type -->
        <xsd:simpleType name="xdYesNo">
                <xsd:restriction base="xsd:NMTOKEN">
                        <xsd:enumeration value="yes" />
                        <xsd:enumeration value="no" />
                </xsd:restriction>
        </xsd:simpleType>
        <!-- xdFileName type -->
        <xsd:simpleType name="xdFileName">
                <xsd:restriction base="xsd:string">
```

```xml
                    <xsd:minLength value="1" />
                    <xsd:maxLength value="64" />
            </xsd:restriction>
      </xsd:simpleType>
      <!-- xdScriptLanguage type -->
      <xsd:simpleType name="xdScriptLanguage">
            <xsd:restriction base="xsd:NMTOKEN">
                    <xsd:pattern
value="((([Jj][Aa][Vv][Aa])|([Jj])|([Vv][Bb]))([Ss][Cc][Rr][Ii][Pp][Tt]))" />
            </xsd:restriction>
      </xsd:simpleType>
      <!-- xdSolutionVersion type -->
      <xsd:simpleType name="xdSolutionVersion">
            <xsd:restriction base="xsd:string">
                    <xsd:pattern value="(([0-9]{1,4}.){3}[0-9]{1,4})" />
            </xsd:restriction>
      </xsd:simpleType>
      <!-- xdEmptyString type -->
      <xsd:simpleType name="xdEmptyString">
            <xsd:restriction base="xsd:string">
                    <xsd:maxLength value="0" />
            </xsd:restriction>
      </xsd:simpleType>

      <!-- xdErrorMessage type -->
      <xsd:simpleType name="xdErrorMessage">
            <xsd:restriction base="xsd:string">
                    <xsd:maxLength value="1023" />
            </xsd:restriction>
      </xsd:simpleType>
      <!-- xDocumentClass -->
      <xsd:element name="xDocumentClass">
            <xsd:complexType>
                    <xsd:all>
                            <xsd:element ref="xsf:package" minOccurs="1" />
                            <xsd:element ref="xsf:views" minOccurs="1" />
                            <xsd:element ref="xsf:scripts" minOccurs="0" />
                            <xsd:element ref="xsf:schemaErrorMessages" minOccurs="0" />
                            <xsd:element ref="xsf:documentSchemas" minOccurs="0" />
                            <xsd:element ref="xsf:applicationParameters" minOccurs="0" />
                            <xsd:element ref="xsf:fileNew" minOccurs="0" />
                            <xsd:element ref="xsf:customValidation" minOccurs="0" />
```

D

```xml
                    <xsd:element ref="xsf:domEventHandlers" minOccurs="0" />
                    <xsd:element ref="xsf:importParameters" minOccurs="0" />
                    <xsd:element ref="xsf:listProperties" minOccurs="0" />
                    <xsd:element ref="xsf:taskpane" minOccurs="0" />
                    <xsd:element ref="xsf:documentSignatures" minOccurs="0" />
                    <xsd:element ref="xsf:dataObjects" minOccurs="0" />
                    <xsd:element ref="xsf:query" minOccurs="0" />
                    <xsd:element ref="xsf:submit" minOccurs="0" />
                    <xsd:element ref="xsf:documentVersionUpgrade" minOccurs="0" />
                    <xsd:element ref="xsf:extensions" minOccurs="0" />
                </xsd:all>
                <xsd:attribute name="name" type="xsd:string" use="optional" />
                <xsd:attribute name="author" type="xsd:string" use="optional" />
                <xsd:attribute name="description" use="optional">

                    <xsd:simpleType>
                        <xsd:restriction base="xsd:string">
                            <xsd:maxLength value="255" />
                        </xsd:restriction>
                    </xsd:simpleType>
                </xsd:attribute>
                <xsd:attribute name="solutionVersion" type="xsf:xdSolutionVersion"
use="optional" />
                <xsd:attribute name="productVersion" type="xsd:string" use="optional"
/>
                <xsd:attribute name="solutionFormatVersion"
type="xsf:xdSolutionVersion" use="required" />
                <xsd:attribute name="dataFormSolution" type="xsf:xdYesNo"
use="optional" />
                <xsd:attribute name="requireFullTrust" type="xsf:xdYesNo"
use="optional" />
                <xsd:attribute name="publishUrl" type="xsd:string" use="optional" />
            </xsd:complexType>
        </xsd:element>
        <!-- UIContainer -->
        <xsd:group name="UIContainer">
            <xsd:choice>
                <xsd:element ref="xsf:toolbar" />
                <xsd:element ref="xsf:menu" />
                <xsd:element ref="xsf:menuArea" />
            </xsd:choice>
        </xsd:group>
```

```xml
<!-- schemaErrorMessages -->
<xsd:element name="schemaErrorMessages">
        <xsd:complexType>
                <xsd:sequence>
                        <xsd:element ref="xsf:override" minOccurs="0"
maxOccurs="unbounded" />
                </xsd:sequence>
          </xsd:complexType>
</xsd:element>
<!-- override -->
<xsd:element name="override">
        <xsd:complexType>
                <xsd:sequence>
                        <xsd:element ref="xsf:errorMessage" />
                </xsd:sequence>
                <xsd:attribute name="match" type="xsd:string" use="required" />
        </xsd:complexType>
</xsd:element>
<!-- applicationParameters -->
<xsd:element name="applicationParameters">
        <xsd:complexType>
                <xsd:all>
                        <xsd:element ref="xsf:solutionProperties" minOccurs="0" />
                </xsd:all>
                <xsd:attribute name="application" use="required">
                        <xsd:simpleType>
                                <xsd:restriction base="xsd:string">
                                        <xsd:enumeration value="InfoPath Design Mode" />
                                </xsd:restriction>
                        </xsd:simpleType>
                </xsd:attribute>
        </xsd:complexType>
</xsd:element>
<!-- solutionProperties -->
<xsd:element name="solutionProperties">
        <xsd:complexType>
                <xsd:attribute name="allowCustomization" type="xsf:xdYesNo"
use="optional" />
                <xsd:attribute name="lastOpenView" use="optional" />
                <xsd:attribute name="scriptLanguage" type="xsf:xdScriptLanguage"
use="optional" />
                <xsd:attribute name="automaticallyCreateNodes" type="xsf:xdYesNo"
```

D

```
use="optional" />
                    <xsd:attribute name="lastVersionNeedingTransform"
type="xsf:xdSolutionVersion" use="optional" />
                    <xsd:attribute name="fullyEditableNamespace" type="xsd:anyURI"
use="optional" />
            </xsd:complexType>
      </xsd:element>
      <!-- dbInfo -->
      <xsd:element name="query">
           <xsd:complexType>
                <xsd:choice>
                     <xsd:element ref="xsf:adoAdapter" />

                     <xsd:element ref="xsf:webServiceAdapter" />
                     <xsd:element ref="xsf:xmlFileAdapter" />
                </xsd:choice>
           </xsd:complexType>
      </xsd:element>
      <!-- scripts -->
      <xsd:element name="scripts">
           <xsd:complexType>
                <xsd:sequence>
                     <xsd:element ref="xsf:script" minOccurs="0"
maxOccurs="unbounded" />
                </xsd:sequence>
                <xsd:attribute name="language" type="xsf:xdScriptLanguage"
use="required" />
           </xsd:complexType>
      </xsd:element>
      <xsd:element name="script">
           <xsd:complexType>
                <xsd:attribute name="src" type="xsf:xdFileName" use="required" />
           </xsd:complexType>
      </xsd:element>
      <!-- docObjects -->
      <xsd:element name="dataObjects">
           <xsd:complexType>
                <xsd:choice minOccurs="0" maxOccurs="unbounded">
                     <xsd:element ref="xsf:dataObject" />
                </xsd:choice>
           </xsd:complexType>
      </xsd:element>
```

```xml
<xsd:element name="dataObject">
      <xsd:complexType>
            <xsd:choice>
                  <xsd:element ref="xsf:query" />
            </xsd:choice>
            <xsd:attribute name="name" type="xsf:xdTitle" use="required" />
            <xsd:attribute name="schema" type="xsd:string" use="optional" />
            <xsd:attribute name="initOnLoad" type="xsf:xdYesNo" use="optional"
/>
      </xsd:complexType>
</xsd:element>
<xsd:element name="adoAdapter">
      <xsd:complexType>
            <xsd:attribute name="connectionString" type="xsd:string"
use="required" />
            <xsd:attribute name="commandText" type="xsd:string" use="required"
/>
            <xsd:attribute name="queryAllowed" type="xsf:xdYesNo"
use="optional" />
            <xsd:attribute name="submitAllowed" type="xsf:xdYesNo"
use="optional" />
      </xsd:complexType>
</xsd:element>
<xsd:element name="webServiceAdapter">
      <xsd:complexType>
            <xsd:choice>
                  <xsd:element ref="xsf:operation" />
            </xsd:choice>
            <xsd:attribute name="wsdlUrl" type="xsd:string" use="required" />
            <xsd:attribute name="queryAllowed" type="xsf:xdYesNo"
use="optional" />
            <xsd:attribute name="submitAllowed" type="xsf:xdYesNo"
use="optional" />
      </xsd:complexType>
</xsd:element>
<xsd:element name="operation">
      <xsd:complexType>
            <xsd:choice>
                  <xsd:element ref="xsf:input" minOccurs="0" />
            </xsd:choice>
            <xsd:attribute name="name" type="xsd:string" use="required" />
            <xsd:attribute name="soapAction" type="xsd:string" use="required"
/>
```

D

```
                                    <xsd:attribute name="serviceUrl" type="xsd:string" use="required" />
                </xsd:complexType>
        </xsd:element>
        <xsd:element name="input">
                <xsd:complexType>
                        <xsd:choice minOccurs="0" maxOccurs="unbounded">
                                <xsd:element ref="xsf:partFragment" />
                        </xsd:choice>
                        <xsd:attribute name="source" type="xsd:string" use="required" />
                </xsd:complexType>
        </xsd:element>
        <xsd:element name="partFragment">
                <xsd:complexType>
                        <xsd:attribute name="match" type="xsd:string" use="required" />
                        <xsd:attribute name="replaceWith" type="xsd:string" use="required" />
                </xsd:complexType>
        </xsd:element>
        <xsd:element name="xmlFileAdapter">
                <xsd:complexType>
                        <xsd:attribute name="fileUrl" type="xsd:anyURI" use="required" />
                </xsd:complexType>
        </xsd:element>
        <!-- documentSchemas -->
        <xsd:element name="documentSchemas">
                <xsd:complexType>
                        <xsd:sequence>
                                <xsd:element ref="xsf:documentSchema" maxOccurs="unbounded" />
                        </xsd:sequence>
                </xsd:complexType>
        </xsd:element>
        <xsd:element name="documentSchema">
                <xsd:complexType>
                        <xsd:attribute name="location" type="xsd:string" use="required" />
                        <xsd:attribute name="rootSchema" type="xsf:xdYesNo" />
                </xsd:complexType>
        </xsd:element>
        <!-- customValidation -->
        <xsd:element name="customValidation">
                <xsd:complexType>
                        <xsd:sequence>
                                <xsd:element ref="xsf:errorCondition" minOccurs="0"
maxOccurs="unbounded" />
```

```xml
              </xsd:sequence>
          </xsd:complexType>
      </xsd:element>
      <xsd:element name="errorCondition">
          <xsd:complexType>
              <xsd:sequence>
                  <xsd:element ref="xsf:errorMessage" />
              </xsd:sequence>
              <xsd:attribute name="match" type="xsd:string" use="required" />
              <xsd:attribute name="expression" type="xsd:string" use="required" />
              <xsd:attribute name="expressionContext" type="xsd:string"
use="optional" />
              <xsd:attribute name="showErrorOn" type="xsd:string" use="optional" />
          </xsd:complexType>
      </xsd:element>
      <xsd:element name="errorMessage">
          <xsd:complexType>
              <xsd:simpleContent>
                  <xsd:extension base="xsf:xdErrorMessage">
                      <xsd:attribute name="type" use="optional">
                          <xsd:simpleType>
                              <xsd:restriction base="xsd:NMTOKEN">
                                  <xsd:enumeration value="modal" />
                                  <xsd:enumeration value="modeless" />
                              </xsd:restriction>
                          </xsd:simpleType>
                      </xsd:attribute>
                      <xsd:attribute name="shortMessage" use="required" >
                          <xsd:simpleType>
                              <xsd:restriction base="xsd:string">
                                  <xsd:maxLength value="127" />
                              </xsd:restriction>
                          </xsd:simpleType>
                      </xsd:attribute>
                  </xsd:extension>
              </xsd:simpleContent>
          </xsd:complexType>
      </xsd:element>
      <!-- domEventHandlers -->
      <xsd:element name="domEventHandlers">
          <xsd:complexType>
              <xsd:sequence>
```

D

```
                            <xsd:element ref="xsf:domEventHandler" minOccurs="0"
maxOccurs="unbounded" />
                    </xsd:sequence>
            </xsd:complexType>
        </xsd:element>
        <xsd:element name="domEventHandler">
            <xsd:complexType>
                    <xsd:attribute name="match" type="xsd:string" use="required" />
                    <xsd:attribute name="handlerObject" type="xsd:string"
use="required" />
            </xsd:complexType>
        </xsd:element>
        <!-- importParameters -->
        <xsd:element name="importParameters">
            <xsd:complexType>
                    <xsd:sequence>
                        <xsd:element ref="xsf:importSource" minOccurs="0"
maxOccurs="unbounded" />
                    </xsd:sequence>
                    <xsd:attribute name="enabled" type="xsf:xdYesNo" use="required" />
             </xsd:complexType>
        </xsd:element>
        <xsd:element name="importSource">
            <xsd:complexType>
                    <xsd:attribute name="name" type="xsd:string" use="required" />
                    <xsd:attribute name="schema" type="xsf:xdFileName" use="required" />
                    <xsd:attribute name="transform" type="xsf:xdFileName" use="required" />
            </xsd:complexType>
        </xsd:element>
        <!-- listProperties -->
        <xsd:element name="listProperties">
            <xsd:complexType>
                    <xsd:all>
                        <xsd:element ref="xsf:fields" />
                    </xsd:all>
            </xsd:complexType>
        </xsd:element>
        <xsd:element name="fields">
            <xsd:complexType>
                    <xsd:sequence>
                        <xsd:element ref="xsf:field" minOccurs="0" maxOccurs="unbounded"
/>
```

```
                    </xsd:sequence>
                </xsd:complexType>
            </xsd:element>
            <xsd:element name="field">
                <xsd:complexType>
                    <xsd:attribute name="type" type="xsd:NMTOKEN" use="required" />
                    <xsd:attribute name="name" type="xsf:xdTitle" use="required" />
                    <xsd:attribute name="columnName" type="xsf:xdTitle" use="required" />
                    <xsd:attribute name="required" type="xsf:xdYesNo" use="optional" />
                    <xsd:attribute name="viewable" type="xsf:xdYesNo" use="optional" />
                    <xsd:attribute name="node" type="xsd:string" use="required" />
                    <xsd:attribute name="maxLength" type="xsd:byte" />
                    <xsd:attribute name="aggregation" use="optional">
                        <xsd:simpleType>
                            <xsd:restriction base="xsd:NMTOKEN">
                                <xsd:enumeration value="sum" />
                                <xsd:enumeration value="count" />
                                <xsd:enumeration value="average" />
                                <xsd:enumeration value="min" />
                                <xsd:enumeration value="max" />
                                <xsd:enumeration value="first" />
                                <xsd:enumeration value="last" />
                                <xsd:enumeration value="merge" />
                                <xsd:enumeration value="plaintext" />
                            </xsd:restriction>
                        </xsd:simpleType>
                    </xsd:attribute>
                </xsd:complexType>
            </xsd:element>
            <xsd:element name="submit">
                <xsd:complexType>
                    <xsd:all>
                        <xsd:element ref="xsf:useHttpHandler" minOccurs="0" />
                        <xsd:element ref="xsf:useScriptHandler" minOccurs="0" />
                        <xsd:element ref="xsf:useQueryAdapter" minOccurs="0" />
                        <xsd:element ref="xsf:webServiceAdapter" minOccurs="0" />
                        <xsd:element name="successMessage" type="xsd:string"
minOccurs="0" />
                        <xsd:element name="errorMessage" type="xsd:string"
minOccurs="0" />
                    </xsd:all>
                    <xsd:attribute name="caption" type="xsd:string" use="optional" />
```

D

```
                        <xsd:attribute name="onAfterSubmit" use="optional">
                            <xsd:simpleType>
                                <xsd:restriction base="xsd:NMTOKEN">
                                    <xsd:enumeration value="close" />
                                    <xsd:enumeration value="keepOpen" />
                                    <xsd:enumeration value="openNew" />
                                </xsd:restriction>
                            </xsd:simpleType>
                        </xsd:attribute>
                        <xsd:attribute name="showStatusDialog" type="xsf:xdYesNo"
use="optional" />
                        <xsd:attribute name="showSignatureReminder" type="xsf:xdYesNo"
use="optional" />
                        <xsd:attribute name="disableMenuItem" type="xsf:xdYesNo" use="optional"
/>
                </xsd:complexType>
        </xsd:element>
        <xsd:element name="useHttpHandler">
            <xsd:complexType>
                    <xsd:attribute name="method" use="required">
                        <xsd:simpleType>
                        <xsd:restriction base="xsd:NMTOKEN">
                                <xsd:enumeration value="POST" />
                            </xsd:restriction>
                        </xsd:simpleType>
                    </xsd:attribute>
                    <xsd:attribute name="href" type="xsd:anyURI" use="required" />
            </xsd:complexType>
        </xsd:element>
        <xsd:element name="useScriptHandler"></xsd:element>
        <xsd:element name="useQueryAdapter">
            <xsd:complexType></xsd:complexType>
        </xsd:element>
        <!-- fileNew -->
        <xsd:element name="fileNew">
            <xsd:complexType>
                <xsd:sequence>
                    <xsd:element ref="xsf:initialXmlDocument" />
                </xsd:sequence>
        </xsd:complexType>
        </xsd:element>
        <xsd:element name="initialXmlDocument">
```

```
            <xsd:complexType>
                    <xsd:attribute name="caption" type="xsf:xdTitle"
use="required"></xsd:attribute>
                    <xsd:attribute name="href" type="xsf:xdFileName" use="required" />
            </xsd:complexType>
    </xsd:element>
    <!-- package -->
    <xsd:element name="package">
            <xsd:complexType>
                    <xsd:sequence>
                            <xsd:element ref="xsf:files" />
                    </xsd:sequence>
            </xsd:complexType>
    </xsd:element>
    <xsd:element name="files">
            <xsd:complexType>
                    <xsd:sequence>
                            <xsd:element ref="xsf:file" minOccurs="0" maxOccurs="unbounded"
/>
                    </xsd:sequence>
            </xsd:complexType>
    </xsd:element>
    <xsd:element name="file">
            <xsd:complexType>
                    <xsd:sequence>
                            <xsd:element ref="xsf:fileProperties" minOccurs="0" maxOccurs="1"
/>
                    </xsd:sequence>
                    <xsd:attribute name="name" type="xsf:xdFileName" use="required" />
            </xsd:complexType>
    </xsd:element>
    <xsd:element name="fileProperties">
            <xsd:complexType>
                    <xsd:sequence>
                            <xsd:element ref="xsf:property" minOccurs="0" maxOccurs="unbounded"
/>
                    </xsd:sequence>
            </xsd:complexType>
    </xsd:element>
    <xsd:element name="property">
            <xsd:complexType>
                    <xsd:attribute name="name" type="xsd:string" use="required" />
```

D

```
                        <xsd:attribute name="value" type="xsd:string" use="required" />
                        <xsd:attribute name="type" type="xsd:QName" use="required" />
                </xsd:complexType>
        </xsd:element>
        <!-- View and Context-Driven Editing definitions -->
        <!-- attributeData -->
        <xsd:element name="attributeData">
                <xsd:complexType>
                        <xsd:attribute name="attribute" type="xsd:string" use="required" />
                        <xsd:attribute name="value" type="xsd:string" use="required" />
                </xsd:complexType>
        </xsd:element>
        <!-- button -->
        <xsd:element name="button">
                <xsd:complexType>
                        <xsd:attribute name="caption" type="xsf:xdTitle" />
                        <xsd:attribute name="icon" type="xsd:string" />
                        <xsd:attribute name="tooltip" type="xsf:xdTitle" />
                        <xsd:attribute name="name" type="xsd:NMTOKEN" />
                        <xsd:attribute name="xmlToEdit" type="xsd:NMTOKEN" />
                        <xsd:attribute name="action">
                                <xsd:simpleType>
                                        <xsd:restriction base="xsd:NMTOKEN">
                                                <xsd:enumeration value="xCollection::insert" />
                                                <xsd:enumeration value="xCollection::insertBefore"
/>
                                                <xsd:enumeration value="xCollection::insertAfter"
/>
                                                <xsd:enumeration value="xCollection::remove" />
                                                <xsd:enumeration value="xCollection::removeAll"
/>
                                                <xsd:enumeration value="xOptional::insert" />
<                                                xsd:enumeration value="xOptional::remove" />
                                                <xsd:enumeration value="xReplace::replace" />
                                        </xsd:restriction>
                                </xsd:simpleType>
                        </xsd:attribute>
                        <xsd:attribute name="showIf">
                                <xsd:simpleType>
                                        <xsd:restriction base="xsd:NMTOKEN">
                                                <xsd:enumeration value="always" />
                                                <xsd:enumeration value="enabled" />
```

```
                                          <xsd:enumeration value="immediate" />
                                </xsd:restriction>
                          </xsd:simpleType>
                    </xsd:attribute>
              </xsd:complexType>
      </xsd:element>
      <!-- chooseFragment -->
      <xsd:element name="chooseFragment">
              <xsd:complexType mixed="true">
                    <xsd:sequence>
                          <xsd:any minOccurs="0" maxOccurs="unbounded"
processContents="skip" />
                    </xsd:sequence>
                    <xsd:attribute name="parent" type="xsd:string" />
                    <xsd:attribute name="followingSiblings" type="xsd:string"
use="optional" />
              </xsd:complexType>
      </xsd:element>
      <!-- editWith -->
      <xsd:element name="editWith">
              <xsd:complexType>
                    <xsd:sequence>
                          <xsd:element ref="xsf:fragmentToInsert" minOccurs="0"
maxOccurs="1" />
                    </xsd:sequence>
                    <xsd:attribute name="component" use="required">
                          <xsd:simpleType>
                          <xsd:restriction base="xsd:NMTOKEN">
                                      <xsd:enumeration value="xCollection" />
                                      <xsd:enumeration value="xOptional" />
                                      <xsd:enumeration value="xReplace" />
                                      <xsd:enumeration value="xTextList" />
                                      <xsd:enumeration value="xField" />
                                      <xsd:enumeration value="xImage" />
                              </xsd:restriction>
                          </xsd:simpleType>
                    </xsd:attribute>
                    <xsd:attribute name="caption" type="xsf:xdTitle" use="optional" />
                    <xsd:attribute name="autoComplete" type="xsf:xdYesNo"
use="optional" />
                    <xsd:attribute name="proofing" type="xsf:xdYesNo" use="optional" />
                    <xsd:attribute name="type" use="optional">
```

D

```
                    <xsd:simpleType>
                            <xsd:restriction base="xsd:NMTOKEN">
                                <xsd:enumeration value="plain" />
            <xsd:enumeration value="formatted" />
            <xsd:enumeration value="plainMultiline" />
            <xsd:enumeration value="formattedMultiline" />
            <xsd:enumeration value="rich" />
                            </xsd:restriction>
                    </xsd:simpleType>
                </xsd:attribute>
                <xsd:attribute name="field" type="xsd:string" use="optional" />
                <xsd:attribute name="removeAncestors" type="xsd:nonNegativeInteger"
use="optional" />
                <xsd:anyAttribute
namespace="http://schemas.microsoft.com/office/infopath/2003" processContents="skip" />
            </xsd:complexType>
        </xsd:element>
        <!-- unboundControls -->
        <xsd:element name="unboundControls">
            <xsd:complexType>
                <xsd:sequence>
                    <!-- button -->
                    <xsd:element name="button" minOccurs="0"
maxOccurs="unbounded">
                        <xsd:complexType>
                            <xsd:attribute name="name" use="required">
                                <xsd:simpleType>
                                    <!-- type of name is non qualified
name, but it also accepts . and - so this characters
    disabled by pattern restriction -->
                                    <xsd:restriction base="xsd:NCName">
                                        <xsd:pattern
value="[^\.\^-]*" />
                                    </xsd:restriction>
                                </xsd:simpleType>
                            </xsd:attribute>
                        </xsd:complexType>
                    </xsd:element>
                </xsd:sequence>
            </xsd:complexType>
        </xsd:element>
        <!-- editing -->
```

```
        <xsd:element name="editing">
            <xsd:complexType>
                <xsd:sequence>
                    <xsd:element ref="xsf:xmlToEdit" minOccurs="0"
maxOccurs="unbounded" />
                </xsd:sequence>
            </xsd:complexType>
        </xsd:element>
        <!-- fragmentToInsert -->
        <xsd:element name="fragmentToInsert">
            <xsd:complexType>
                <xsd:sequence>
                    <xsd:element ref="xsf:chooseFragment" minOccurs="1"
maxOccurs="unbounded" />
                </xsd:sequence>
            </xsd:complexType>
        </xsd:element>
        <!-- mainpane -->
        <xsd:element name="mainpane">
            <xsd:complexType>
                <xsd:attribute name="transform" type="xsf:xdFileName"
use="required" />
            </xsd:complexType>
        </xsd:element>
        <!-- printSettings -->
        <xsd:element name="printSettings">
            <xsd:complexType>
                <xsd:attribute name="orientation">
                    <xsd:simpleType>
                        <xsd:restriction base="xsd:NMTOKEN">
                            <xsd:enumeration value="portrait" />
                            <xsd:enumeration value="landscape" />
                        </xsd:restriction>
                    </xsd:simpleType>
                </xsd:attribute>
                <xsd:attribute name="header">
                    <xsd:simpleType>
                        <xsd:restriction base="xsd:string">
                            <xsd:maxLength value="255" />
                        </xsd:restriction>
                    </xsd:simpleType>
                </xsd:attribute>
```

D

```
                        <xsd:attribute name="footer">
                                <xsd:simpleType>
                                        <xsd:restriction base="xsd:string">
                                                <xsd:maxLength value="255" />
                                </xsd:restriction>
                                </xsd:simpleType>
                        </xsd:attribute>
                </xsd:complexType>
        </xsd:element>
        <!-- toolbar -->
        <xsd:element name="toolbar">
                <xsd:complexType>
                        <xsd:sequence>
                                <xsd:group ref="xsf:UIItem" minOccurs="0" maxOccurs="unbounded"
/>
                        </xsd:sequence>
                        <xsd:attribute name="name" type="xsf:xdTitle" use="required" />
                        <xsd:attribute name="caption" type="xsf:xdTitle" use="required" />
                </xsd:complexType>
        </xsd:element>
        <!-- menu -->
        <xsd:element name="menu">
                <xsd:complexType>
                        <xsd:sequence>
                                <xsd:group ref="xsf:UIItem" minOccurs="0"
maxOccurs="unbounded" />
                        </xsd:sequence>
                        <xsd:attribute name="caption" type="xsf:xdTitle" use="required" />
                </xsd:complexType>
        </xsd:element>
        <!-- menuArea -->
        <xsd:element name="menuArea">
                <xsd:complexType>
                        <xsd:sequence>
                                <xsd:group ref="xsf:UIItem" minOccurs="0" maxOccurs="unbounded"
/>
                        </xsd:sequence>
                        <xsd:attribute name="name" use="required">
                                <xsd:simpleType>
                                        <xsd:restriction base="xsd:NMTOKEN">
                                                <xsd:enumeration value="msoFileMenu" />
                                                <xsd:enumeration value="msoEditMenu" />
```

```
                                    <xsd:enumeration value="msoInsertMenu" />
                                    <xsd:enumeration value="msoViewMenu" />
                                    <xsd:enumeration value="msoFormatMenu" />
                                    <xsd:enumeration value="msoToolsMenu" />
                                    <xsd:enumeration value="msoTableMenu" />
                                    <xsd:enumeration value="msoHelpMenu" />
                                    <xsd:enumeration
value="msoStructuralEditingContextMenu" />
                        </xsd:restriction>
                    </xsd:simpleType>
                </xsd:attribute>
            </xsd:complexType>
    </xsd:element>
    <!-- UIContainer -->
    <xsd:group name="UIItem">
            <xsd:choice>
                    <xsd:element ref="xsf:button" />
                    <xsd:element ref="xsf:menu" />
            </xsd:choice>
    </xsd:group>
    <!-- taskpane -->
    <xsd:element name="taskpane">
            <xsd:complexType>
                    <xsd:attribute name="caption" type="xsd:string" use="required" />
                    <xsd:attribute name="href" type="xsd:string" use="required" />
            </xsd:complexType>
    </xsd:element>
    <!-- views -->
    <xsd:element name="views">
            <xsd:complexType>
                    <xsd:sequence>
                            <xsd:element ref="xsf:view" minOccurs="1" maxOccurs="unbounded"
/>
                    </xsd:sequence>
                    <xsd:attribute name="default" type="xsd:string" />
            </xsd:complexType>
            <xsd:unique name="views_name_unique">
                    <xsd:selector xpath="./xsf:view" />
                    <xsd:field xpath="@name" />
            </xsd:unique>
            <xsd:key name="view_name_key">
                    <xsd:selector xpath="./xsf:view" />
```

D

```
                    <xsd:field xpath="@name" />
            </xsd:key>
            <xsd:keyref name="view_printView" refer="xsf:view_name_key">
                    <xsd:selector xpath="./xsf:view" />
                    <xsd:field xpath="@printView" />
            </xsd:keyref>
            <xsd:keyref name="views_default" refer="xsf:view_name_key">
                    <xsd:selector xpath="." />
                    <xsd:field xpath="@default" />
            </xsd:keyref>
    </xsd:element>
    <!-- ViewContent -->
    <xsd:group name="ViewContent">
            <xsd:choice>
                    <xsd:element ref="xsf:editing" minOccurs="0" />
                    <xsd:element ref="xsf:mainpane" minOccurs="0" />
                    <xsd:element ref="xsf:printSettings" minOccurs="0" />
                    <xsd:group ref="xsf:UIContainer" minOccurs="0"
maxOccurs="unbounded" />
                    <xsd:element ref="xsf:unboundControls" minOccurs="0" />
            </xsd:choice>
    </xsd:group>
    <!-- view -->
    <xsd:element name="view">
            <xsd:complexType>
                    <xsd:group ref="xsf:ViewContent" minOccurs="0"
maxOccurs="unbounded" />
                    <xsd:attribute name="caption" type="xsf:xdViewName" />
                    <xsd:attribute name="name" type="xsf:xdViewName" use="required" />
                    <xsd:attribute name="printView" type="xsd:string" />
            </xsd:complexType>
            <xsd:unique name="toolbar_name_unique">
                    <xsd:selector xpath="./xsf:toolbar" />
                    <xsd:field xpath="@name" />
            </xsd:unique>
            <xsd:unique name="menuArea_name_unique">
                    <xsd:selector xpath="./xsf:menuArea" />
                    <xsd:field xpath="@name" />
            </xsd:unique>
            <xsd:unique name="xmlToEdit_name_unique">
                    <xsd:selector xpath="./xsf:editing/xsf:xmlToEdit" />
                    <xsd:field xpath="@name" />
```

```
            </xsd:unique>
            <xsd:key name="xmlToEdit_name_key">
                  <xsd:selector xpath="./xsf:editing/xsf:xmlToEdit" />
                  <xsd:field xpath="@name" />
            </xsd:key>
            <xsd:keyref name="button_xmlToEdit_reference"
refer="xsf:xmlToEdit_name_key">
                  <xsd:selector xpath="./xsf:menuArea/xsf:button |
./xsf:menu/xsf:button | ./xsf:toolbar/xsf:button" />
                  <xsd:field xpath="@xmlToEdit" />
             </xsd:keyref>
      </xsd:element>
      <!-- xmlToEdit -->
      <xsd:element name="xmlToEdit">
            <xsd:complexType>
                  <xsd:sequence>
                        <xsd:element ref="xsf:editWith" minOccurs="0" maxOccurs="1" />
                  </xsd:sequence>
                  <xsd:attribute name="name" type="xsd:NMTOKEN" use="required" />
                  <xsd:attribute name="item" type="xsd:string" use="required" />
                  <xsd:attribute name="container" type="xsd:string" />
                  <xsd:attribute name="viewContext">
                        <xsd:simpleType>
                              <xsd:restriction base="xsd:string">
                                    <xsd:pattern
value="((\.|\#|[a-zA-Z0-9_])[a-zA-Z0-9_]*)(\s((\.|\#|[a-zA-Z0-9_])[a-zA-Z0-9_]*))*" />
                              </xsd:restriction>
                        </xsd:simpleType>
                  </xsd:attribute>
            </xsd:complexType>
      </xsd:element>
      <!-- docDigitalSignatures -->
      <xsd:element name="documentSignatures">
            <xsd:complexType>
                  <xsd:attribute name="signatureLocation" type="xsd:string"
use="required" />
            </xsd:complexType>
      </xsd:element>
      <!-- Upgrade -->
      <xsd:element name="documentVersionUpgrade">
            <xsd:complexType>
                  <xsd:choice>
```

D

```
                              <xsd:element ref="xsf:useScriptHandler" />
                              <xsd:element ref="xsf:useTransform" />
                       </xsd:choice>
                 </xsd:complexType>
     </xsd:element>
     <xsd:element name="useTransform">
           <xsd:complexType>
                 <xsd:attribute name="transform" use="required">
                       <xsd:simpleType>
                             <xsd:union memberTypes="xsf:xdFileName xsf:xdEmptyString"
/>
                       </xsd:simpleType>
                 </xsd:attribute>
                 <xsd:attribute name="minVersionToUpgrade" type="xsf:xdSolutionVersion"
use="required" />
                 <xsd:attribute name="maxVersionToUpgrade" type="xsf:xdSolutionVersion"
/>
           </xsd:complexType>
     </xsd:element>
     <!-- XSF Extensions -->
     <xsd:element name="extensions">
           <xsd:complexType>
                 <xsd:sequence>
                       <xsd:element ref="xsf:extension" minOccurs="0"
maxOccurs="unbounded" />
                 </xsd:sequence>
           </xsd:complexType>
     </xsd:element>
     <xsd:element name="extension">
           <xsd:complexType mixed="true">
                 <xsd:sequence>
                       <xsd:any minOccurs="0" maxOccurs="unbounded"
processContents="skip" />
                 </xsd:sequence>
                 <xsd:attribute name="name" type="xsd:NMTOKEN" use="required" />
                 <xsd:anyAttribute processContents="skip" />
           </xsd:complexType>
     </xsd:element>
</xsd:schema>
```

D

Index

INTERNATIONAL CONTACT INFORMATION

AUSTRALIA
McGraw-Hill Book Company
Australia Pty. Ltd.
TEL +61-2-9900-1800
FAX +61-2-9878-8881
http://www.mcgraw-hill.com.au
books-it_sydney@mcgraw-hill.com

CANADA
McGraw-Hill Ryerson Ltd.
TEL +905-430-5000
FAX +905-430-5020
http://www.mcgraw-hill.ca

GREECE, MIDDLE EAST, & AFRICA
(Excluding South Africa)
McGraw-Hill Hellas
TEL +30-210-6560-990
TEL +30-210-6560-993
TEL +30-210-6560-994
FAX +30-210-6545-525

MEXICO (Also serving Latin America)
McGraw-Hill Interamericana Editores
S.A. de C.V.
TEL +525-1500-5108
FAX +525-117-1589
http://www.mcgraw-hill.com.mx
carlos_ruiz@mcgraw-hill.com

SINGAPORE (Serving Asia)
McGraw-Hill Book Company
TEL +65-6863-1580
FAX +65-6862-3354
http://www.mcgraw-hill.com.sg
mghasia@mcgraw-hill.com

SOUTH AFRICA
McGraw-Hill South Africa
TEL +27-11-622-7512
FAX +27-11-622-9045
robyn_swanepoel@mcgraw-hill.com

SPAIN
McGraw-Hill/
Interamericana de España, S.A.U.
TEL +34-91-180-3000
FAX +34-91-372-8513
http://www.mcgraw-hill.es
professional@mcgraw-hill.es

UNITED KINGDOM, NORTHERN, EASTERN, & CENTRAL EUROPE
McGraw-Hill Education Europe
TEL +44-1-628-502500
FAX +44-1-628-770224
http://www.mcgraw-hill.co.uk
emea_queries@mcgraw-hill.com

ALL OTHER INQUIRIES Contact:
McGraw-Hill/Osborne
TEL +1-510-420-7700
FAX +1-510-420-7703
http://www.osborne.com
omg_international@mcgraw-hill.com

Sound Off!

Visit us at **www.osborne.com/bookregistration** and let us know what you thought of this book. While you're online you'll have the opportunity to register for newsletters and special offers from McGraw-Hill/Osborne.

We want to hear from you!

Sneak Peek

Visit us today at **www.betabooks.com** and see what's coming from McGraw-Hill/Osborne tomorrow!

Based on the successful software paradigm, Bet@Books™ allows computing professionals to view partial and sometimes complete text versions of selected titles online. Bet@Books™ viewing is free, invites comments and feedback, and allows you to "test drive" books in progress on the subjects that interest you the most.

Know How

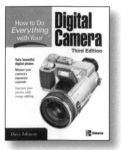

How to Do Everything with Your Digital Camera
Third Edition
ISBN: 0-07-223081-9

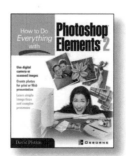

How to Do Everything with Photoshop Elements 2
ISBN: 0-07-222638-2

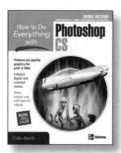

How to Do Everything with Photoshop CS
ISBN: 0-07-223143-2
4-color

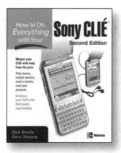

How to Do Everything with Your Sony CLIÉ
Second Edition
ISBN: 0-07-223074-6

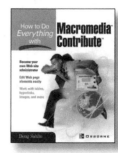

How to Do Everything with Macromedia Contribute
0-07-222892-X

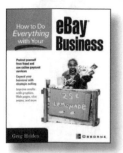

How to Do Everything with Your eBay Business
0-07-222948-9

How to Do Everything with Illustrator CS
ISBN: 0-07-223092-4
4-color

How to Do Everything with Your iPod
ISBN: 0-07-222700-1

How to Do Everything with Your iMac,
Third Edition
ISBN: 0-07-213172-1

How to Do Everything with Your iPAQ Pocket PC
Second Edition
ISBN: 0-07-222950-0